Teaching about Television

Teaching about Television

Len Masterman

MACMILLAN
EDUCATION

First published 1980
Reprinted 1982, 1983 (twice), 1984, 1985, 1987, 1988

Published by
MACMILLAN EDUCATION LTD
Houndmills, Basingstoke, Hampshire RG21 2XS
and London
Companies and representatives
throughout the world

Printed in Hong Kong

British Library Cataloguing in Publication Data
Masterman, Len
Teaching about television.
1. Television broadcasting — Study and teaching
I. Title
301.16′1   HE8700.6
ISBN 0-333-26676-5
ISBN 0-333-26677-3 Pbk

For Paula and Edith

Contents

Acknowledgements

To:

The IBA. Without the support of one of their excellent Research Fellowship awards, this book would never have seen the light of day. The book does not, of course, necessarily represent the views of the Authority.

Charles Mayo of the IBA for all of his patience, co-operation and help.

Professor Stuart Hood, for his continual advice and active support.

Ed Buscombe, Manuel Alvarado and Bob Ferguson for their interest in my work and their generous and helpful comments upon early draft material.

Dr John Daniels, Wyn Williams and Dr Paula Allman, three great educators to whom I have a general indebtedness; I have learned more from them than from a library of books.

Adrienne Edwards, Pat Hughes, Audrey Eaton, Jill Cleaver and Marian Anderton, who have provided impeccable secretarial assistance in the face of indecipherable handwriting.

John Wightman for technical and photographic assistance.

The following friends and colleagues, who have all in different ways influenced this book:

Dr John Baggaley	Colin Harrison
Andrew Bethell	Heather Hillier
Terry Dolan	Vale Humble
Gillian Dyer	Douglas Lowndes
Mike English	Andy Mead
Richard Exton	Hugh Morris
George Foster	Chris Mottershead
Brian Glover	Bob Osgerby
Felicity Grant	Alan O'Shea
John Hardcastle	John Thompson
Noel Hardy	Professor Ted Wragg

All of the pupils who participated in my television classes, and who tolerated my mistakes. My debt to them – whether their work is represented here or not – is an obvious one.

My wife, Paula, for her unstinting support and superhuman understanding, and for clarifying many of my ideas for me over a late-night pint.

To all, my gratitude and thanks.

The courtesy of the following is also acknowledged for permission to use copyright material from these sources:

S. M. Jourard and the Cambridge University Press for Figure 1 from the *British Journal of Social and Clinical Psychology*, vol. 5 (1966) p. 229; Dr Barnardo's for Plate 1; *TV Times* for Plate 3; John Timbers and *Radio Times* for Plates 2 and 4; TOPIX (Thomson Regional Newspapers Ltd) for Plate 5; Michael Simons and Cary Bazalgette, with Simon Clements and Andrew Bethell, for Plates 6, 7, 8, 9; Richard Hoggart and Chatto and Windus Ltd for *Speaking to Each Other (i) About Society*; Sheed and Ward Ltd and Penguin Books Ltd for *Pedagogy of the Oppressed* by Paulo Freire; Eamonn McCann for 'The British Press in Northern Ireland'; Dennis Potter and *New Statesman* for 'Lost Horizons'; Richard Collins and the BFI for *Television News*; Tom Burns and Macmillan, London and Basingstoke, for *The BBC*; John Dearlove and *Index on Censorship* for '*The BBC and the Politicians*'; Times Newspapers Ltd for my own pieces on 'The Burke Special' and 'Mastermind'; and, with Albert Hunt, for 'When to Say No'; Trevor Griffiths and Faber and Faber Ltd for *Comedians*; Random House Inc. for *Culture Against Man*; Dr Desmond Morris and Jonathan Cape Ltd for *The Naked Ape*.

November 1978   LEN MASTERMAN

Introduction

by Stuart Hood

Why teach about television?

One answer is that television can be used as a substitute for literature. If pupils read little and watch television instead, some teachers argue, then perhaps television may provide surrogate material for 'appreciation' and for content analysis. Others see in the use of television a means of self-expression or self-discovery; it has to be added, however, that the first enthusiasm for electronic equipment has waned somewhat. Others still, aware of the growth of media studies at centres of higher education, respond by teaching about television in the context of the wider study of other media: film, the press, photography, advertising. It is part of that inevitable process whereby what has been incorporated in the syllabus at a higher level finds its way down into the secondary schools. Len Masterman belongs to none of these tendencies. What inspires him to propose that we teach children about television is the view that television has replaced film as the most important mass medium; the knowledge that children, who may go to the cinema twice a year, view for more hours per week than they spend in school; and the conviction that these children can only benefit from an understanding of the medium from which they will derive, over their lives, the greater part of their information and entertainment.

To those who object that much of television is trivial and suggest that school time might be better employed than discussing, for instance, situation comedy or football on television, Masterman replies that, in crucial ways, what is said on television is less important than how it is said. What pupils who are taught about television should become aware of is that television has a language of its own with which values are suggested, attitudes reinforced and statements conveyed about society, the family, male–female relationships. The language is a complex one consisting not only of words but of gestures, the way a shot is framed, the way opening titles are designed, the way an announcer is dressed, the way a studio is furnished. In short, he sees television as a conveyor of ideology – an ideology which is the more effective, the less easy to challenge, if the viewer is convinced that the medium is transparent. For ideology on television depends to a large degree on the impression that its images are as apparently unmediated as water, gas or electricity appear to be when we turn on a tap or switch on a light.

Granted the desirability of teaching about television, how does one set about it? Are the concepts basic to a critical theory of the medium – for that is what Masterman is propounding – not too sophisticated for school children who will not necessarily go on to media studies at a polytechnic or university or seek careers in the mass media? They are children who are likely, as he points out, to have been discouraged by the schooling process from believing in their own judgements even when, as is the case with television, they are highly familiar with the subject matter. His answers to the question are concrete – accounts of teaching methods, of exercises in perception and in visual analysis from which teacher and pupils can proceed together to a discussion of the television image and its connotations. The examples he gives of work in this area by children, even when their capacity for formal expression is limited, show that they are – if well taught and rightly encouraged – capable of discussing some of the fundamental questions dealt with in courses on media studies. It is not the subject matter itself that presents the difficulty but the teaching method to be adopted.

One of the pedagogic problems posed by teaching about television is that the children are likely to be familiar with a wider range of the subject matter than the teacher. It is a situation which Masterman sees as capable of positive exploitation in that it permits the teacher to adopt a new and fruitful role – not that of a source of authority who knows the 'right' answers but of a collaborator in the exploration of an area of knowledge. It is at this point that his views on the importance of television as a subject mesh with his desire to see educational methods radically altered. Masterman believes that many of the techniques practised in schools and taught in colleges of education are calculated not to educate but to cut children off from learning. A system which is based on the retrieval from memory as quickly as possible of the 'right' answer is allied to a competitive ethos of which marks and 'places' are the rewards and expression. It is a system which is calculated to produce in a number of children a block that inhibits learning. Thus for most of my schooldays I was unable to count because of fear and embarrassment at not being able quickly and readily to produce 'correct' solutions and of frustration at not being able to ask what seemed to me to be highly relevant questions; it was only much later that I found that it was possible to think about numbers as one thinks about words. Anyone who has shared this experience will concur with Masterman in opposing competitiveness and what he calls the 'banking' system – the injection of knowledge by the teacher for retrieval at some later date when the proper stimulus is applied – and in opposing an educational system which tends to produce citizens who are as unquestioning about society as they are about the nature and import of the messages they receive each evening on their television screens.

It is important, however, not to fall into extremes of pessimism when discussing the television audience. There is probably – this is not an area much explored by audience research – a rather widely diffused scepticism in parts of that audience about what they see on their screens. Men and women workers from Fords who had taken part in mass meetings and voted there were, when interviewed by a student from a London polytechnic, highly critical of the way in which an event in which they had participated was filmed, presented and commented on in television news. It was clear from their responses to questioning that they had a clear understanding of the nature of mediation, of the power of editing and of the importance of the shot. What they lacked were the concepts to allow them to analyse their reactions. What Masterman would like to see is a generation of school-leavers going out into the world already armed with these concepts and accustomed to forming independent judgements not only about television but about the society in which they live. His proposals are innovatory in terms of pedagogy and society, admirably interesting on both counts, and, unlike much current work on the media, they have the virtue of being lucidly written and easy to read.

1

Television, Film and Media Education

Precisely how is television studied in schools and colleges at the present time? How should the study of television relate to already established courses in film studies, and the growing development of general mass-media courses in secondary schools and colleges? What problems surround the independent study of television as a viable intellectual discipline? And on what basis has the study of television and the mass media been urged by educational reports and media experts? This chapter attempts to answer these questions, and to clarify some of the theoretical problems underlying the study of the mass media. It ends with a critical survey of discriminatory approaches to mass-media teaching.

1. The present situation

At the present time there are two major trends apparent in the development of media education. First of all, more than a decade after the Newsom Report, the problems and difficulties of establishing film as an autonomous study within the secondary school curriculum are now becoming quite apparent. Secondly, a general movement has already taken place within schools towards the umbrella discipline of media studies. The situation was nicely summarised in a report by the Television Commission of a recent conference of film and television educators at York University:

> The most positive and perhaps, in terms of its importance for the future direction of work, the most significant of the Commission's conclusions is that the existing separation of TV and Film studies is no longer tenable.
> The Commission is generally agreed that we ought to think of all these areas (Film, TV, Radio, Music, the Press, Advertising, etc.) in terms of media studies. All these various media are interrelated within society, in terms of structures of ownership and means of organisation. And if they were approached from the other end, in terms of their aesthetic systems, they would also be found to have much in common.
> However, the Commission goes further than this. Not only is TV part of

a wider area of study; it also ought to form the core of that study. Film, which has been pre-eminent so far, can no longer sustain that position, certainly within secondary education. TV is by almost every criterion (with the dubious exception of 'quality') more centrally important.[1]

2. Film studies

The Commission's advocacy of television as a more centrally important medium than film at least in part reflects a number of practical problems encountered by teachers of film during the last decade. Far from being the liberating, radicalising experience which they had in mind, many teachers discovered that the subject, through its institutionalisation, became, willy-nilly, an instrument of control. The Commission on CSE Film Studies at the York conference noted that

The problem of pupil alienation from the school situation is as serious for the teacher of Film as it is for any other subject. Indeed, the pupil brings to the Film class a history of attitudes and experiences which shape his expectations of the work to be engaged in.[2]

Once film became a subject on the timetable, and formally examinable, the teacher did not simply face the problem of the pupil bringing into the film class alienating attitudes and expectations *from outside*. When files needed to be kept up to date, marks given, mock examinations set; when the examination was used as a threat, and assessment – in spite of the teacher's better judgement – became a prime instrument of control; when the teacher found that he had to judge as well as teach his pupils, discriminate between them, grade, order and rank them on grounds which he knew had little validity and which said nothing of the ways in which he valued them as individuals; and when the teacher finally realised that the compulsion for using these mechanisms of control arose from his knowledge that it was *he* who was being assessed by his pupils' results, his subject had already become reified, inert and instrumental before his very eyes.

It was not simply accommodation to the constraints of the examination system which caused problems for film teachers however. My own experience of teaching film to low-stream disenchanted secondary school pupils revealed that the medium itself was more remote from any of them than I had ever imagined – not one of them went to the cinema more than a couple of times each year, for example, and their experience of films was gained almost exclusively through watching television. Conventional approaches to the study of film cut no ice. There was no interest in genre, while Ford and even Hitchcock were as remote from them as Shelley and Keats. Discussion, when it occurred, was at a low, generally uninterested level, though it often raised unexpectedly important issues. From the teaching point of view, there were a surprising number of additional obstacles. No foreign films could ever be used since no one in the group could read quickly enough to catch even the simplest of subtitles as they flashed by; extracts inevitably provoked disappointed reactions, while features raised *too many* issues and complexities, caused timetabling problems and left no time for discussion immediately after viewing.

Apart from my own pedagogic inadequacies, many of the difficulties encountered with this group could be directly attributed to a rigidly streamed school organisation. At the age of eleven, on their first day in their new school, most of the group had been publicly placed in the lowest 'F' stream. It was a day they could all vividly remember. They responded to this calculated insult to their spirit by making life impossible for most teachers with whom they had come into contact ever since. Nevertheless the logic of my experience led me to the conclusion that film might be a less immediate, relevant and appropriate medium for classroom study than television. It was, as we have seen, a conclusion also reached by many other teachers who have recognised that it is time to redress the balance, to respond more sensitively to the direct viewing experiences of pupils and to acknowledge the greater significance and potency of the television medium.

3. Media studies

The study of television, where it finds a place at all in schools at the moment, is characterised by its heterogeneity and *ad-hocery*. The most common solution has undoubtedly been to treat television as a component part, lasting perhaps a half or one term, of a media studies course, an approach advocated as we have seen by the BFI/SEFT national conference on media education. There are, however, major conceptual and pedagogic difficulties involved in the notion of media studies. What insights or understandings would a one- or two-year course (the time-span of most media studies courses) give pupils in each of the media mentioned by the conference ('Film, TV, Radio, Music, the Press, Advertising, etc.' One wonders about the additional media suggested by that 'etc.' Books, perhaps? Telephones? Photographs? Cars?)? What would a half-term component in television or music look like? Could it be anything but superficial? And if so, is it worth doing at all? What would give coherence to the course's constituent units? A particular mode of enquiry? The examination of important cross-media concepts? Or what? And what would be the subject-matter under scrutiny – which of the many aspects of each of the media? What would be the status of this content? Would its acquisition be a desirable end in itself or a means of understanding general principles? Is there an essential body of knowledge or information? If so, what is it? And embracing all of these questions: what would constitute student learning? The acquisition of particular unnamed abilities, attitudes, information, techniques, methodologies or what? These are basic questions to which teachers will need to have answers before they can begin to set up coherent courses in media studies. They are questions which when raised at all have been answered with a resounding silence. As a result media studies courses invariably run the risk of being superficial and fragmented rag-bags, covering arbitrary issues, orientated towards content rather than process, asking different questions of different media and developing no consistent line of enquiry.

The difficulties of developing a coherent and organic framework which would comprehend each and all of the mass media are only too evident. Why then the compulsion to crowd them under the same umbrella? There are a number of reasons. Richard Collins has argued[3] the folly of regarding television and radio as discrete media, and there is obvious sense in this. Simply in terms of their organisational structures – particularly since the advent of commercial radio and the evolution of the Independent Television Authority to the Independent Broadcasting Authority – they ought to be considered together under the heading of broadcasting. But, the argument continues, the broadcasting institutions hold so many functions, attitudes and practices in common with newspapers and magazines – they may even cover the same events – that there is a kind of perversity about ignoring these connections and inter-relationships. Indeed, it is the establishment of valid cross-media generalisations which can give to media studies its worthwhileness and academic respectability. There is a further important argument, put forward by Graham Murdock, Douglas Lowndes and others for considering the mass media together: they are *industries* which are connected with each other, and linked to a vast range of service and consumer industries through their structures of ownership and control. EMI, for example, which has a substantial shareholding in Thames Television, is the country's largest record manufacturer and owns approximately one-quarter of the nation's cinemas as well as live theatres and restaurants (including the Golden Egg restaurant chain). The Rank Organisation, with a substantial shareholding in Southern Television, controls the country's largest cinema chain and owns Butlin's holiday camps, large numbers of bingo and dance halls, hotels and a group of radio, television and hi-fi manufacturers (Bush, Murphy and Dansette). The International Publishing Corporation (owners of the *Daily Mirror, Sunday Mirror* and *Sunday People*) is part of the giant multinational combine Reed International, which has interests in bathroom and sanitary ware (it owns Twyford's), wallpapers, paints, do-it-yourself products, fabrics, building products and publishing.[4] And so one could go on. The mass media are not isolated phenomena but significant links in a vast capitalist chain.

The study of mass-media *products*, which is what generally takes place in any educational study of the media, if it is to be of any value at all, cannot be done in isolation. There are *industrial, professional* and *organisational* constraints upon what appears in newspapers, magazines or on the television screen. The *values* of mass-media products are not likely to be very much at variance with the values of capitalism and consumerism, and the pattern of values and constraints (and of the individual communicator's ability to break free from them) is likely to hang together in a coherent way throughout all of the mass media.

There are then plausible arguments for the collective study of the media; but how strong are such arguments? To take Collins' first: the institutional and functional connections between the media ought not to blind us to the fundamental *distinctions* which exist between them. There is much that relates to the study of television to which radio and newspapers are an irrelevance, and vice versa, and I have seen no evidence in visiting schools that cross-media work within a media studies framework has illuminated either the specificity of a particular medium, or generated cross-media generalisations in a way that the study of an individual medium could not have done equally well. To argue for the detailed study of a particular medium is not to argue against the value of cross-media comparisons. Indeed such comparisons are inevitable. In studying television news, as we shall see, one continually needs to move outwards from the details of a particular news transmission to the interrogation of particular stories, journalistic practices or sources of bias as they exist in other media. 'Interrogation' is the key word, however; students examine with particular questions in mind, questions which have already been raised by the study of television news. Such questioning either pinpoints media specificities (where differences arise) or draws attention to general principles (where there are congruencies). It is this very *sharpness of focus* which is so often missing when pupils attempt to study news coverage across the media in a generalised way. Quite simply there is too much ground to cover, too much information, and no agreed methodological tools for processing it. Since the field must be delimited each teacher will do it in his own largely arbitrary way. As a result the content and procedures of media studies vary widely from school to school, syllabuses tend to be information-laden rather than question-orientated, and the ultimate outcome is to obscure cross-media principles rather than illuminate them.

All of the arguments in favour of studying the media collectively stem from a *prior* commitment to uncover for students either the institutional bases or the structures of ownership and control of the media. I have a great deal of sympathy with these commitments but there are great difficulties in urging their centrality to the study of media *in schools*. The major problem lies in the distinct differences which are likely to exist between what is considered important and interesting by the teacher, and what is of interest to his pupils. Like most articulate people who don't possess much of it, teachers and lecturers tend to be fascinated and even preoccupied with questions of power and control. It is not, by and large, a preoccupation which is likely to be shared by many of their pupils. And even assuming that pupils are able to see its significance there is a genuine difficulty in relating questions of organis-ational structures or patterns of control to the direct experience of the pupil.

Pupils buy records of course; they watch television, read magazines and some of them go to the pictures. Connections can be made and investigations can even be undertaken of who owns local newspapers, cinemas, bingo halls and the like, but the fact remains that media *products*, because they are immediate, concrete and involving are more intrinsically interesting to most pupils than media structures which are necessarily covert and abstract. If media control or the 'consciousness industry' are to become predominant concerns in media studies then proponents of this view will need to work hard to find ways of embedding their concerns within concrete experiences which are familiar, interesting and comprehensible to their pupils. There is no evidence that they have yet found ways of doing this.[5]

In this context, it is necessary to draw attention to an analogous movement which has been taking place within film studies – the movement towards the study of *Film as Industry*[6] in which the financing and distribution of films, and such notions as film 'property' are explored. Notwithstanding the doubts and difficulties articulately expressed by some teachers,[7] setting the study of films firmly within the context of their industrial production has been an undoubted step forward, bringing home

> very forcibly to the students the economic and commercial basis of the film industry and throwing light on aspects such as the collaborative industrial nature of film, constraints on film directors, the reasons for the existence of certain types of film and the complexities and limitations of the systems of distribution and exhibition in this country.[8]

The promise of the *Film as Industry* unit has undoubtedly provided some of the impetus towards a conception of media studies in which industrial constraints and structures of ownership would play a central part. It is worth stressing therefore that this study was confined to a *single* medium, and that even within this context teachers were clearly worried by the sheer volume of information which needed to be processed by pupils and by the difficulties of 'keeping the students away from content' during the discussion of films (it is ironic that one of the prime advantages of using visual material, its concreteness, should here be seen as obstructive). Finally it ought to be said that the *Film as Industry* unit was designed for and studied by 'examinable' pupils, many of them sixth formers. One can, to say the least, foresee difficulties in working out an approach to the study of the industrial bases of more than one of the mass media which might be appropriate for mixed-ability or low-stream groups.

This is not to denigrate the importance of this area of study, but to suggest that it can be most appropriately handled in the classroom if it is examined – as it is with *Film as Industry* – within the framework of a particular medium. Even within this circumscribed orbit however pedagogic procedures are by no means clear, and access to simple information by no means easy. What the television teacher can do is to work outwards from the concrete television images themselves towards a recognition of and feeling for – if not always a precise understanding of – the institutional and industrial contexts within which they are manufactured. This process begins with a reading of the total communication of the television image and an exploration of the values implicit within it, and ends with speculation upon four questions. Who is producing the images? For whose consumption? For what possible purposes? and What alternative images are thereby excluded? The teacher and his pupils must tread with care. Glib answers – the kind of crude determinism which equates commercialism with cynical audience manipulation for example – are easy; accurate ones more elusive and complex. We still know alarmingly little about the ways in which the major communication institutions operate; our knowledge of the sociology of the communicating professions is scant; and as laymen we are still very largely in the dark about the precise nature of the process which ends with one version of reality upon the screen rather than others.[9]

4. The case for television studies

So far I have tried to draw attention to two observable trends in media education. First of all an increasing awareness by teachers of the problems associated with the use of film material in the classroom, an awareness which has led to a growing feeling that television might be a more appropriate and important medium for study. The second trend concerned an observable movement towards the umbrella subject of media studies in which the study of television would play an important part. I have attempted to draw attention to the epistemological fuzziness surrounding media studies, to point to some of its deficiencies in existing classroom practice and to look at some of the problems raised by one version of the subject in which the study of the media as consciousness industries would provide the containing framework. It now remains to ask whether the medium of television itself can offer to the teacher a framework for disciplined study.

The need for a sound theoretical base capable of standing close scrutiny is paramount. At the moment the study of television in schools lacks not only intellectual coherence but even very much in the way of simple mechanical co-ordination. There are exceptions,[10] but, whether television is taught independently or within the context of the mass media, the tendency appears overwhelmingly to be for teachers to go very much their own way, guided principally by their own tastes and judgements and by a generalised desire to encourage discrimination and visual literacy. The proliferation of Mode III examinations, while bringing tremendous advantages in its encouragement of teacher independence and initiative, has tended to contribute to the current chaotic heterogeneity. As a result television courses at the moment are largely uninfluenced by one another, and good practice remains isolated within individual schools. The lack of course co-ordination, together with the familiar difficulty for overworked teachers of making space for themselves in which they can seriously reflect upon their own practice, has been responsible for television being taught in something of an intellectual vacuum. Yet there is evidence that some teachers are moving away from 'discriminatory' television teaching towards new approaches and that if only the right questions could be posed it might be possible to find a surprising amount of agreement about what might constitute the way ahead. The purpose of the rest of this chapter is to pose these questions and to suggest answers which might illuminate the way in which television teaching might develop in schools within the next decade.

*   *   *

To what extent can the study of television be constituted as a viable intellectual discipline? Before we can answer this question we must ask another: what is it that constitutes any discipline? Most fundamentally a discipline is characterised by *an agreed field of study or enquiry*, and is further defined by an *intellectual framework which delimits the questions to be asked*. Information is elicited from the field through a *distinctive mode of enquiry* and the purposes of this enquiry must be *'important'* or *'serious'* in ways which need no elaborate justification. Jerome Bruner has also argued that at the core of any discipline lie *concepts* and *principles* 'as *simple* as they are *powerful*' which 'may be taught to anybody at any age in some form'.[11] Can these considerations lead us to a more disciplined study of television? It is to this question which we must now turn.

a. *The field of study*

The primary object of study in television studies is observable and circumscribed; it is the continual flow of information which is communicated to us by television. What are the characteristics of this body of information? Most importantly the study of television is based upon the premiss that televisual information is *non-transparent*. As Nell Keddie has pointed out[12] this is also true of film studies, but the need to emphasise and demonstrate non-transparency is even more urgent in television since it is an apparently less synthetic medium than film with an apparently closer relationship to 'real' events. A 'window on the world' view of the medium would make the study of television impossible; one would not be studying it but other things – news, sport or light entertainment. The case for the study of television rests upon the significance and potency of a mediating process which exists independently of the existence of the event being televised.

Televisual communication is also characterised by its great diversity – it serves the functions of the newspaper, theatre, cinema, sports arena and music hall all rolled into one. This apparent hindrance to its disciplined study (it is difficult to imagine any but the woolliest of conceptual structures being able to comprehend such diverse functions) again forces attention upon a major generic function of television which is to provide a field for the embodiment and revelation of beliefs, values and attitudes. This it must inevitably do. In practice one can say much more – that in every country in which it operates *television has an ideological function*, as James Halloran has succinctly pointed out:

> Generally throughout Europe television serves the nation state, whatever the politics of the state . . . On the one side there are the broadcasters with their professional ideologies, occupational routines, and self-protecting mythologies, who have been socialised into a profession within given socio-economic systems. These professionals select, process and present the message. On the other side, there are individuals who make up the non-participating audiences and who receive the messages in relative isolation. It is seen by many as an elitist, literary set-up where a small group of educated, articulate people who more or less share the same codes of the dominant culture – encode messages for consumption by others who have different codes . . . generally the receiver will not be in a position to recognise all the professional rules and practices.[13]

Stuart Hood has drawn the connection between television's ideological function and the carefully fostered illusion of transparency:

> Since one of the principal functions of television is to convey the dominant ideology of society, the impression of immediacy or lack of intervention is important. What appears to be immediate is less likely to be questioned.[14]

Roland Barthes' notion of myth – 'depoliticised speech' – takes the logic of the argument a stage further. When constructed meanings operate under the guise of 'givens', when ideological dimensions are suppressed, and speech depoliticised, then 'Nature seems to spontaneously produce the represented scene'.[15] Myth transforms ideological representations into natural ones. The study of television necessarily becomes the study of myths through the suppression of ideological functions and mediating processes. *Television education is therefore a demythologising process which will reveal the selective practices by which images reach the television screen, emphasise the constructed nature of the representations projected, and make explicit their suppressed ideological function.* Such an education will also necessarily be concerned with alternative realities – those constructions implicitly rejected, suppressed or filtered out by the images which appear on the screen.[16]

If this theoretical formulation seems remote from the kinds of activities which are normally considered to be within the capabilities of a mixed-ability comprehensive school class, it is because the sphere of ideology is one which pupils will approach as the final stage of a three-level process of analysis. The teacher's first task is to encourage his pupils to generate from images *descriptions* of what they see at a *denotative* level. This, it is suggested, may be achieved by increasing awareness of the multiplicity of ways in which television images communicate their meanings (see Chapter 3). Secondly he may encourage pupil *interpretation* by drawing attention to the *connotative* levels of meaning in cultural images and objects. What does each denotative quality *suggest*? What associations do that colour, that shape, that size, that material have? Discussion, at first free-flowing and open-ended, will gradually become less so as definite patterns and clusters of associations become evident and the group move into interpretation at the *third* level, that of *ideology*, 'the final connotation of the totality of connotations of the sign' as Umberto Eco has described it. What does this programme *say* through its complex of signs and symbols? What values are embodied here, and what does it tell us of the society in which it finds a place? Who is producing this programme, for what audience and with what purpose?

To recapitulate: in television studies the field of investigation is constituted by the flow of information communicated to us by the medium. In spite of the apparent transparency, neutrality and diversity of function of this information it is both mediated and ideological. Mediation and ideology are themselves inextricably intertwined. Mediation is an ideological process, whilst ideology becomes 'visible' the moment that mediation processes are pinned down. The nature of that mediation and ideology can be partly revealed by a three-step process of analysis in which television information is examined at the levels of its denotative and connotative meanings before revealing itself as an ideological construct. For a fuller understanding of the constructed nature of the television image, however, further interrogation is necessary both of the images themselves and of the contexts within which they are embedded. Attention will need to be drawn to such diverse containing frameworks as the contextualising remarks of announcers, linkmen, comperes and presenters; articles relating to television programmes in the press or in *Radio Times* and *TV Times*; the visual codings and conventions of the medium; and the routine professional practices of those who work within it.

Of all of the questions that can be asked of the television image it is those which reveal it as a mediated and ideological construct which provide the most significant structures within television studies' conceptual framework. Many other questions can, and often will, be asked by the student of the television image; for example,

What other programmes are like this one? What connections can be made between this programme and others featuring the same star/production team/writer? What insights does this programme give us into the problems and people it depicts? How does this programme compare with the novel or play it derives from? Do I like this programme? Does the programme/film/play/documentary have any kind of organic unity? Is it of greater or less value than comparable programmes?

These questions simultaneously open out further perspectives and delimit additional areas of enquiry. They are questions of *secondary significance* however since they are most properly applied only to part of the total output of television and not to all of it.

This is perhaps an appropriate point to stress that the discussion of questions ought in itself to play a significant role in television education. How many questions is it possible to ask of a television picture? What are the differences between these questions? Can they be categorised? Or arranged into a hierarchy? These and other methodological problems ought not simply to be the concern of the teacher, but should be thought through and understood by pupils as well, for it is they who will ultimately be confronting the primary source material and who will need to be aware of the wide variety of tools at their disposal for making sense of it.[17] (See Chapter 3.)

b. The mode of enquiry

Some indication has already been given of the kind of enquiry in which television studies will engage. What will be the process of this enquiry? The task of the student of television is to *observe* and *describe* the images he sees, and *interpret* them at their connotative and ideological levels. This will involve the *analysis* of the codings, conventions and mediating processes which shape television images. As I have stressed, however, this mode of enquiry cannot reveal mediating frameworks which exist outside of the medium itself; it cannot directly disclose those images which have been excluded from the screen, and it cannot inform us directly of the many constraints and influences operating upon the form of a particular communication, though in both areas legitimate inferences can often be made on the basis of the images themselves. Our mode of enquiry will need to incorporate a sensitivity to its own limitations, and an awareness that these less accessible strands will need to be woven into any coherent understanding of television images. Hence the importance attached in this book to simulations in which pupils themselves become mediators and the acts of selection which make the television image a 'preferred' one can be replicated in the classroom.

c. Core concepts and principles

Teachers of the mass media will find it a useful exercise to try to formulate the 'simple' and 'powerful' concepts which lie at the heart of their work. The difficulties of achieving this *across* the media have already been touched upon. Central to the study of television there seem to me to be a number of core concepts: total communication, connotation, mediation and ideology; and a number of subsidiary ones such as genre, iconography and coding. Most of these – the concepts if not necessarily the words – seem to me to be capable of being passed on to the youngest of pupils in intellectually respectable versions via a spiral curriculum of the kind suggested by Bruner. The brief for television education in primary and early secondary education must be to find ways of introducing and deepening these concepts through the use of material appropriate to different age ranges. Chapter 3 of this book describes my own attempts to introduce them to secondary school pupils.

d. The importance of television studies

One of the most persistent arguments which the television teacher will meet from colleagues and parents is this: 'I find your work very interesting, most stimulating, etc., but do you *really* think it's important? I mean a lot of the material you're handling is pretty trivial stuff; and kids watch too much of it anyway without our needing to bring it into the classroom. Surely there are more important things for them to be doing in school.' According to Murdock and Phelps' survey[18] this view is still widely prevalent in schools, let alone amongst parents: 80 per cent of grammar schools and 42 per cent of the comprehensive schools surveyed felt that the study of the mass media had little or no legitimate claim to classroom attention. This whole question then is neither remote nor academic, but one that the television teacher will meet every day in the course of his work. In the last resort, any answer to the question 'Why is the study of television important?' must be a personal rather than a definitive one; in offering my own answer I do so in the recognition that the individual teacher will wish to add arguments of his own, and delete those with which he cannot agree.

The study of television is important because the medium itself is important. The Bullock Report is simply the latest of a number of sources to draw attention to the fact that most pupils spend far more time watching television than they do in the classroom.[19] To teach about television is to value this important and concrete part of pupils' experience and to assume its prime importance in real pupil learning. It is to attack a countervailing tendency in education to distrust the experience and judgement of the pupil, a process which whittles away the significance of his opinions, his dignity and ultimately his identity. One of the most damning indictments of schooling is that it can instil a conviction in pupils that neither they nor their experience are of any importance. A belief that one is not worthy of anything better is of course a precondition for the passive acceptance of slum houses, boring repetitive jobs and social and political subservience. Television studies assumes the prime importance of the experience of the learner, attempts to raise his consciousness by demythologising this experience; encourages him to posit alternatives; demonstrates the importance and strength of group experience; and continually fringes out from what is concrete and 'known' to a consideration of the wide range of social, aesthetic, industrial, political and philosophic issues raised by particular programmes.

Television is a major source of most people's information about the world. Because we live in a socially segregated society with total institutions for deviants, and socially segregated housing and schooling areas the medium is often our *only* source of information about a wide range of social problems and deviancies. Hartmann and Husband[20] have drawn attention to the importance of the frames of reference within which such issues are presented by television, and which need very careful scrutiny before any understanding of the issues involved can be reached. The study of television is vital not simply because it is such a pervasive and influential medium, but, as we have seen, because of its apparent transparency and naturalness. Knowledge of the mediated and constructed nature of the television message, and of the ways in which pictures are used selectively ought to be part of the common stock of every person's knowledge in a world where communication at all levels is both increasingly visual and industrialised. Television education is therefore part of an education for responsible citizenship. The case for its serious study seems to me to be very strong – even unanswerable; the fact that the medium continues to be ignored by vast numbers of schools in spite of a whole string of recommendations from official reports over the last twenty years is indeed an indictment of the conservatism and inflexibility of many educational establishments and of their inability to respond to developments and trends of major significance within society.

e. 'Appreciation' and 'discrimination'

Apart from colleagues, headmasters, advisers and parents who believe there is little educational value in what he is doing, the television teacher will undoubtedly come into contact with many supporters and well-wishers who will need no convincing of the importance of his work. They will see it as an admirable attempt to foster 'discrimination' in pupils, and such colleagues, he may find, will occasionally refer to his work as 'television appreciation'. The appropriateness of the aim of fostering discrimination in media work has come under a good deal of critical scrutiny in recent years but its influence upon teachers and the general public remains so widely pervasive that it may be helpful to examine the concept in some detail, and to clarify some of the issues surrounding its use.

The birth of the whole discrimination argument in media education lay in a profound distrust of the media themselves. Traditionally ignored by the educational system, the mass media were drawn to the attention of teachers when they came to be identified as aspects of cultural decline, seducers of the innocent, and creeping diseases whose baleful influence clearly needed to be actively fought by the teacher and counterbalanced by doses of 'inoculative' education. The Spens Report on Secondary Education in 1938, for example, spoke of 'The hoarding, the cinema and . . . the public press . . . subtly corrupting the taste and habit of a rising generation', and advocated speech training as a way of combating 'the infectious accent of Hollywood' and of abolishing class barriers.[21] Twenty-one years later, the Crowther Report on the education of fifteen- to eighteen-year-olds suggested that

> Because they [the mass media] are so powerful they need to be treated with the discrimination that only education can give. There is . . . a duty on those who are charged with the responsibility for education to see that teenagers . . . are not suddenly exposed to the full force of the 'mass-media' without some counterbalancing assistance.[22]

The classic, and almost certainly the most influential argument of the case for inoculative education was put by F. R. Leavis and Denys Thompson in *Culture and Environment*, first published in the 1930s but still widely influential amongst English readers in the 1950s and 1960s:

> those who in school are offered (perhaps) the beginnings of education in taste are exposed, out of school, to the competing exploitation of the cheapest emotional responses; films, newspapers, publicity in all its forms, commercially-catered fiction – all offer satisfaction at the lowest level, and inculcate the choosing of the most immediate pleasures, got with the least effort . . . We cannot, as we might in a healthy state of culture, leave the citizen to be formed unconsciously by his environment; if anything like a worthy idea of satisfactory living is to be saved he must be trained to discriminate and to resist.[23]

The importance and impact of Leavis and Thompson's little book for the educationalist lay not only in its moralistic stance but in the practical examples from advertisements, newspapers and journals which crowded its pages. *Culture and Environment* was essentially a handbook for teachers with an immediately practical application, and for all its antipathy to the media it was instrumental in bringing media texts out from the cold and into the classroom. It was a movement which was to be irreversible, opening the way in the 1960s for the classroom use of a wide range of materials derived from books which cast a much more informed and sympathetic eye upon popular culture – Richard Hoggart's *The Uses of Literacy* (1958 in its paperback edition), Vance Packard's *The Hidden Persuaders* (1960) and Whannel and Hall's *The Popular Arts* (1964).

The movement towards the increasing availability and use of popular texts was paralleled by an intellectual and emotional movement away from discrimination *against* the mass media towards discrimination *within* them. The strength and pervasiveness of this movement can be gauged from the fact that in 1960 it provided the theme for a national conference held by the

National Union of Teachers on *Popular Culture and Personal Responsibility*.
Old attitudes however continued to co-exist uneasily alongside the new.
Denys Thompson could still write in his introduction to *Discrimination and
Popular Culture*, a book arising directly out of the 1960 conference, and
whose contents typify the stances and attitudes of the new movement, that
'The aim of schools is to provide children with standards against which the
offerings of the mass media will appear cut down to size.'[24]

By now however this was coming to be seen as an unproductively elitist
stance by many teachers and other voices were beginning to articulate more
clearly what was to become the conventional wisdom for the remainder of the
decade. In Hall and Whannel's words

> In terms of actual quality . . . the struggle between what is good and
> worthwhile and what is shoddy and debased is not a struggle against the
> modern forms of communication, but a conflict within these media.[25]

One way of interpreting this was to assert the existence of a kind of high
culture within the mass media, and there is no doubt that this approach
informed a good deal of mass-media teaching in the 1960s. Discrimination
came to mean a preference for foreign films and 'classics of the cinema' over
the kinds of films shown at the local Odeon (a preference heavily underscored
in Hall and Whannel's work for example);[26] for the *Guardian* rather than the
Mirror; for *Panorama* rather than *Opportunity Knocks*; in short a preference
for the rather high-brow, 'serious' media tastes of teachers rather than the
popular media offerings most avidly consumed by their pupils.

This movement had received its official imprimatur with the publication of
the Newsom Report in 1963. In words directly echoing Crowther, the report
spoke of the need for schools to provide a 'counterbalancing assistance' to the
mass media, and, in a passage well known to all film teachers, of the necessity
of discrimination:

> We need to train children to look critically and discriminate between what
> is good and bad in what they see. They must learn to realize that many
> makers of films and of television programmes present false or distorted
> views of people, relationships, and experience in general, besides producing
> much trivial and worthless stuff made according to stock patterns.
>
> By presenting examples of films selected for the integrity of their
> treatment of human values, and the craftsmanship with which they were
> made, alongside others of mixed or poor quality, we can not only build up a
> way of evaluating but also lead the pupils to an understanding of film as a
> unique and potentially valuable art form in its own right as capable of
> communicating depth of experience as any other art form.[27]

It has often been remarked that Newsom was of immense importance in encouraging the serious study of film in colleges and schools since 1963. Newsom's influence upon the serious study of television has been less rarely scrutinised. It is worth observing in the above quotation that while film *and* television are condemned for presenting 'false or distorted views', television mysteriously disappears when examples of integrity and craftsmanship are mentioned. The report, notice, recommends the *way* in which film studies might develop – as the study of an *art form* comparable with literature, music and painting. Such an approach clearly has its limitations when applied to television, for though the medium might be said to have produced original works of aesthetic merit, it serves many other diverse functions. Newsom then provided the impetus for the establishment of 'high culture' courses in film at the expense of a medium clearly a more potent influence upon pupils, and a more integral part of their experience. It initiated a trend from which schools and colleges have scarcely yet begun to recover. Paradoxically the effect of Newsom was to *arrest* the development of the study of television by linking film and television together and encouraging teachers to think of them both in aesthetic terms, by failing to acknowledge the diverse functions of television and by offering no guidelines to teachers on how television might be studied in order to foster discrimination.[28] When teachers began to glimpse some of the pitfalls awaiting them on this particular route it is little wonder that they became reluctant to take the journey.

Richard Hoggart's attempts to move beyond this position and to interpret discrimination within the media rather more sympathetically clearly illustrate the potency of the concept and the peculiar grip it contrived to hold even upon those educators who could recognise the class basis of the current formulations. Writing in the *Observer* in 1961 he observed the tendency to carry

> . . . into new and confused areas of cultural activity, the old, comfortable grading by height of brow . . . reinforced by an implied social or edu-cational grading . . . 'Mass culture' is that enjoyed by the 80 per cent who have not been to a grammar school . . . The crucial distinctions today are not those between the *News of the World* and *The Observer*, between the Third Programme and the Light Programme . . . between the Top Ten and a celebrity concert . . . The distinctions we should be making are those between the *News of the World* and the *Sunday Pictorial*, between 'skiffle' and the Top Ten; and, for 'highbrows', between *The Observer* and the *Sunday Times*. This is to make distinctions . . . which require an active discrimination, not the application of a fixed 'brow' or educational scale . . . Our job is to separate the Processed from the Living at all levels . . . Processed culture has its eye always on the audience, the consumers, the customers. Living culture has its eye on the subject, the material. It expects the same attention to the subject from the members of its audience. Processed culture asks: 'What will they take? Will this get most

of them?' Living culture asks 'What is the truth of this experience and how can I capture it?'[29]

What Hoggart is arguing here is that old forms of discrimination did not really constitute active discrimination at all. They were rigid preformulated class judgements requiring 'the application of a fixed "brow" or educational scale'. Active discrimination on the other hand is classless and involves separating the Processed from the Living in each thing of its own kind. Hoggart's attempt to raise the concept of discrimination, Phoenix-like from its own ashes is based upon the assumption that class connotations have accreted around the word, and simply need to be hacked from it like limpets from a rock in order for the word to become serviceable again. It seems much more likely however that class consensi are incorporated within the word's denotative meaning, and are ultimately inseparable from it. To see why this is the case it is necessary to turn to a detailed consideration of the concept of discrimination itself.

Attention needs to be drawn at the outset to three important features of the word 'discrimination'. Most obviously – but also most crucially– it is, as Raymond Williams has recently pointed out, 'a split word with a positive sense for good and informed judgment but also a strong negative sense of unreasonable *exclusion* or unfair treatment of some outside groups'.[30] Indeed one meaning of the word still widely employed refers *only* to the process of treating certain groups unfairly.

Secondly the word elevates and generalises specific personal responses and preferences to the status of evident social facts. An example: on radio, film critic Alexander Walker discussing the making of a controversial film on the sex life of Christ says that controversies rarely surround films of any significance. He can think of only two exceptions: *Last Tango in Paris* and *A Clockwork Orange*.

The extensive nature of the 'hidden' exclusions is worth noting here, particularly for those who have followed Walker's public battles with Ken Russell. But it is the confidence, authority and glibness of judgement to which I really want to draw attention. And to its *ordinariness*. This kind of statement is the stock-in-trade of critics of all descriptions. There are no qualifications of the 'It-seems-to-me' or 'In-my-view' variety; the personal judgement is presented as straightforward fact, so that the listener might be forgiven for believing that film criticism had established well-defined and widely agreed criteria of evaluation. That the reverse is true ought to guarantee a degree of tentativeness in judgement which is conspicuously absent from the pronouncements of critics, and not a few media teachers.

Thirdly, 'this form of social development of personal responses to the point where they could be represented as standards of judgement'[31] was dependent on the social authority and confidence of the class making the response and indeed upon the existence of a social consensus of particular evaluations. The odd thing about 'discrimination' is that it is still widely used, yet it is blood brother to words such as 'taste', 'cultivation' and 'sensibility' which have been made virtually obsolete by their clear class overtones and by the fragmentation of the evaluative consensus which legitimised them. Discriminatory approaches in mass-media teaching – even Hoggart's – assume the existence and validity of a bourgeois hegemony. In the classroom the authority which the teacher requires to make his preferences into judgements are provided by his social class and his education. He it is who decides on what counts as discrimination and this remains true whether the struggle is between 'the shoddy and the worthwhile' of Whannel and Hall or 'the Processed and the Living' of Hoggart.

Those elements of exclusion and rejection which tend to be hidden in much of the talking and writing about discrimination *are its very cornerstones in practice*. And what is excluded and rejected, what is being discriminated against, are *inevitably* those aspects of popular culture which are valued and have a potent influence among large numbers of pupils. If this were not so – if the 'shoddy and debased' or 'the Processed' had no hold upon pupils – then discriminatory approaches would be unnecessary. Discriminatory teaching is premissed by the assumption that genuine differences are likely to exist between the teacher's view of what is Living and Processed, and the pupil's. (Again, if this were not so discriminatory teaching would be unnecessary.) These differences carry unequal weight in the classroom however. By the sleight of hand outlined above teacher views become discriminatory judgements, while pupil preferences, lacking either authority or an acceptable language code, remain at the low-level status of preferences.

Teaching discrimination therefore involves attacking the personal preferences of many pupils. It is a practice as socially divisive and individually destructive as attacks upon (i.e. attempts to 'improve') a pupil's language. A working-class pupil who has been taught discrimination has almost certainly also been taught that his own judgement is unreliable, and no basis for the development of aesthetic sensitivity. Taught to distrust or even despise the television programmes and magazines habitually watched or read at home, the danger is that he may come finally to despise his parents, friends and indeed himself. Fortunately I have seen no evidence to suggest that discrimination cuts very much ice with large numbers of comprehensive school pupils who obstinately persist in asserting the validity of their own tastes.

In addition to all this it needs to be said that there are particular problems associated with applying the notion of discrimination to the study of television. It is clearly an inappropriate tool for handling a good deal of television material: there seems little point in trying to discriminate between televised news bulletins, weather forecasts, football matches, race meetings, quiz programmes or chat shows. And even when it might seem to make sense – with plays or comedy series for example – how does one begin to do it? Little consensus exists on what constitutes 'good' and 'bad' television, and attempts to erect and defend generally agreed criteria for judgement have been singularly unsuccessful.[32] Finally any criteria which were widely agreed would have no universal validity but simply be part of that society's dominant ideology.[33]

It has been necessary to outline the historical development, and some of the theoretical problems and practical difficulties of teaching 'discrimination', for in spite of the recent development of alternative semiological approaches to media studies the concept continues to have a powerful hold upon the minds of educators.[34] Even commentators as sympathetic to the media and sensitive to the needs of pupils as Murdock and Phelps could say in 1973 that:

> In even the simplest, most mechanical production there may be something worth salvaging, and it is with this elementary act of salvage that any attempts to encourage appreciation and discrimination must begin. There will of course be a sizeable gap between the tastes and experiences of the pupils and those of the teachers. This is inevitable, given the differences in social class background, age and training. Nevertheless if teachers are prepared to understand their own experience of popular culture and to take seriously the judgments and discriminations of their pupils, then a constructive dialogue can begin.[35]

To see media education in terms of a somewhat desperate salvaging operation is hardly far removed from the old inoculation theories which Murdock and Phelps profess to deplore; nor is it likely to generate in teachers the high degree of commitment and energy necessary to establish the serious study of the media within the school curriculum. It is worth drawing attention too to a familiar theme in our analysis of discrimination – the way in which Murdock and Phelps manage to slide over the implications of exclusion and rejection inherent within a discriminatory approach. The final sentences of the quotation ironically suggest a final argument against the value of teaching discrimination. For the barriers to classroom dialogue which do exist within media studies are not only a result of the gap between teacher and pupil tastes and experiences, but grow inevitably out of the element of rejection of pupil tastes *and* the teacher's view of his task as salvage operation implicit in most discriminatory approaches. The writers are glimpsing what every practising teacher knows: that the objective of arriving at value judgements closes up rather than opens out discussion; that it is too *easy* to obtain evaluative responses from pupils, and thereafter too difficult to move beyond them; that as soon as a programme is evaluated as bad (or Processed) or good (or Authentic) then the impetus for further investigation disappears and is likely to be seen by pupils as an unnecessary 'pulling to pieces'; that evaluative responses force students to make individual stands and take personal positions, a more threatening procedure and ultimately one less productive of dialogue than say a systematic group exploration; that one of the keys to unlocking responses is to move students towards making statements which seem to them to have some validity, *irrespective* of their own personal feelings and tastes. If judgement can be suspended and mass-media material simply examined – *seen* more clearly – so that a wider and more complex range of meanings and values can become apparent, then discussion can flow and the necessity for discrimination, an irrelevance to the process of understanding, withers away.

The movement advocated here from appreciation to investigation is underpinned by a shift away from an elitist definition of *culture* – 'the best that has been thought and written in the world' – to a view of culture which is *descriptive* of the values manifest in the arts and institutions of a society and the behaviour of its groups and individuals. The gain is intellectual as well as obviously social and political. For under the first definition of culture very little can be said about a wide range of television programmes; they are simply 'trivial', 'processed' and unworthy of serious reflection. Yet such programmes all need elucidation, all need to be read as cultural texts, iconic in character, which can be decoded to reveal large numbers of meanings. The codings themselves will reveal and embody the ideology and professional practices of the broadcasting institutions, demonstrate the constructed and mediated nature of the 'normal' world of the programmes, and invite a comparison with other possible, but suppressed codings. It is with cultural criticism in this sense that the study of television should be concerned.

2
The Methodology and Organisation of Television Studies

1. The significance of methodology

Perhaps the single most important development in educational thinking within the past decade has been the elevation of the status of methodology within the learning process. Good primary school practice has for years been based upon the premiss that children learn most effectively by 'doing', but the full implications of the truism have not been clearly articulated until very recently even in relation to primary education, while secondary school practice still continues to function as though methodology were a form of pill-sugaring, a way of making palatable what is really being learned, the subject content itself. Media education has been no exception to this general trend. Overwhelmingly, writing on media studies has been concerned with questions of content. There are syllabuses, prescriptions and blueprints aplenty. There are, less frequently, accounts of classroom practice, though suggestions for classroom activities tend to be treated in a partial and fragmented way. And even on those rare occasions when problems of classroom organisation and methodology are explicitly discussed, the primacy of 'content' is rarely seriously questioned.

No anecdote about life in classrooms more succinctly summarises the way in which the most effective learning within schools is conveyed implicitly through classroom methodology and practice than the story of Boris recounted by the American sociologist, Jules Henry. It is a practice which is powerfully reinforced by the school's formal organisation and its social rituals to form a 'hidden curriculum' which is far more effectively learned, because daily *enacted*, than formal subject content, most of which is 'learned' for regurgitation and quickly forgotten:

> Boris had trouble reducing 12/16 to the lowest terms and could only get as far as 6/8. The teacher asked him quietly if that was as far as he could reduce it. She suggested he 'think'.
> Much heaving up and down and waving of hands by the other children, all frantic to correct him. Boris pretty unhappy, probably mentally

paralysed. The teacher quiet, patient, ignores the others and concentrates with look and voice on Boris. After a minute or two she turns to the class and says, 'Well, who can tell Boris what the number is?' A forest of hands appears, and the teacher calls Peggy. Peggy says that four may be divided into the numerator and the denominator.[1]

Henry comments:

Boris's failure made it possible for Peggy to succeed; his misery is the occasion for her rejoicing. This is a standard condition of the contemporary American elementary school. To a Zuni, Hopi or Dakota Indian, Peggy's performance would seem cruel beyond belief, for competition, the wringing of success from somebody's failure, is a form of torture foreign to those non-competitive cultures.

Looked at from Boris's point of view, the nightmare at the blackboard was, perhaps, a lesson in controlling himself so that he would not fly shrieking from the room under enormous public pressure. Such experiences force every man reared in our culture, over and over again, night in, night out, even at the pinnacle of success, to dream not of success, but of failure. In school the external nightmare is internalized for life. Boris was not learning arithmetic only; he was learning the essential nightmare also. To be successful in our culture one must learn to dream of failure.[2]

Two further points are worth making about the story. First of all this is a good class. Boris's teacher is no ogre, but 'quiet, patient' and obviously compassionate. She is however completely unaware of the dimensions of the situation to which Henry alludes. With an unsympathetic teacher the situation would be made even worse. Secondly the situation is as disastrous for Peggy as it is for Boris, encouraging in her feelings of superiority which when multiplied over a school career seem designed to engender the kind of arrogance and elitism all too common in 'successful' school pupils. The crux of the matter, however, is that here Boris and Peggy are learning less about reducing fractions than they are about a whole range of appropriate social attitudes and behaviour patterns. Boris is in no position to learn anything other than that fractions can be used as instruments for his discomfort; in the future he will be slightly more effective in his avoidance of so public an exposure of his ignorance.

The work of John Holt, that great anatomist of pupil strategies for avoiding failure, graphically describes to us what schooling looks like from the pupils' point of view. The fear of displeasing the teacher, the fear of being made to look a fool in front of his peers, and the fear of having his ignorance exposed all make life for the pupil a matter of survival rather than learning. He becomes skilful above all in adopting techniques which will keep the teacher happy by producing right answers fast. The teacher's addiction to the right answer has been elaborated by David Hargreaves:

> The teacher's instructional role was defined as the task of getting the pupils to learn and to *show evidence of that learning* . . . This is a surprisingly difficult task . . . At root the evidence on which the teacher relies is the child's ability to produce, in written or oral form, the right answer to the problems imposed by the teacher.
>
> The teacher's reliance on right answers, and his desire to obtain plenty of them, indicates that from the pupil's point of view much of his behaviour is answer-centred. The teacher sets the problems and the task of the pupils is to find the right answer which will please the teacher. They know that the teacher knows the answer; it is there in the teacher's mind. Their job is to hunt around until it can be found. The focus is not so much on the problem itself as a problem, but on chasing the answer. The result is that schools encourage producers, the pupils who can get the 'right answers', and may thus be discouraging places for thinkers.[3]

The object of education for students then becomes not learning but the production of *presumed evidence* of learning, that is, right answers, and this remains true both of the primary school pupil engaged in a class discussion with his teacher, and the university student sitting his final examinations. Alienated learning – learning whose real purpose and meaning lie outside of itself – exists on a truly massive scale, and is firmly institutionalised, from the degrees and diplomas of universities to the 'stars' and marks of the primary school. *Instrumentalism*, 'The elevation of otherwise meaningless activities into worthwhile goals because of the rewards which successful performance brings'[4] is one of the things most effectively taught by schools and learned by pupils. Douglas Holly:

> In many schools, for instance, great emphasis is placed on 'marks'. No one asks the worth of the tasks which are performed or whether they are educative: what matters is whether they can earn points. For this purpose, knowing how to spell Othello is of greater moment than understanding what is at stake in Shakespeare's play, since the orthographical knowledge though humble is easy to score while conceptual awareness is a complex matter and difficult to assess . . . To object to any given system of marking, though, is to miss the point. It is the idea of marking itself which is in question. Pupils working for marks are working for something external, not only to themselves but to the very subject-matter they are dealing with . . . This is essentially instrumental thinking. It is also essentially alienated, separating the meaning of the activity from the activity itself.[5]

It is an interesting sign of the times that so many books now written about education begin by assuming the pointlessness of what goes on in classrooms. Here are two passages written not by theoreticians or academic de-schoolers but by practising teachers, the first a former grammar school teacher in Norfolk, the second a Scottish headmaster with a lifetime of teaching behind him:

> None of these Norfolk boys saw any point in learning French: I didn't see much point in teaching them French. But that was what I was qualified to do and what I was paid for. And it was on the timetable.
>
> So we went through all the right rituals. I gave them homework and most of them did it. I counted the exercise books when they were handed in and pretended to make a fuss about the ones that were missing. I gave them tests: they ostentatiously stopped each other from copying. Then they swopped papers, and marked each other's answers, and argued about half-marks. And I wrote down the marks in a big book, and totted up the positions each term.
>
> We got on very well together. And every French period we waited eagerly for the bell to go. Nobody learnt much French.[6]

As far as secondary modern children of our own day are concerned, what is the effect and what are the advantages of this bumbling educational tradition? Almost nil. The evidence grows that their ten years of desk-sitting makes little positive impression on our pupils. All those sums and interpretation exercises, the causes and results of wars, the imports and exports – where has all the knowledge gone? Down the drain, mostly. If all our schools, primary and secondary, were wiped out tomorrow, apart from a little temporary inconvenience, the country would hardly know the difference.

At first, anyway. Later there would be such an upsurge of cultural interest, released from the pressure of school education, that half our major problems would be solved within a decade.[7]

Why is it that the explicit content of the curriculum contributes so little to what is actually learned by students in educational institutions? Perhaps the most coherent answer has been provided by the Brazilian educator Paulo Freire who has drawn attention to three crucial features of conventional institutionalised learning: it is essentially conceived of in terms of the *depositing* of knowledge via a *narrative* mode within a *hierarchical* teacher–pupil relationship. This has been astutely termed by Freire, the 'banking' concept of education:

> Banking education maintains and even stimulates the contradiction [between teacher and student] through the following attitudes and practices, which mirror oppressive society as a whole:

1. The teacher teaches and the students are taught.
2. The teacher knows everything and the students know nothing.
3. The teacher thinks and the students are thought about.
4. The teacher talks and the students listen – meekly.
5. The teacher disciplines and the students are disciplined.
6. The teacher chooses and enforces his choice, and the students comply.
7. The teacher acts and the students have the illusion of acting through the action of the teacher.
8. The teacher chooses the programme content, and the students (who were not consulted) adapt to it.
9. The teacher confuses the authority of knowledge with his own professional authority, which he sets in opposition to the freedom of the students.
10. The teacher is the subject of the learning process, while the pupils are mere objects . . .

It follows logically from the banking notion of consciousness that the educator's . . . task is . . . to 'fill' the students by making deposits of information which he considers constitute true knowledge. And since men 'receive' the world as passive entities, education should make them more passive still, and adapt them to the world. The educated man is the adapted man, because he is more 'fit' for the world. Translated into practice, this concept is well suited to the purposes of the oppressors, whose tranquility rests on how well men fit the world the oppressors have created, and how little they question it.[8]

For Freire the student–teacher 'contradiction' can be resolved through a dialogue which makes both simultaneously teachers and students. The relationship between material and learner should be an active and dynamic one, and knowledge not a deadening deposit to be accommodated to but an instrument whose cutting edge can at once express individuality and transform reality. The precondition of this development has been termed by Freire 'conscientization', an awareness of one's own political situation and a recognition that far from being a 'given' which must be accommodated to, reality is negotiable, the result of human choices and decisions which should be subject to scrutiny, criticism, intervention and change. The implications of this are of course far-reaching, and reveal such labels as 'language deprivation' and 'compensatory education', such practices as streaming, and even the concept of 'subjects', as instruments of oppression and control, all aspects of seeing reality as something outside of the individual, part of an a-political and knowable world to which he must adapt.

How does all of this relate to the study of television? One answer to that question can be found in the remainder of this chapter. But from the outset it ought to be stated clearly that the introduction of television studies into the school curriculum will serve little useful purpose if it is taught in the same kind

of way as other school subjects since the essential messages passed to students
will remain the same as they always were. This, in effect, is what has happened
to film studies in schools. John Ford and westerns may have replaced
Shakespeare and tragedy, but the curriculum remains a course determined by
the teacher and jumped by the pupils, transmission continues to be
hierarchical with the teacher very much the expert (I see no evidence that film
teaching is any less authoritarian than other kinds; in practice it often seems
more doctrinaire), and the crucial relationship of pupil to subject-matter
remains much the same. The liveliest educational discussion revolves around
the most effective ways of examining the knowledge deposited and a
'demystification' is attempted which never confronts the material educational
mystifications within which teacher and students are alike ensnared. The time
has come for media teachers to recognise, as they above all others should, that
in education too the medium is the message, and that the most powerful
meanings are carried not by the content of what they teach but by its form.

One of the most important implications of this for the television teacher has
already been touched upon. A central aim in television teaching is demystification – an examination of the rituals, conventions and practices through
which a dominant ideology is disseminated via the medium. But, as I have
suggested, to attempt to achieve this within a content-orientated, teacher-
dominated, examination-assessed structure which itself goes unexamined is
to be peculiarly perverse. Because the educational system is precisely the
point at which mystification and alienation are woven most closely into the
experience of students, it follows that the content of any course aiming at
demystification must include an examination of the educational process itself.
What is to be learned, how it is to be learned, and how evaluated must be the
subjects of constant and continuing dialogue between teacher and students.
Why is this a success? Why did this approach fail? Why isn't this discussion
getting off the ground? are questions which teachers tend to ask of themselves
but which might more helpfully be recognised as group problems which
teacher and students will need to hammer out together. Intelligence,
knowledge and what counts as knowledge, the function of examinations,
streaming, and the nature of subjects should all be the subject not of forced
and predetermined discussion, but of serious analysis as they arise from the
concrete situations within which students and their teachers find themselves.
Understanding television as a 'consciousness industry' can best be fostered by
bringing an ideological awareness to bear upon school situations. In this
respect collective school rituals such as assemblies, house-meetings, speech
days and the like are especially susceptible to observation and analysis, and
Everett Reimer has suggested models through which this kind of analysis
might be carried out.[9]

There is a further reason for attaching particular importance to the
discussion of organisational and methodological principles. Because education is itself the subject of a good deal of attention by television, educational

assumptions and alternatives will inevitably be of some importance in studying the medium; the teacher will constantly find that media insights are simply transmutations of earlier educational analyses. One of the three classic functions of television is to instruct, and the nature of televisual instruction as well as the semantic and philosophic problems relating to possible definitions of instruction, entertainment and information will play an important part in most television courses. But apart from this, programmes such as *University Challenge, Mastermind* and *Top of the Form* (which link actual educational institutions to the medium) all make statements about what counts as expertise and knowledge and the same could be said of programmes as diverse as *Match of the Day, The Nine O'Clock News* and *Tomorrow's World.* In addition there is the 'official' educational output of programmes for schools and colleges which all students will have seen but which can now be examined not so much for their content but for their values and assumptions. There are hours of Open University and pre-school transmissions to say nothing of the perennial discussions, news stories, interviews and talk-ins on educational topics on magazine programmes such as *Nationwide* and *Tonight.* There are, too, myriad dramatisations of educational problems and issues from the full and complex treatment of a play like Barry Hines' *Speech Day* to incidental characters in series and soap operas like Ken Barlow, the teacher-turned-business-executive of *Coronation Street.* All of this represents a massive output to which students will only respond critically if they are engaged in a simultaneous dialogue about their own education. Only dialogue can enable them to develop perspectives within which they can place the mediated view of education presented to them by television.

2. Television studies: some principles of organisation and methodology

What, then, are the most important methodological and organisational principles to be adduced for the study of television?

Methodology itself is of prime importance and must be constantly discussed and reviewed since:

1. it is integral to what the group will really be learning.
2. demystification of television images is likely to be more successful if it is carried on alongside an examination of more concrete examples of mystification which lie within the immediate institutional experience of pupils.
3. insights developed in this area can feed directly into the analysis of a great deal of television material.

There should be as little competition, grading and examination as possible, and when these devices are used they should always have as their prime purpose the facilitation of the pupil's own learning and self-evaluation. It might be possible to replace alienated learning by real learning: (i) if *pupils* can come to see tasks as relevant ends in themselves rather than as ways of achieving marks; and (ii) if *teachers* can place the development of the mind of the individual pupil rather than the depositing of subject material at the centre of the educational experience.

The nature of television studies makes it particularly important for the teacher to resolve the teacher–pupil dichotomy. The role of 'expert' would be very difficult for the teacher to sustain even if he wished to, since what constitutes 'good and bad' television, or 'right' and 'wrong' in television practice is not only highly problematic, but, as I have suggested in Chapter 1, a sterile area for exploration. Furthermore the teacher does not control his subject material, does not *possess* it in the way that traditional subject teachers do. Most of the information within the television studies class will inevitably be transmitted laterally, from the medium across to pupils rather than hierarchically from teacher down to pupils. For these reasons *the teacher might best regard himself as a senior colleague* – older and more experienced in analysis – *working with junior colleagues, rather than as an expert who will make all the important decisions and through whom all communications will pass.*[10]

The teacher's own resources will actually compare poorly with those of his group who will quite literally see more than he does, and bring to what they see a range of backgrounds, perspectives and understandings which will be beyond the wit of any individual teacher or student. *The focus of learning within television studies should therefore be the group rather than the individual.* Attention is transferred away from the teacher's problem of traditional education ('How can I transmit and make palatable this information?') towards the problems facing, and only soluble by, the group (for example, 'How can the flow of information within the group be improved?').

Television studies should be taught in mixed-ability groups. Streaming is not simply a method of organisation but *a way of valuing* some pupil responses over others. Learning is a highly individualised activity however – even within streamed groups – and the television teacher in particular needs to value all genuine responses, and to understand that from the point of view of the learner each has an equal validity. In addition, of course, it needs to be stressed that the most potent learnings of streamed groups are social in nature and permeate, with disastrous consequences, every aspect of the nation's social, political and industrial life, encouraging an individualistic and often arrogant elitism in top groups, and a destructive 'delinquescent' group solidarity in low streams.[11] In heterogeneous television studies groups, social, political, aesthetic and intellectual development have the opportunity of growing apace.

Learning should be active wherever possible and emerge from group activity and dialogue. Hence the importance placed in this book upon simulation exercises, games, practical activities and discussion. The acquisition of information will play very little part in television studies but developmental processes will. Ostensible content is merely a means to an end and options as to which aspects of television are to be studied should be left as open as possible, so that particular enthusiasms and topical interests can be fully tapped. What is of prime significance is the *critical interaction of the mind of the student and the material*, rather than the particularity of the material itself. It should be added here that television studies itself ought not to be compulsory but part of a wide-ranging option system within the school curriculum.

* * *

The principles outlined here are not offered as a theoretical blueprint, but as descriptive generalisations of an ongoing television studies practice. Some of the problems which these principles attempt to meet have already been discussed, but this methodology in turn gives rise to a number of practical difficulties within the classroom. It is to a consideration of these problems that we must now turn.

3. Organisation and methodology: practical difficulties

a. Marking and assessment

Jettisoning marks is the first step towards a more human and organic approach to learning. When marks disappear so, by magic, do some of the most obnoxious kinds of classroom behaviour – cheating, copying, mark-grubbing and other immature manifestations of competition. Whenever I have suggested to pupils that the necessary first step towards real learning is a greater degree of self-evaluation and a concentration upon abilities really developed rather than marks gained by fair means or foul, an animated discussion has inevitably followed. It is a discussion of some importance, for it is probably the first in which pupils have participated about the nature of their own education and learning. It is the first but it will not be the last for when marks have been removed, attention inevitably focuses upon the real processes of learning. It ought to be axiomatic in any teaching based upon developmental processes rather than content transmission that pupils themselves should have some idea at each stage of the process they are passing through, and of the abilities they are acquiring. Strangely, this rarely seems to happen. Even amongst those teachers who think of content as a means to an end, and are more concerned with the development of transferable abilities and attitudes which will remain long after the course content has been forgotten, the number who have actually thought of communicating this view of the curriculum *to their pupils* is miniscule. Pupils are, apparently, expected to acquire abilities of which they have never been made explicitly aware. Yet there needs to be a high degree of pupil awareness of the processes with which he is involved if there is to be any significant movement towards self-evaluation and if the processes are to be related to his own development. It is not only the teacher, but most crucially the student himself who will need to reflect upon the ways he has developed and changed, upon what he thinks he has learned and upon what the strengths and weaknesses of a particular unit of work have been, so that self-evaluation actually merges into an ongoing course evaluation. Paradoxically, placing pupil attitudes and skills at the centre of the educational process forces attention back to the subject-matter itself and to the problems which arise when students encounter it. Traditional questions about content which demand simple regurgitation can now, however, be replaced by questions demanding content evaluation in personal terms by each pupil: What sense did you make of this material? How does it relate to previous understandings? How has it affected you in terms of awareness, knowledge, motivation or attitudes?

Of the pupil's own work, prime importance should be attached to the way in which it is regarded by the pupil himself. Does it represent a real step forward, a real commitment, a real interest? Or is it merely going through the motions, fulfilling the requirements of the course, but empty of personal involvement? Ultimately evaluation can be filtered down to a single criterion – the extent to which a piece of work exhibits any intellectual interest or commitment to its subject – and a single question: Is there any real purpose to this communication or are the requirements of the course its sole *raison d'être*? The person best placed to answer that is the student himself, and it is the value *he* places upon his own work which is of prime importance. The teacher will not withhold comments (indeed because he does not award marks, there is an *extra* burden upon him to try to assess the strengths and weaknesses of the work), but they should be constructive, helpful and express an honest opinion. If a student really hasn't done himself justice in a piece of work the teacher should say so. But this is a comment upon the work and not the *person* of the student, and the teacher must talk about this distinction with his group, and act upon it himself in his contact with them. The purpose of a teacher's comments should be to help his pupils' learning, and not to judge, rank or discriminate between them. What he offers above all is a personal opinion, and not an ultimate truth, and his comments should be seen as the beginning of a dialogue rather than as the final authoritative word.

There are of course institutional and outside pressures upon teachers to discriminate between pupils as finely as possible. The dilemma facing all teachers who can see clearly enough the harm done by the examination system is a familiar one: if the subject is not examined, however important it is seen to be by the teacher and his pupils, it will enjoy low status within the school and have little prestige amongst pupils and parents. And if pupils are doing genuinely worthwhile work, why should they be penalised? Why not devise a 'liberal' Mode III CSE or GCE examination, compromising as few principles as possible, so that pupils can have the best of both worlds – a sound education and an examination certificate at the end of it? Such thinking is largely illusory. Examinations exist to divide and discriminate between people; they create and institutionalise failure; important qualities that ought to be at the centre of any worthwhile education – self-understanding, aesthetic and social sensitivity, intellectual curiosity and creativity – get pushed to the fringes because they are not conventionally examinable and wither away when they are measured not in personal terms, but against other people's or a mythical norm. Examinations affect the way in which the teacher regards his students (making his relationship primarily a judgemental one) and the way in which the students regard him and each other. Co-operative learning becomes difficult if not impossible to achieve, and the important purposes of learning come to be seen as irrelevant as teachers teach and students 'learn' with the examination in mind. Finally, it is possible to see Mode iii examinations not merely as reformist, masking their true function under a seemingly liberal patina, but as an enormous confidence trick which is being played upon both teachers and students alike. Most employers seem to know little about CSE and often care even less. The influence of a Grade 3 or 4 pass in CSE is negligible, yet it is used as an instrument of control, both stick and carrot, as teachers persuade recalcitrant students that the meaningless charade they are playing out for the final two whole years of their school lives is of some importance.

In this situation what can teachers realistically do? As I shall suggest later in this chapter, on an *institutional* level, realistic possibilities exist for those schools who wish to do so to break with the examination system. But what can be achieved by the *individual* television teacher who is working within an examination-orientated school? First of all he can encourage critical scrutiny by his pupils of the issues raised here, making them aware of what the examination system is and what it does; they themselves have a great deal of responsibility in deciding how to respond to it. Secondly he can initiate discussions in his own institution about the function of examinations and grading systems within it. Thirdly he can attempt to turn the examination system into a medium for self-evaluation. Is this idealistic pie-in-the-sky? Here is part of one pupil's course evaluation. Typical of the responses received it does indicate I think that our students can develop the ability, sensitivity and self-awareness to undertake their own self-assessment:

Before this course I had never really criticised a television programme properly except by saying it was good or bad. I had never really thought about the effects of television or how it communicates ideas. I now know a little about how to evaluate or criticise a television programme which I think is an art that has to be learned. My first attempts at writing about television programmes were not as good as the later ones. At first I tended to write about my own feelings regarding the programmes instead of writing something that was true of everybody.

We spent a lot of time in discussion after watching programmes. The group would talk about the programme together rather than just sit down and write or answer questions. In this way a lot of different ideas came together. The other members of the group sometimes had different ideas to mine and by discussing I managed to get some subjects clearer in my mind. Although this meant that we had to do most of our written work at home I think I gained quite a lot from these discussions. My ideas on education, for example, have changed. I think that the most important part of the course for me was when we went out of school to interview people. We had to go up to people we had never seen before and talk to them. I think that these interviews showed me how nice it was to communicate with people although I found it quite difficult to ask the right questions and keep the conversation going. I'm still shy sometimes but before the interviews I think I was too defensive and reserved when talking to people. At least I want to get on with people more now. (Kathryn Stuart)

The lines between course evaluation and self-assessment are already becoming blurred here. The step towards handing these pupils full responsibility for their own final assessment is not a radical measure but a logical one. How will students respond to the challenge of self-grading? Reactions will vary with each individual. In the case of one pupil it produced an effective result of stunning immediacy. Likeable, but scarcely hard-working, he suddenly realised that his immediate future lay in his own hands. He wanted a high-grade CSE pass and worked unstintingly in the final part of the course to achieve it, writing essays with skill, commitment and alacrity in order to justify his own grading. In retrospect it is difficult to imagine any teaching device or method which could have produced so startling and instant an effect. The vast majority of pupils reacted less spectacularly but nevertheless seriously and responsibly. If they had worked with interest and commitment they graded themselves highly (though frequently not highly enough in my opinion); a few, recognising that their real interests lay elsewhere, awarded themselves lower grades.

Other problems relating to self-evaluation exist in theory, though I have never encountered them in fact. A common hypothesis is: 'What if a weak student grades himself high?' The terms of the question betray an inherent bias: the normative 'weak' here really means 'considered weak by the teacher'. Clearly the student doesn't consider himself weak. An area of disagreement exists which needs to be brought out into the open and discussed by both student and teacher. It could well be, for example, that the student has spent more time, effort and energy upon his work than the teacher can discern. Given the fact that both parties are open to persuasion, however, most conflicts ought to be easily resolvable. It needs to be repeated that I have never encountered a situation of this kind with any pupils though a common problem is of a pupil *undergrading* himself by the teacher's evaluation. Again dialogue quickly resolves this discrepancy.[12]

(Self-evaluative procedures of the kind described above are probably the best that can be hoped for by the individual teacher working within the state system. But I cannot help feeling that the first state schools to break completely with formal examinations and concentrate their attention on giving a good education and turning out questioning, interested, articulate and creative pupils, who have some self-understanding and who have produced real work will have a tremendous advantage over schools whose students spend vast quantities of time preparing for examinations which encourage none of these qualities. If a courageous headteacher and his staff can work hard to convince parents, and make known the policy of their school both locally and nationally, their students, backed by detailed reports and perhaps examples of work, would, far from suffering, have a head start in seeking employment or university and college entry over the familiar 'successes' of the present school system, those thousands of leavers with O and A levels, who seem to have scarcely an interest or idea in their heads, and who know neither where they are at, nor where they are going. 'Official' entry requirements can be by-passed by professors, college principals and employers if it means holding on to outstanding people, for the purpose of these requirements is not to exclude the able. Indeed the appearance of self-evidently capable students who have not taken GCE or CSE upon a market in which institutions are chasing an ever-decreasing number of good students is an obvious pressure upon institutions to review the effectiveness of their own admission policies.)

I have retained the above paragraph in parenthesis as a graphic example of how much education has regressed since early 1977 when it was first written. Then it seemed a realistic assessment of what was possible in schools; some institutions indeed were already well-embarked upon such a course. At the present time, the almost universal popular equation of educational standards with examination passes, the protection of educational privilege under the banner of freedom for all, the winning over of large numbers of parents to an increasingly instrumental view of education, the prevalence in the popular press of stories in which 'any angle that shows state education, in particular comprehensive schools, up in a bad light is taken', have combined to produce a cultural climate so hostile to progressive teaching as to make such hopes seem Utopian. This, however, may be too pessimistic a view. Joanna Mack in a survey of recent press coverage of schools concludes that 'if a school is not a bad school, and most importantly has the confidence of the parents, bad publicity cannot damage the school and may even strengthen it by bringing in the parents'. Even sustained hostility of the kind shown by the *Leicester Mercury* towards Countesthorpe College, in which any information that could discredit the school would be given large coverage, had the effect of demonstrating a real depth of support among the mass of parents. Indeed, at one famous public meeting, 'the parents spent the whole meeting in a bitter, vehement and prolonged attack on the *Leicester Mercury's* correspondent who was present about what they considered to be the *Mercury's* blatantly unfair coverage. The parents had first-hand experience of the school; they knew their children enjoyed school and schoolwork and worked hard. Reading second-hand accounts cannot change views that are based on experience.'[13]

The message here is clear. Schools need to take public relations much more seriously than they have traditionally done, and the television teacher, in particular, will need to work very hard to keep parents, and indeed his own colleagues, informed about and supportive of his own innovative work. Failure to do so will create an ideological gap which may, as the past few years have shown, be all too eagerly filled by less informed, less sympathetic and more strident voices than his own.

b. Discussion problems

One of the dangers of television studies is that it can easily degenerate into a viewing-discussion-writing pattern of activity which is limited and stereotyped. For this reason the emphasis in the pages which follow will be upon *activities* and participatory exercises. Nevertheless there will be, inevitably, a good deal of discussion within television studies and the teacher will want these classes to go well. In my own experience they have all too often gone badly. There are a number of very good reasons for this. If students are unaccustomed to discussing problems in other classes, if their opinion counts for nothing during most of their school life then whole classes can literally lose their voice, becoming part of a passive 'culture of silence' which an individual teacher working in isolation will find extremely difficult to break through. Even given a willingness amongst students to participate in discussion, they may simply lack the skills to make the exercise work; they may fail to listen to the arguments of others perhaps, or be unable to see the relationship between evidence and conclusions. Simple difficulties of this kind virtually sabotaged the Schools Council's Humanities Curriculum Project, which produced at considerable expense multimedia discussion 'starters' and stimuli for 'injection' when discussion faltered. The assumption upon which the material was based – that students were in fact able to conduct a discussion under the guidance of a neutral chairman – alas proved to be too often without foundation.[14]

A third factor, and a very pertinent one to film and television work, is the difficulty inherent in articulating a response to a very recent aesthetic experience – particularly one which is largely non-verbal. Articulating an immediate yet coherent response to a film or television programme which has just been seen isn't easy for anyone and to expect this of school pupils may be demanding more than ought reasonably to be asked. As I shall suggest (Chapter 10), an aesthetic experience needs to be lived with and worked through until the individual achieves his own synthesis in his own good time. Time is the important factor however, and it is the very ingredient of which the teacher deprives the student if he precipitates him into discussion immediately after viewing.

This lesson, like most in this chapter, was taught to me by my own pupils about three years ago. In those days studying television, to me, simply meant discussing programmes after watching them. I remember on one occasion that after watching *This Is Your Life* nobody in the group had anything to say about it. This was very much part of a recurring pattern. I tried not to impose my own framework upon discussion but left it as open as possible for general reactions. Neither this, nor more positive attempts to structure discussion provoked much response. I have since discovered that this kind of situation is not uncommon. Here is Albert Hunt's description of his experiences of running a film course with art college students in Bradford:

> One morning I'd been looking at a comedy with a group of second-year textile students, and I'd tried to open up a discussion about different kinds of humour. The usual two or three students talked aimlessly for a while – some of them got involved in a meaningless wrangle. Suddenly, a girl said: 'Why do you have to spoil everything for us? The film was all right. Why do we have to sit here taking it to pieces?'
>
> We broke for coffee. After the break there would still be an hour and a half to go. I too felt that I couldn't stand another session of aimless talk. I went into the library and found a few copies of Brecht's *The Caucasian Chalk Circle*.[15]

Albert Hunt then describes how the group ingeniously improvised a short scene from the play and followed this with a discussion in which everyone was 'involved and interested'. *Hopes for Great Happenings* is a testament both to Hunt's inventiveness as a teacher and to the quality of his relationships with his students; but attention needs to be paid to the assumptions lying behind his resolution of the problem. Hunt conceives of his difficulty as a *teacher* problem, and it is ultimately resolved through his own initiative in going to the library and picking up Brecht. By his action the students are transformed from passive to happy and more active consumers. But they remain consumers, and they will remain happy for only so long as the teacher is able to entertain and involve them. In my own situation I tended to conceive of the situation from the outset as a *group* problem. After all, the students were wasting their time just as much as I was wasting mine. I assumed from the beginning that it must be possible for a group of people to discover ways in which they could spend their time together more profitably. The initiatives were in their hands as much as mine.

As soon as the problem had been stated in those terms, ideas and possible solutions flowed freely. The real difficulty, the group said, had been caused by my expectation of an immediate response to unfamiliar material. What they needed was time; time to think, digest and talk about the material in their own way: 'Leave us alone for twenty minutes. Let us talk about the programme amongst ourselves and then we will be ready for you.' And this was the procedure we followed thereafter. It was a process in which 'progress' was much slower than I had anticipated, but the progress was at least genuine and the group generally seemed more responsible, mature and sensitive in their attitude towards the tasks they were engaged in than they had been before. The key of course lay less in their solution than in the fact that they had formulated it themselves. In subsequent impasses and blockages with groups I have asked the same question ('What are we as a group going to do about this problem?') and I have, without exception, been surprised at the seriousness of the response and the fertility of the solutions which it has stimulated. To ask the question, however, is to turn a significant portion of the power and responsibility for what goes on in the classroom over to the group as a whole. It is their learning, their time, their lives which are at stake here, and they should have as much responsibility for determining it as the teacher dares to give. This is no abdication of teacher responsibility for he is a significant member of the group, older and more experienced, in many ways genuinely wiser, than his students and he will find inevitably that his opinions will count for a great deal.[16] Finally it should be stressed that group resolution of discussion problems as advocated here should not be regarded as an isolated way of solving particular problems but should form part of a whole pattern of group responsibilities of the kind discussed throughout this chapter.

c. Organisational minutiae

In the daily life of a school, philosophical questions play a less important part than such mundane and apparently trivial matters as room allocations, timetabling arrangements, departmental allowances, pupil option systems and the like. A coherent philosophy of television education is a threadbare garment for a teacher exposed, on the last period of a Friday afternoon, to an F stream who don't want to be there, in a room, cold in winter and hot in summer, which is filled with rows of desks, and a videotape recorder which doesn't work. To a degree rarely acknowledged by educational writers, successful teaching largely depends upon the ability of the teacher to manipulate the minutiae of school life to prevent such situations arising and to produce for his pupils the best possible working conditions.

Upon what principles should the television teacher proceed in order to accomplish this task? First of all it is of immeasurable importance to establish a base and an identity for the subject. A television room is needed in which all television classes will be taught, all television equipment centralised, and upon which the television teacher will have the first claim. Because television studies is a new curriculum area and because the television teacher is unlikely to be exclusively identified with television studies (he will teach other subjects as well) pupils may tend to regard the activity as nebulous, impermanent and lacking an identity, a feeling which will only be heightened if the television teacher is habitually seen on the move, haunting the corridors like a ubiquitous spook, risking hernias and slipped discs as he drags his inordinately heavy equipment to a far-off classroom. The existence of something called a television room, whatever its contents, establishes the permanent existence of a particular kind of activity which is quite different from those which go on inside other rooms. A television studies room should ideally contain:

1. At least one large television set, preferably coloured, for viewing by entire groups.
2. At least one, but preferably two, reel-to-reel videotape recorders, and if possible a colour cassette-recorder with pre-set timing device (a teacher would be ill-advised to begin a television studies course with only one VTR).
3. A portable television camera and pack.
4. Equipment for simple studio work. What this consists of will depend entirely upon the ambitions of the teacher and the amount of money at his disposal. Most teachers will need to seek specialist advice on how best to meet their specific needs.
5. An acoustic area – carpeted and curtained.
6. Apart from acoustic efficiency, the room should be carpeted for dramatic purposes, as well as for comfort.
7. Blackout facilities.
8. A 16 mm film projector.
9. A screen.
10. A slide projector.
11. A large supply of videotapes and videocassettes.
12. A trolley for transporting equipment.
13. A blackboard.
14. Comfortable easy chairs for every pupil in the group.
15. Functional and easily stackable chairs and tables.
16. A large notice board for displays of work and items of interest.
17. A good aerial system running into a convenient place.
18. A plentiful supply of electric wall plugs.
19. Six cassette tape recorders and as many cassettes as there are pupils in a group.
20. A good reel-to-reel tape recorder, preferably one upon which tape can be edited.

21. Adequate space for storing equipment and furniture.
22. A television resources area including:
    (a) videotapes;
    (b) sound tapes;
    (c) a library containing not only books of the kind suggested in the bibliography to this book, but also popular paperback spin-offs from television shows;
    (d) boxed material on issues such as censorship, advertising, television and violence, etc.;
    (e) slides from television programmes.
23. A still camera.
24. Space for movement and flexible seating arrangements.

The television teacher has a strong case for a generous departmental allowance as well as the assistance of a technician or technical teacher. He also has a case for special timetable provision. The nature of his work makes single periods of little value to him. Double periods, preferably during the morning, should be arranged (avoid Friday afternoons if possible), and block periods of full and half days should be secured at the end of school terms for practical work.

Having acquired a usable room, a capitation allowance and a workable timetable the television teacher should try to ensure that the pupils who come to him do so out of *some* interest, and are reasonably well informed about the nature of the work they will undertake. He should try to ensure, that is, that his class is part of a subject option system and that all pupils are well informed of what goes on in the television class before they make their choice of subjects. Having achieved all of this, he is now ready to receive his class. What he can do with them when they arrive is the subject of the rest of this book.

3

Towards Teleliteracy—1: Exercises in Perception and Non-Verbal Communication

The following two chapters present some possible components of a visual literacy programme with special reference to television literacy. The exercises in this chapter do not relate directly to television at all, but attempt, using much simpler material, to develop awarenesses and abilities which might later be applied to the much more complex amalgam of sounds and images which constitute television programmes. Chapter 4 introduces a number of concepts important for an understanding of television programmes through the use of simple television material.

The exercises in this chapter developed out of a series of unsuccessful attempts to encourage a group of students to respond to television programmes they had just seen. Uninterested in moving beyond a few evaluative responses, they also seemed to lack the skills and abilities to take these responses any further. What could be done to improve the situation? One of the major reasons why discussion proved difficult was that the group regarded television images as unproblematic ('There's nothing to discuss'). For them television images were presented within a logical sequential or narrative format whose meanings were clear and unambiguous. This sequence or narrative was 'seen' by viewers and almost universally understood by them. What indeed was there to discuss?

This chapter contains exercises designed to challenge these notions. It has two main objectives:

1. To demonstrate that the process of perception itself is fraught with problems and uncertainties, which need to be reflected upon.
2. To demonstrate that television images are overloaded with information and meaning through increasing awareness of the variety of non-verbal channels along which information and meaning may be carried.

1. Some problems of perception

a. Exercises in perception

'We are so familiar with seeing that it takes a leap of imagination to realise that there are problems to be solved.'[1] The opening words of R. L. Gregory's *Eye and Brain* suggest the appropriateness of drawing attention from the outset of a television course to some of the problems inherent in visual perception, for, as this book will continually emphasise, though visual evidence appears seductively 'open' and innocent it is invariably ambiguous, partial and open to interpretation. More, there will *inevitably* be differences, and sometimes major discrepancies, between the perceptions of any two people of the same visual evidence. The topic makes an excellent 'starter' for a visual curriculum too since a good deal of interesting and visually stimulating material is available in the form of pictures, puzzles and games which are fun to work through, encourage a high degree of class participation and will generally result in high motivation which can, with luck, be carried over into the exercises described in the rest of this chapter.

Space does not permit reproduction of the many examples of ambiguous figures and pictures available, but the sources listed below contain scores of examples which can be used directly in the classroom. Most of the figures are simple enough to copy on to coloured card; a colleague in the Art Department or a student with artistic flair might be prevailed upon to copy the more complex pictures. Each figure should have a question attached to it, requiring the viewer to interpret what he sees. The more cards you have the better, though about fifteen should be enough to keep most classes busy. Covered with laminating film the cards should remain serviceable for many years. Once a basic collection has been made it is surprisingly simple to add topical examples of your own as they are discovered in newspapers and magazines. (Packs of perception cards are available from the author at the School of Education, Nottingham University.)

Sources   By far the most fertile source of recent and original perceptual problems which has not yet become widely known is *Recent Progress in Perception: Readings from Scientific America* (W. H. Freeman, 1976) and especially the following articles:

F. Attneave	'Multistability in perception'
M. L. Teuber	'Sources of ambiguity in the prints of Maurits C. Escher'
I. Rock	'The perception of disoriented figures'
R. Buckhout	'Eyewitness testimony'
J. B. Deregowski	'Pictorial perception and culture'

More traditional examples can be found in the following books:

M. L. J. Abercrombie *The Anatomy of Judgement* (Hutchinson, 1960; Pelican, 1969)
R. L. Gregory *The Intelligent Eye* (Weidenfeld & Nicolson, 1970)
R. L. Gregory *Eye and Brain* (Weidenfeld & Nicolson, 1966)
E. H. Gombrich *Art and Illusion* (Phaidon, 1960)
D. Huff *How to Lie with Statistics* (Pelican, 1973) See especially Chapter 6 on Pictographs.
F. Perls,
  R. F. Heffeline
  and P. Goodman *Gestalt Therapy* (Delta, 1951)
M. D. Vernon *The Psychology of Perception* (Pelican, 1962)

Periodicals Two issues of *Screen Education*, no. 13 (Winter 1974–5) and no. 23 (Summer 1977), have been devoted to image analysis. Both contain articles which reproduce examples of perceptual problems and give accounts of their use in the classroom.

In working through perceptual problems, pupils will need to respond flexibly, jettisoning conventional ways of seeing, experimenting with and acquiring new ones, and in general loosening up their observational 'sets' so that their judgements become less dogmatic and the imperative to 'close' on interpretation, and to resolve ambiguities becomes less pressing. One ought not to attend too rigorously to what each problem 'proves', for even a cursory glance at the literature will reveal that they are used to demonstrate or give substance to an astonishingly wide range of theories and hypotheses. It is perhaps enough to draw attention to the selective and individual nature of perception and to the significance of the individual's previous knowledge and experience in perceiving new information in 'preferred' and often unique ways.

In summary then, perceptual exercises, puzzles and games can underwrite in a general way two of the most important premisses of the work which is to follow. They can establish at the outset of the course both the validity and significance of each student's perceptions, and the highly problematic nature of visual evidence.

b. Visual games and puzzles

1. Show one half of the class a card containing capital letters, and the other half a card containing digits. Now write the ambiguous figure '13' on the board, and ask each individual in turn what he sees. Can the class deduce the reason for any discrepancies? Can they devise exercises themselves in which different people will interpret the same figure differently?

2. The group sits in a semi-circle and the teacher arranges four or five matches

in a pattern upon the floor, saying 'That's eight'. He rearranges the matches and says that this arrangement signifies another number, and repeats this process until everyone in the group has cracked the code. The code itself should never be given away by those who have guessed it; they should simply call out the right answers to the different arrangements of matches until everyone has succeeded in getting it right. The secret is that the 'code' has nothing to do with the matches; the teacher signifies the number he wishes to be called by placing the appropriate number of fingers upon the floor beside the matches.

3. A similar kind of game. The group sits in a circle and a pair of scissors is passed from hand to hand. The scissors can either be opened or closed by each person before he passes them on. As he passes them on he must use the words 'crossed' or 'uncrossed'. Those who know the code will tell him whether he is correct or not. This is another 'trick' game. The 'crossed—uncrossed' refers not to the scissors but to whether the person has his legs crossed or uncrossed. Again the essence of the game lies in those who 'crack' the code not divulging it to those still in the dark.

4. A game which can be played orally or written upon a board. The teacher begins: 'It's summer but not spring; a lampoon but not a satire; a carrot but not a parsnip; butter but not marge; football but not cricket; beer but not ale' etc. Those who think they have cracked the code can test out their theory by supplying their own examples. The distinction between the words lies in their possession or lack of a double letter.

These games can be very frustrating to those unable to break the codes so the teacher should not let them go on for too long.

5. 'Without looking at your watch, describe how the number four is depicted on it.' Although most people look at their watches quite frequently, very few are at all certain of the answer to this question. It is quite possible for someone to have owned the same watch for ten or twenty years and not know the answer to the question, a fact which tells us a great deal about the selective nature of perception. The number four is chosen because on most clocks and watches using Roman numerals, four is represented as IIII rather than the expected IV.

6. Simple observational exercises and games relating to the immediate environment can be tried out, e.g. Without looking around can you say how many people in the group are wearing spectacles? Where is the nearest fire extinguisher/fire alarm? What colour is the main hall painted? etc.

2. Non-verbal communication

a. Introduction

Because the study of non-verbal communication is, particularly in the field of social psychology, a 'growth' area of academic study in its own right, it is tempting to think of attention to paralinguistic levels of communication as being something new. This is far from the case. Such traditional forms of communication as music, painting, mime and sculpture communicate entirely through their different non-verbal systems while drama and song derive their textural richness from the often complex relationships which exist between their linguistic and paralinguistic levels of meaning. What *is* new however is that attention to non-verbal communication should be breaking through the predominantly literary-based curricula of educational institutions, though it is likely that for some time yet the study (as opposed to the practice) of drama, to take one example, will continue to consist of the study of the printed text rather than the tensions which may exist between linguistic text and paralinguistic subtexts. The study of more recent forms of visual communication such as film and television will necessarily involve the study of ways in which meanings are communicated non-verbally. For this reason, as well as a number of others outlined below, an introductory exploration of some very basic aspects of non-verbal communication is perhaps an appropriate way to begin the study of television.

The work described in this section has two main strands. First, it attempts to encourage an awareness of the sheer richness and variety of the channels along which non-verbal meanings may be carried. Television pictures present the viewer with an enormous amount of information most of which he processes at a level where he does not see it as having 'meanings' at all. It is this very fact which, as we have seen, makes the discussion of television programmes difficult, and even meaningless, for most pupils. Before a problem can be reflected upon it must first be identified as a problem; if the television image is seen as unproblematic, and programmes as having only one meaning – that embodied within their narrative of events – then discussion becomes superfluous. On the other hand, an awareness that television messages are *overloaded* with meaning is of itself enough to make the medium fit subject for reflection and discussion. The development of such an awareness is therefore one of the primary aims of the work described in this section.

Secondly, this work will also pay particular attention to one of the most compelling characteristics of non-verbal communication – its apparent 'innocence'. A gesture or mode of dress appears to be the spontaneous, inevitable and natural expression of a particular attitude rather than the result of considered human choice. Yet the way in which one sits, or the tie one wears, embody decisions over which one has the fullest control. It is this fact which makes non-verbal communications prime agents of mystification for they tend to work against a rational understanding of society, elevating particular choices and the values implicit within them to the status of natural events, and masking the element of choice and control behind them. It is of some importance then that students should regard this area not simply as a complex amalgam of different communication systems worthy of study in their own right, but as inextricably connected with the political, economic and social systems which originally gave them life.

b. Visual comprehension: a conceptual framework

As I have said, the origin of the work described in this chapter lay in the difficulties encountered by pupils when they attempted to talk about television programmes. My earliest formulation of the problem was this:

> Can the complex of skills which I am expecting pupils to exercise when they view a television programme be more clearly identified and separated out? Do discrete 'visual-literacy' skills exist which can be isolated and practised by pupils in specially designed exercises? And are such skills developmental and hierarchical? Is it possible for pupils to move through 'primary' skills demanding simple cognitive responses to more complex skills which would call for progressively higher levels of thinking?

My hope was that having isolated, practised and acquired individual skills pupils would be able to use them to make more sense than they could at present of more complex television images. Armed with these skills, pupils would be able to understand more clearly how visual meanings communicate themselves, see 'underlying' structures and meanings in programmes, and perhaps even be prepared to discuss what they saw. So it was that I devised a visual skills programme in which pupils were given the opportunity to practise decoding skills in all of those areas of non-verbal communication outlined in this chapter.

The urge to feel that this was a 'distinct advance' was almost irresistible. It was after all bringing some developmental structure into a curriculum area of hitherto chaotic growth. The work had a definable purpose and direction and it became perfectly possible to diagnose particular weaknesses in the responses of individual pupils and to begin to apply remedies. Moreover the exercises clearly worked; they were tackled with general enthusiasm and interest, and it was even possible for pupils to chart their own progress in terms of the skills they were acquiring. While the emphasis upon intellectual processes rather than subject content certainly seemed correct, I was far from happy with my conceptualisation of the problem. The models projected both of communication and learning seemed essentially false. To begin with the notion of separable *skills* did not seem to me to be actually applicable to anything that I had ever learned myself. In the first place the most significant, most organic learning that people ever achieve – within, say, a personal relationship, or through being involved in a particular occupation or task – did not seem best characterised by the use of the word 'skill' at all; a purely technical or mechanical mastery, a very limited notion of learning and one that I had never been especially interested in, is suggested by the word. And even in those areas where it seemed appropriate to speak of 'skills'; and where individual skills could be isolated, such as in learning to drive a car for example, they were not *learned* separately – clutch one week, steering the next, accelerator the next – but in their essential relationships with one another.

I had always been highly opposed to any conceptual framework which regarded most pupils as deficit systems, who could be saved if they were 'topped' up to the standards of their more privileged (middle-class) counterparts. Such concepts as a 'restricted' language code, or 'compensatory education' had always seemed to me to be clearly class-based, providing teachers with a framework for defining their working-class pupils in terms of what they *lacked* rather than what they already possessed which could be respected and developed. Yet my skills-deficit model fell into precisely this trap. The model may have been an advance on what had gone before, but it did not really describe the nature of the processes at work in our television studies classes.

A 'skills' curriculum actually hardens the teacher–pupil hierarchy; the teacher possesses the skills and passes them down to his pupils. But we were involved in something completely different. As one girl put it: 'We're not really learning anything new; you're just making us more aware of what we really know already.' I had certainly been responsible for increasing *awareness* of the multiplicity of ways in which television pictures communicate their meanings, but the abilities developed by a student were not copied from or passed down by me, but emerged *from the student himself* through the way in which he shaped and handled his growing awareness. And this growth was not mechanistic in the way posited by skills-models. It didn't emerge through doing the right things in the right order at the right time, but much more haphazardly through the sparking of an interest or the kindling of an enthusiasm from which pupils would wish to 'take off' on their own. My prime aim as a teacher had always been to kindle this kind of enthusiasm. For the development of skills and abilities had always seemed to me to be the inevitable by-products of involvement. To begin by trying to teach skills as my model prescribed was to place the teacher in the position of the man who seeks happiness. If it becomes his primary aim he will never succeed, for like skill, it emerges out of involvement in something else. The task of every teacher is to seek that 'something else'.

This analysis of the concept of visual literacy skills has an interesting and informative parallel in the field of literacy itself. Skills-based approaches to teaching, postulating the existence of *independent* reading and comprehension skills, are now widely influential.[2] While it is of course possible to delineate particular reading or comprehension skills it seems at least possible that competence in performing them is a unitary ability. Recent reading research has indeed confirmed this belief. A current Schools Council reading research project[3] has found that pupils who are weak at summarising a passage will also be weak at recognising word meaning, detecting irony or interpreting metaphors. Comprehension, in other words, is a single competence which one researcher has defined as 'the ability and willingness to reflect on matter that is read'.[4] The definition does I think have profound implications both for reading and visual literacy.

In terms of visual literacy and comprehension, as we have seen, the 'ability to reflect' emerges from a general awareness of the channels through which meanings are produced. The crucial point at which comprehension develops is when the 'aware' mind of the student confronts the material under analysis. It is not something passed down, or deposited by the teacher. Furthermore in the above definition, the emphasis upon the pupil's 'willingness' to reflect recognises the primary importance of pupil motivation for comprehension. The movement away from a skills-deficit model is of some importance for it is a movement away from a mechanistic hierarchical learning towards a more organic and humanistic one in which the critical abilities of both teacher and pupils alike develop through dynamic interaction with the visual texts which confront them.

c. Methodology

Many of the activities suggested in this section will be new to both teachers and pupils, and some – those on eye-contact and touch for example – demand a combination of maturity and lack of inhibition not customarily found in English society let alone school classrooms. For this reason, how the teacher handles this material is left to his own discretion. He can gauge best the feelings and mood of his group and knows best his own strengths and weaknesses as a teacher. Drama, role-play and games can play an important part in these activities for those teachers who feel happy using such techniques, and for those who don't, co-operation and help might be enlisted from the drama department, who could well be exploring many of the ideas suggested in this chapter in their own work. On the whole, teachers are best advised to do what they normally do with such material – adapt it as best they can to their own strengths as teachers, to the specific needs of their own pupils, and to the situation as it exists in their own schools. One piece of firm advice can be offered however: the conventional classroom is not the best environment for this kind of work; a more flexible, but not necessarily large room, in which chairs can be pushed back and space created is preferable, though a hall or studio would also do.

A final note: television itself is not used a great deal in this part of the course, the emphasis being very much more upon examples of non-verbal communication already existing within the group. The relevance of the study of 'total communication'[5] patterns to the study of television may be questioned by some pupils, and will need to be clarified by the teacher at every point. The study of television will necessarily have as a primary aim the fullest possible explication of the 'total communication' of television images. The exercises which follow are designed to encourage a generalised awareness of the non-verbal channels along which communication can flow, and to provide pupils with some simple practice in analysis from which they may experience success and develop enough confidence in their own judgement to attempt more complex analytical tasks later.

d. Introducing non-verbal communication in the classroom

One simple way of introducing the topic is to ask the group to write down as many ways as they can think of in which it is possible to communicate without using words.

Communication systems which are removed from but still *dependent* upon words such as Morse code and semaphore are likely to figure more prominently here than anything else, but if so this will simply be indicative of the narrowness of the group's concept of what constitutes non-verbal communication. The teacher's task is to open out the concept by suggesting the richness and variety of the field, and to clarify any difficulties arising from this. For instance some pupils may feel that one's choice of clothing or hair style cannot really be considered as communication, and the teacher will need to elaborate upon the precise nature of the processes involved here. Bodily communication may be introduced by asking each member of the group in turn to communicate something different by using one part of the body (the fingers, the feet or the mouth, for example), the rest of the group guessing what is being communicated.

On the basis of the group's original list and the subsequent discussion a list of some of the principal means by which people communicate to others without using words may be drawn up. These should include:

Eye-contact
Facial expression
Touch
Body movement and posture
Positional communication
Physical appearance

e. Eye-contact and facial expression

Some classroom experiments

1. Divide pupils into pairs. Eye-contact exercises will prove inhibiting to many pupils, so it is perhaps best to begin by making the initial exercise into a game. Try to 'stare out' your partner.
2. Now, look at your partner without aggression for two or three minutes.

The difficulties and embarrassments this causes ought to be fully discussed. What possible meanings of eye-contact and eye-avoidance can be arrived at by the group?

3. Arrange a series of objects around the room and explain that pupils should stand as close as is comfortable to each object to see it well. This is best described to pupils as 'an experiment in vision'. One of the 'objects' should include a person who will be viewed by some people when his eyes are closed, by others when his eyes are open. When this experiment was conducted by Argyle[6] observers stood 8 inches further away from the 'open-eyed' than the 'closed-eyed' person. Why should this be so?
4. Have each pupil-pair act out a mini-drama to illuminate a range of meanings communicable by eye-contact or eye-avoidance; e.g.:
   a. A busy waiter avoiding eye-contact with a hungry customer who seeks it.
   b. A person talking to someone who is bored.
   c. A boy talking about football to a girl, uninterested in football, who has a crush on him.
   d. An adolescent returning home very late one night tells lies to his parents about where he has been.
   e. A police interrogation of a suspect. In the first half of the interview the detective wears dark glasses; in the second he takes them off.

After each 'incident', the class should discuss the implications of the eye-contact and eye-avoidance within it.

5. Divide into groups of three. Appointing one person as observer, ask the remaining pair to hold a conversation upon anything with which they are both familiar (school; sport; clothes – the subject-matter is immaterial). Before the conversation begins hand each observer a sheet containing the following questions. The questions should be hidden from the speakers.
   a. Who looks most at the face of the other, the listener or the speaker?
   b. When one person is about to speak does he tend to look at or away from his partner?
   c. Just as he finishes speaking does he tend to look at or away from his partner?
   d. Is the direction of gaze connected to the pattern of the conversation?

The observer should discuss his findings with the two speakers.

6. Ask each pupil to analyse and report back on the eye-contact patterns of:
   (i) a particular teacher of his choice; (ii) a person with whom he comes into
   contact between now and next lesson.[7]

Note: A large number of posters and photographs depicting a wide range of
facial expressions have been produced by the Schools Council Moral
Education 8–13 project under the title *Startline*. Numerous suggestions for
activities and games accompany the materials, which are quite suitable for use
with older students.[8]

Eye-contact and television   Of what relevance are such exercises as these to
the study of television? The hypothesis that sensitivity to meanings expressed
at these levels might lead to a greater awareness of their employment within
television images proved to be true to the extent that pupils used these
concepts a good deal in their analyses of programmes as we shall see.

In plays, films, documentaries and studio discussions person-to-person eye-
contact or avoidance very frequently carries very significant subtextual
meanings. Eye-to-camera contact is a slightly different field and worthy of
study in its own right. The relationship between the eye of the 'performer' and
the eye of the viewer may be: (i) non-existent, as in most sporting events,
plays, films and some discussion; (ii) intermittent – discussion, current affairs,
magazine programmes; (iii) very close, as with comperes, newsreaders and
announcers.

Even within (iii) the patterns may vary widely. Michael Barratt in
Nationwide used to lean forward and fearlessly *stare* at us – an eye-
relationship in no way resembling those of normal social interactions.
Newsreaders, compelled to look occasionally at the papers on their desk in
fact adopt a more normal eye-relationship with the viewer. Appearances are
deceptive here however. The seemingly close eye-to-camera relationship of
newsreaders is an illusion, for they are actually staring at the autocue beside
the camera. It is the *consistency* of the newsreader's eye-line which maintains
the illusion. Interestingly, performers who do look at camera may ruin the
eye-contact illusion through failing to maintain a consistent eye-line. Max
Bygraves is a good example of this; his eyes, flicking backwards and forwards
between camera and autocue, can have an unsettling effect upon the viewer. It
is worth observing too that in general, eye-to-camera patterns will vary a good
deal between: (i) *scripted shows*, where an autocue is used, and *unscripted* or
semi-scripted ones (most quiz or panel shows) where it is not; and (ii) shows
with a *live audience*, where there is often a reluctance by stars to use the
autocue (it blunts their charisma with the audience; the popular name for the
autocue is in fact the 'idiot-board'), and shows *without an audience* where the
autocue generally prevails.

Many writers have suggested that there is a hierarchy of authority implicit in different eye-contact codings:

> If we switch on our sets and see someone addressing us directly, we know he is a narrator or presenter. If his gaze is directly slightly off-camera, we know he is an interviewee, a talking head. If he is turned away from us by an angle of more than about 15° he is a part of an action sequence. It is clear that there is a hierarchy of authority implicit in this code. The talking head is permitted to gaze into the sacred sector only through the priest-like intercession of the interviewer: and, if he should speak directly to the camera, he will create an impression of insolence.[9]

The hierarchy of eye-contact codings is clearly relevant to the question of 'access'. Codings suggesting the highest degree of authority are the almost exclusive preserve of those who are *agents* of broadcasting institutions rather than *sources*. Raymond Williams elaborates the distinction:

> A man offering an opinion, a proposal, a feeling, of course normally desires that other persons will accept this, and act or feel in the ways he defines. Yet such a man may be properly described as a source, in distinction from an agent whose characteristic is that his expression is subordinated to an undeclared intention.[10]

Sources rarely have direct eye-contact with the viewer. And those who do are quite rigidly confined to the same social class as those who control broadcasting. Reith's reprimand sent to all radio station directors back in 1924 still largely defines, albeit negatively, the range of those who have access to television in the 1970s: 'In some stations I see periodically men down to speak whose status, either professionally or socially, and whose qualifications to speak seem doubtful.'[11]

In terms of television, if working-class people ever appear on the screen they will almost inevitably be compelled to adopt the eye-contact code which gives them the least authority with the viewer.

f. Touch and body contact

Begin with a discussion and analysis of the patterns which exist within the room.

1. Are individuals in the room separate or touching? Why? What meanings exist here?
2. What kinds of physical contact are there? Make a list of them, and the different meanings they have, and try to establish connections between them.

3. Who was the last person with whom each member came into physical contact? What were the meanings of that contact?

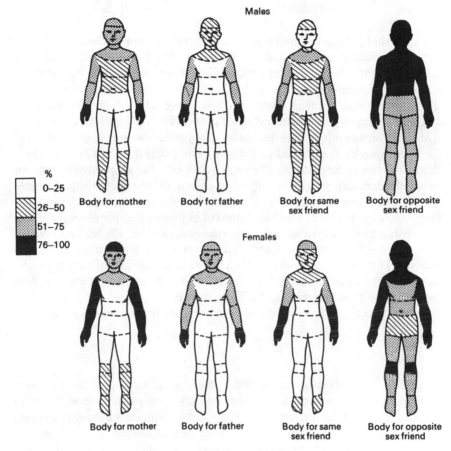

Figure 1

These questions should raise the whole question of touch taboos and cultural variations in touch patterns. The group might, for example, like to discuss some of the implications of Figure 1.[12] The percentages represent the number of subjects who reported being touched *at some time* by the person indicated below each figure. The subjects were young American adults, and it seems likely that touch taboos are even more widely operative in Britain since the psychologist who gathered the data, Jourard, also conducted an experiment in which, sitting in coffee bars in four different cities, he observed pairs of people engaged in conversation and noted on average how many times they touched each other in an hour. His figures reveal how deeply embedded within our society the touch taboo is:[13]

San Juan (Puerto Rico)	180
Paris	102
Gainesville (Florida)	2
London	0

Pupils should be made aware of the fact that there seems to be a correlation between touching and physical and mental health. I discovered in teaching adults in mental hospitals that almost all of them had become incapable of expressing themselves through any kind of physical contact. They were people who scarcely ever touched others, and who were untouched themselves.

There are many games and encounter group experiences which can be used within the classroom to sensitise pupils to a greater awareness of touch, and their reactions to it. It should go without saying that this is an area in which there are likely to be great inhibitions and that even the simplest exercises can only be undertaken with the willing co-operation of the entire group. A simple 'game' (the game format tends to reduce self-consciousness) is to instruct everyone to memorise by touch the hands of as many other people in the group as possible, so that he is able to distinguish between them. The task is to match up the face with the way the hands feel. Allow about fifteen minutes for this activity. The whole group should then stand in the middle of the room and close their eyes. The teacher pairs them off, and their task is to guess who their partner is by touching his hands. They then open their eyes to see if they guessed correctly. When this is done, the teacher makes new pairings.

g. Kinesics

Kinesics – the study of communication through gesture, posture and body movement – is becoming such an increasingly (and perhaps unnecessarily) complex field that the teacher must be content to skim the surface in this area, introducing his pupils to the field, increasing their awareness of its possibilities and allowing them to practice kinesic analysis as quickly as possible. Again it will invariably be most effective to begin with the here-and-now concrete experience of sitting in a group, each member of which is communicating many things without speaking. Since sensitivity to non-verbal cues is part of the art of teaching, most teachers will be able to surprise and impress the group from the outset by describing what individuals within the group have been communicating non-verbally from the moment they entered the room.

Introductory exercises   Discuss as a group, in turn, the way in which each member is sitting. It is enough here to bring out in a general way the signs of boredom, interest, relaxation or tension and the extent to which the body is 'open' or 'closed' to reception.

It should now be possible to move on to dramatic demonstrations of open and closed groupings, and the ways in which territorial considerations may affect body language:

1. What is being communicated in the playground when a circle of boys stand around talking?
2. What is communicated if a boy walks straight through the circle?
3. How does your body language change if you are:
   (i) at home (on your own territory)
   (ii) at school (on familiar territory, but not your own). Do you react differently in different parts of the school?
   (iii) on unfamiliar territory (for example, going to a library for the first time; entering a strange house)?

Devising additional exercises involving the playing out and interpretation of gesture and mime is not difficult:

convey by a single gesture (a) happiness, (b) anger, (c) boredom, (d) elation.
mime how (a) an angry parent, (b) the headmaster, (c) a new boy, might enter the room.
the teacher enters the room in six different ways. The class must interpret his mood.
analyse what is communicated by the body language of people in photographs.

Longer-term observation As a final exercise to draw together the work done so far on non-verbal communication, each group member should be asked to bring along to the next meeting a list of three different types of non-verbal behaviour which he/she believes to be typical of him/her.

Next, the names of each group member should be placed in a hat. Everyone draws a name, keeping the identity of his 'subject' a secret. Each person's task is to observe his subject as closely as possible between now and the next meeting, bringing along to that meeting a list of four or five non-verbal characteristics *typical of the subject*.

At the next meeting each person demonstrates or impersonates the different non-verbal characteristics of his subject, describing the contexts in which such behaviour occurs and suggesting possible meanings. The group must guess who the subject is. When the subject has been identified, he can give his own list relating to his own behaviour for purposes of comparison.

h. Positional communication (proxemics)

This can cover a wide range of phenomena.

Personal and social space Experiments with what constitutes 'comfortable' personal space can be attempted. Cultural differences in definitions of what constitutes comfortable space may be known by some pupils, particularly in multiracial classes. The whole question of the importance of territorial factors in determining human and animal behaviour can be raised, and again pupils, particularly those with pets, will have something to offer here. The ways in which both humans and animals mark off territorial boundaries and resent intrusion into them by outsiders can be linked with examples of the uncomfortable and aggressive feelings we may have when someone intrudes onto our personal space.

Furniture arrangements   The way that chairs and tables are arranged in an empty room tells us a good deal about the relative positions which people are likely to take up when they enter it. Most people seem to take the positioning of furniture for granted and, without realising it, allow it to structure the relationships which can exist within the room. In running courses and conferences one quickly realises that the choice of room and the arrangement of furniture within it are very important determinants of what can go on there.

The meanings implicit within different arrangements of chairs, tables and desks can be demonstrated by an examination of the present seating arrangements of the group. Furniture can be rearranged to suggest different meanings, and the layout of different rooms in the building can be examined in terms of the way in which it predetermines the behaviour of those who enter them. Links can be made here with the layout of studio sets on television, particularly for magazine-type programmes. What is the physical relationship between interviewer and interviewee? What kind of desks and chairs are there and how are they used to structure the interaction? etc.

Distance   Situations can be set up to illustrate the ways in which the physical positioning of people in relation to each other conveys meaning. Divide the group into pairs. Choose different pairs to illustrate *through physical closeness*

  (i) equality
 (ii) intimacy
(iii) hostility
(iv) indifference

by their relative position to each other; and to convey through *physical distance*

  (i) respect
 (ii) remoteness
(iii) superiority/inferiority.

The possible meanings and nuances of physical *highness* and *lowness* might also be considered.

If these exercises prove too complex, an easier way to begin is by setting up pairs in physical relationship to each other and then asking the class to interpret what their positions suggest, e.g.:

  (i) two people standing back to back.
 (ii) two people standing side by side.
(iii) two people facing each other. One looks at the other, the other looks straight ahead.
 (iv) three or four people standing very close to each other (as on a tube) but ignoring each other.
  (v) two people sitting close together on an otherwise empty bench, etc.

A useful way of demonstrating the relevance of the work covered so far to television is to try and make sense of a videotaped programme with its sound turned off. This can be especially fruitful if the programme happens to be dramatic. In a programme from a detective series for example the class might like to work out what the plot is about, and if the programme is stopped before the end it can also become a prediction exercise in which the pupil must forecast the probable outcome. After full discussion the whole programme is replayed complete with sound.

i. Physical appearance

People can be regarded as quite complex communication networks, their clothes, hair style, posture, even fingernails all revealing something about them. After pupils have practised some of the interpretive exercises outlined above, they will be ready to analyse a particular individual and a very stimulating exercise is to introduce to the group two or three total strangers who are prepared to undergo the experience for the purpose of analysis.

Split the group into as many subgroups as you have 'visitors', and rotate the visitors to each subgroup in turn. There must be no verbal communication between the groups and the visitors. Members of each group must write down as much as they can observe and logically deduce from their observations about the stranger. Time can be allowed for subgroups to discuss their findings and reach a consensus without the visitor present. Finally all groups come together and the analyses of each visitor in turn are discussed. Each visitor is finally allowed to speak to reveal the accuracy of the conclusions reached. Visitors are generally very surprised by the perceptiveness of the groups' observations.

An interesting aspect of this exercise is that the 'subject' who is ostensibly under analysis can be briefed to observe and analyse each subgroup he visits. Since the groups are unaware of the fact that they are under scrutiny a description of their non-verbal communication patterns by the subject can have considerable impact, demonstrating graphically the revelatory qualities of their own largely unconscious behaviour.

j. Analysing objects

For the most part television pictures depict complex inter-relationships of objects and people within space. So far in this chapter we have examined some of the many ways in which people communicate both consciously and unconsciously, and we have explored some of the ways in which spatial relationships may confer meaning. Now we must turn to the ways in which physical objects communicate to us both in a literal and overt way, and through their more subtle suggestions. By giving pupils practice in observing and analysing the 'meanings' of single objects it should be possible to heighten their powers of perception and increase their confidence when they come to examine the dynamic conglomeration of objects which make up the television picture.

Introducing connotations The group will need to be introduced to the distinction between denotative and connotative meanings (one or two people are likely to have some inkling of the distinction). Connotations have such a particular potency in visual communication that some practice needs to be given to pupils in analysis at this level of meaning.

Exercise: Explore the connotations of these different objects and their characteristics in group discussion:
(Provide actual examples for observation wherever possible.)
e.g.   (a) the colour red   (d) a pair of jeans
        (b) a book   (e) a paper cup
        (c) the figure X   (f) a one pound note

The group may need considerable help and coaxing at first. Improvement soon comes with practice however, and by the time the end of the list is reached, answers should be quite fluent. The teacher will need to prompt the group with questions however, and he should attempt to link his questions with television images wherever possible: What is suggested about a person if you see him interviewed on television while surrounded by books? What impression would be given if someone reading the news was wearing jeans? Apart from physical objects, photographs, slides and posters can all be used to explore the meanings of objects at a connotative level.

The purpose and process of object analysis Artefacts are cultural. Their existence is not accidental, any more than their particular qualities are. The shape, size, colour and every other quality of the objects which we see around us are so by design, and represent the result of conscious human choices. Because that chair, that glass or that home is the final outcome of a process of selection, because it is *that* way rather than any other, it embodies meanings and reveals something of the values of the society in which it finds a place. The purpose of analysing objects is to unmask the choices implicit within them and most fundamentally to reveal them as the outcome of human rather than natural processes. Sophisticated examples of the possibilities of this kind of analysis may be seen in Roland Barthes' *Mythologies*.[14] Barthes' work also clarifies what the process of analysis might be. Students should first of all *describe* what they see as closely as possible. From description they can then move to an interrogation of the *purpose and function* of the qualities they observe: Why is it that shape and size? What difference would it make were it of another colour or material? From here a further movement should be encouraged towards exploring the *values* implicit within the object: What does the object *say* through its complex of signs and symbols? How would the world be different if this object did not exist? What does its existence tell us of society's values? The movement here from observation to an interrogation of *function* and *values* is one of which students should be consciously aware. It is one which will be carried over to the study of television itself.

This kind of analysis may sound like a tall order for young adolescents, but teachers, I think, will be pleasantly surprised by the results which pupils can achieve and by the quality of their insights. Here is a typical example, from a fourteen year old:

A Biro Pen

A long trasperant object with a regular shape and size and the shape is small and long which is easy to hold in your hand. There are diferent ways of holding a pen but it can be held easily between your thumb and your fingers in several diferent styles it has to be quite long so as to get a lot of ink in it which is why it is transparent so that you can se if the ink is runing out or not. The pen has two blue ends to it one a cover so that the ink dos'ent spill out in your pocket or bag the other end is a stopper to stop the refill falling out. These ends are blue so that you can tell the colour of ink inside which is blue. Black ink has black ends, green has green ink etc. It is also small so you can cary it anywhere you want without any case of any kind. Pens have to be used almost everywhere so this is handy and you dont have to carry cartriges or an ink bottle. It is a method of communication wich can be used enywhere without sound and a sentence of importance can be kept for years. It is made of hard plastic wich is cheap and easy to make, it is quite strong but can be crushed if dropped and trod on. It suggests school because its cheap and can be brought with pocket money. A Buissness man working in an office or travelling a lot will use one because it is quick and easy. (Malcolm Parnham)

Malcolm manages to make quite a lot out of a not very promising object. There are some surprising omissions in observation (he nowhere mentions the ball-point) and some errors in assigning function (the stopper *doesn't* stop the refill from falling out), but Malcolm clearly understands the relationship between quality and function and draws out a number of examples to prove it. The movement towards the values inherent in the object is flirted with but never quite clinched. Convenience and cheapness are certainly pointed out, but the most significant attempt to grapple with values lies in the leap made from the object itself to the method of communication it embodies – 'a method of communication wich [*sic*] can be used anywhere without sound and a sentence of importance can be kept for years'. Poor expression vitiates the first part of this sentence, and the significance of the second part is not elaborated, but the shift in cognitive gear is unmistakable.

Games with objects   The potency of objects in suggesting and expressing meanings can be explored in other exercises:

1. The observation of the qualities of objects can take on a 'pure' and creative form in this improvised game. The group sits in a circle and an object is passed around. The aim is for each person to use the object as a prop and to communicate through mime what the object is being used as. The object must not be used as itself. The cleverer and more ingenious uses found for the object the better. The object is passed to the next person when its meaning has been guessed by anyone in the group.

2. A variation on the first game in which each student is given a different object, told he is an archaeologist and that his object has been discovered in an archaeological dig. He must explain what unlikely function it served in the past. The further divorced this function is from its present one, the funnier this becomes. Both of these games can be played with quite young secondary school children and with growing sophistication by adolescents and adults.

3. Place a pile of objects on a table in the middle of the group, explaining that they are the contents of a particular person's handbag or pockets. (Ideally, this is what they should be if the teacher can arrange it.) The task of group members is to deduce as much as they can about the person's age, interests and character from these contents. This is perhaps best done as an individual exercise at first, with individuals then comparing their findings. This game is useful in moving pupils on from the analyses of individual objects towards an exploration of the possible connections between disparate objects, a task integral to the ultimate goal of these exercises, the analysis of television programmes.

k. Analysing photographs

The analysis of photographs is a particularly appropriate activity at this point for pupils have now reached an intermediate stage between the earlier a-contextual analysis of objects and aspects of non-verbal communication, and the more complex analysis of the dynamic, constantly fluctuating movements and objects of the television picture, which will ultimately be undertaken. It is the paradoxical 'frozen movement' quality of photographs, their depiction of a fully contexted, yet static world which makes them particularly useful to the teacher at this point. No less significant is that the photograph's existence is dependent upon one who never appears, a hidden mediator who has his own aims and designs, and whose structuring and selection of the 'reality' of the photograph severely modifies the 'way-things-really-were' aspect of the representation.

Consequence analysis   So called for its passing resemblance to the game of Truth and Consequences, and a technique I have frequently found useful with pupils at all levels. Distribute a photograph and large sheet of paper to each pupil. Each photograph will have pinned to it a specific instruction requiring the pupil to analyse particular aspects of non-verbal communication within the photograph. A few instructions may draw attention to the hidden presence of the photographer (for example, 'What impression of this man is the photographer trying to convey?'). About two or three minutes should be allowed for written analysis, then each pupil should cover his answer by folding over the paper and pass it and the photograph on to the next pupil. When, and only when, each pupil has completed his own analysis of a particular photograph, is he allowed to look at the preceding comments. The photographs rotate until each pupil finally receives his original photograph and the comments of the entire group upon it. His task is to write a final analysis of his own photograph using the perceptions of others as he thinks fit. The exercise demonstrates the possibilities of peer-group rather than teacher-deposited learning and provides evidence for all pupils of the advantages to each individual of co-operative learning. The most perceptive pupils recognise that group perceptions are much wider than their own; pupils who see little can begin to learn by using and organising the perceptions of others to produce very coherent pieces of their own. A finished answer will look something like this.

Comment upon the body-language of the man (Dr Barnardo) in Plate 1 (opposite p. 112).

From looking at the picture Dr Barnardo seems a rather dominant and self-centred man. The girl on his knee looks too old to be treated like a baby as she is in the picture. Dr Barnardo probably only had her on his knee to create an impression of him being a very considerate gentleman. But the girl's horrified expression as she looks up at him disproves that theory.

Dr Barnardo's mousetache is carefully 'twirled' at the ends showing personal pride in his appearance. His boots are also carefully polished. The girls all look slightly uncomfortable and the seated girl in the centre is smiling only with her mouth – the eyes are not smiling, making it a false smile.

The seated girl in the corner has a secretive smile – it seems as though she understands what is happening – she knows Dr Barnardo is giving a false impression.

His hat does not look very neat – it looks a bit worn. A strange thing about him is that he does not seem to be wearing a tie. (Kerri Parke)

This is a genuine 'reading' of the picture in that it is almost entirely subtextual, subverting both the overt text of the picture (Dr Barnardo, the father of 'nobody's children' with some of the girls, who but for him would have been destitute waifs and strays) and the myth of the man ('modern saint') by hypothesising, on the basis of observation, ambiguities and complexities in the relationships which existed between Barnardo and his children. Observation here then can be seen as a primary tool in the demystification process; for mystification is in part a product of not-seeing or ignoring what is manifestly there. It is important to stress again though that this particular reading, written by a fourteen-year-old girl, was not the result of her own observations but of her organisation of the perceptions of the group.

1. Conclusion: a note on texts

For pupils, *Identity Kits* by G. Facetti and A. Fletcher[15] is a beautifully illustrated introduction to a wide range of signs and symbols; it makes an ideal class book. Scheflen's *Body Language and The Social Order*,[16] a general introduction to kinesics, has much useful visual material which compensates for the somewhat off-putting American academic jargon. Both of these books circulated around the class while the exercises in this chapter were being worked through. Much useful visual material and some of the text of an Open University's Social Sciences Course Unit on *Interpersonal Communication*[17] were distributed to the group, who were flattered and highly motivated by the expectation that they were capable of university-level work.

For the teacher, Roland Barthes' *Mythologies*[18] with its brief but penetrating analyses of a wide range of cultural objects is essential reading; so too is the widely-known *Ways of Seeing*[19] by John Berger, while his shorter piece, 'From today art is dead',[20] provides a general theoretical underpinning of much of the work undertaken here. M. Argyle's *The Psychology of Interpersonal Behaviour*[21] is an easily accessible text on interpersonal communication, and Stuart Hall's 'The determinations of news photographs'[22] is an invaluable background text for work on photograph analysis.

Curriculum project materials from other subjects may be available within the school, and these can often be a very fertile source of photographs and posters. *The Humanities Curriculum Project*[23] materials contain large numbers of useful photographs while the Schools Council Moral Education 8–13 Project materials, published under the name *Startline*,[24] contain photographs, posters and games relating to many of the aspects of non-verbal communication discussed in this chapter.

Reference should finally be made to two aspects of visual literacy which might have been included in this chapter, but which, for different reasons, were not.

The study of 'the image'   A good deal of work has been done on image study over the past few years, but much of it remains only marginally relevant to the study of television. Guy Gauthier's paper, *The Semiology of the Image*,[25] with its accompanying slides is a useful resource for teachers, but concentrates its analysis on the more formally composed images of advertising and magazines. Conventional television material receives no attention, a characteristic of image analysis as it is presently conceived. In addition Gauthier's paper assumes that photographic images represent the simplest starting point available – a kind of base-line for analysis. The assumption of this chapter, on the other hand, has been that the *constituents and referents* of photographs (that is, objects, gesture, dress, etc.) are themselves in need of prior investigation. To assume that they are not is to court classroom disaster as much in the field of images as it would in the study of television.

The relationship of image to text   This important aspect of visual literacy is discussed in Chapter 9. Because it is of critical significance to an understanding of television, however, many teachers may wish to introduce this work much earlier as part of an initial teleliteracy programme, incorporating it into the work described in this chapter.

4

Towards Teleliteracy–2: Beginning Television Analysis and Introducing Television Concepts

This chapter describes a number of early steps in the analysis of television images, introduces such concepts as iconography, narrative structure, spectacle, genre and mediation, and raises in an explicit way questions of analytical methodology. It begins with pupil analyses of *Top of the Pops* and *Gardeners' World* based upon the programmes' iconography, and then describes exercises in which the title sequences of a number of television programmes were analysed. The concept of genre is then introduced and a unit of work on one of television's simplest and most accessible genres, the television cartoon, is described, in which, *inter alia*, questions of narrative structure were explicitly raised. Finally, the range of questions to which television images may be subjected is explored with reference to the programme *Young Scientists of the Year*.

1. Iconographic analyses: 'Top of the Pops' and 'Gardeners' World'

a. *'Top of the Pops'*

Having cut their teeth on the kinds of exercises described in the previous chapter the group should now be ready to turn to the more dynamic complex of images and the relationships between them – the iconography – presented by television programmes. Are their objects and the relationships between them susceptible to analysis as sign-systems in the same kind of way as individual objects and people were shown to be in the previous chapter? The teacher will need to stress the experimental nature of the activity to be pursued; this will be a tentative group exploration, whose outcome cannot be known. For the purposes of this exercise any programme will do – a point worth stressing, for what is being sought is a method of analysis which will yield insights across the whole output of the medium. Deciding by majority vote the class choose, unsurprisingly, *Top of the Pops* (BBC 1).

Given the ever-present debate on how schools should react to pop music, the choice is a challenging one. The dichotomy within which the debate is usually framed – between rejection on the one hand and acceptance in the furtherance of discrimination on the other – seems to me unhelpful. Pop music as an important part of pupils' experience needs to be thought about and understood by both pupils and teachers alike, whatever their personal tastes, their likes and dislikes. This thinking can be generated most easily by paying close attention to the phenomenon itself. As with pop music, so with television programmes about pop music: by keeping our collective eyes firmly upon the objects in front of us it may be possible to reach some tentative widely-agreed generalisations about *Top of the Pops* which will clarify the perceptions and deepen the understandings of all of us about the programme.

* * *

After viewing a video-recording of the show, a list of the objects noted by the group is written on the board:

> microphone
> hair
> guitar
> fashionable clothes
> maxi-skirts
> girls
> piano
> young people
> effeminate ('puffy') men
> big house
> flashing lights
> spotlights
> 'No. 1' (flashing on and off)
> breasts
> fast car
> darkness

Seeing the list immediately heightens awareness of the number of levels upon which the programme is communicating, many of them only marginally connected with music. To my surprise the lesson begins to teach itself.

'Fashionable clothes'; 'maxi-skirts' As it turns out, the chief reason for viewing for most girls is to discover what is fashionable not simply in music, but even more significantly in clothes and social manners. *Top of the Pops* performs the same function for them that *Vogue* does for the middle-class woman and the colour supplements for the middle-class family. Are the girls in the audience 'girls-in-the-street'? The group think not; they are more up to

date, modern, fashionable and sexy. Wish fulfilment, the girls admit, plays an important part in their motivation for watching the show.

'Girls'; 'breasts'   If the girls watch the programme for a kind of informal social education, then boys — if this group is typical — watch it primarily for its depiction of girls, whose sexuality is continually emphasised by camera positioning which accentuates their breasts and thighs. This is particularly true of the routines performed by dancing girls like Pan's People, who were seen as having an overtly sexual function ('They can't dance, can they?'), but also applies to the coverage of the girls dancing in the audience. The absence of men amongst the dancers was as conspicuous as the absence of females amongst the performers. In the show we watched all of the artists were men (the symbolism of the guitars and microphones is an established cliché by now of course and needed no elaboration). The stock shots in the show for live numbers being close-ups of the artists, shots of the artists surrounded by dancing girls, and close-ups of the dancers. Girls, in spite of their dancing, serve an almost purely decorative and passive function. The other context in which they are seen in the programme, when between records they surrounded the disc-jockey (again an exclusively male preserve), an easily available, ever-changing commodity, confirms this function.

'Spotlights'; 'flashing lights'; 'darkness'   The attention-grabbing visual effects of the programme have their origin — the class grapple with an established adult cliché — in the difficulty of making interesting television out of music. The variety and pervasiveness of the visual 'effects' becomes even more apparent when an excerpt is viewed again, this time without sound. Then the restlessness of the camera, zooming, panning, circling, never settling, becomes patent.

'Big house'; 'fast car'; 'girls'; 'fashionable clothes'   objects of totemic significance — less the rewards or evidence of success than its pure signs. Film clips of the stars show them conspicuously doing nothing, pensive amid luxury, inhabitants of a mythic world in which material transformations are effected not by work but by ownership.

'Young people'   Writing these words upon the blackboard is to draw attention to *Top of the Pops'* most banal point — that it is a show for and about young people. Like most obvious iconographic features it is easy to miss; yet once observed it raises problems. How is 'youth' defined by the programme? Is Tony Blackburn young? (Class discussion here will resemble a medieval theological dispute.) It isn't a chronological age which has drawn together the blooming young and fast-fading disc-jockeys and stars, but an attitude. To be young in this sense is to exist butterfly-like in an a-causal world to which one has a totally passive relationship. Here-and-now, celebrated because it *is*,

becomes emptied of meaning (cf. the aimless meandering talk of all disc-jockeys everywhere). Whether one views this as a kind of hedonistic existentialism ('now' is unique), a touching belief in progress (this week is better than last), or a debilitating lack of historical perspective (this moment is causeless and uncaused), the attitude locks wonderfully well into the interests of capitalism. Likewise the expression of a tentatively emerging identity, a 'natural' desire to be different, to be an individual is achieved through an ownership, particularly of records and clothes, which presupposes the possession of money, and an absence of adult constraints in spending it. If to be young is to be immersed in the present, to buy the new is to drink at the fountain of youth. *Top of the Pops* does not simply demonstrate the appropriation of youth's 'natural' qualities by the consumer ethic; it holds out the promise of eternal youth through constant consumption.

b. The world of 'Gardeners' World'

Many of the qualities of *Top of the Pops* were thrown into sharp relief by the accidental juxtapositioning of a recording of *Gardeners' World* on the same videotape. It would be difficult to envisage two worlds further apart than those presented by these programmes. Their music, language, iconography and values are at such extremes of the spectrum that each programme curiously throws light on the qualities of the other.

The simple, homely unpretentious music of *Gardeners' World* introduces simple, homely, unpretentious Percy Thrower wearing baggy flannels and an old blazer. Unlike the changing musical and sartorial fashions of *Top of the Pops*, the iconography of the programme gives little clue as to when the programme was made – it could literally have been any time within the past twenty-five years, for even the hair styles and language give nothing away. Percy's regional accent is still unusual enough in straight television pro-grammes to be worthy of comment, though ironically its 'correctness' here derives from the social role and status of the gardener. Its contrast with the mid-Atlantic tones generally favoured by *Top of the Pops* does however emphasise Percy's real roots in a real place. His personality exists in-dependently of the camera, rather than being constructed for it. Particularity of location is the first thing established by the programme.

> This week in Gardeners' World we're back again at Clacks Farm . . . Let's go and see how the vegetables which we planted earlier in the year are coming along.

The maturity of the time perspectives, and the ability to place the moment within a more significant process – the gardener inevitably sees life cyclically – point up their absence in *Top of the Pops*, where the moment is all. Even more crucially in *Gardeners' World* the relationship of man to his environment is not passive but dynamic and creative. The ability to control and change the environment is achieved through two agencies, both conspicuously lacking in *Top of the Pops* – a consciousness of processes and structures which render surface events explicable, predictable and controllable, and *work* through which material transformations are achieved. In the programme Percy is dressed for work, and actually does a good deal of physical digging; in *Top of the Pops* people and actions simply *exist* divorced from any real function; being, owning and consuming make this world turn, but it is a world of inactivity and impotence.

c. 'Top of the Pops': what was learned?

The *Top of the Pops* lesson lasted one double period. What did pupils learn from viewing the programme and discussing it? How much did they absorb and retain, and for how long? Like many teachers I have long learned to expect little recollection of arguments, facts or points raised from a general class discussion, but in order to test what remained from this isolated lesson almost two years later, I asked the group at the *end* of their course to write on an unseen extract from a current *Top of the Pops* programme. A fairly typical response is reproduced below. Since they took no notes at the time, I was surprised at the way in which many of the arguments had lingered on in their minds. I offer these explanations for this phenomenon: many of the points raised were group rather than teacher perceptions – many pupils were simply recalling their own ideas; the perceptions, arguments and analyses discussed were cemented, modified or contradicted by subsequent viewings of the programme itself, an interaction which continued and developed every time the pupil watched it. This then is not a hastily revised or 'got up' response but represents the real understanding achieved by one pupil at a particular point in his life.

As well as being for entertainment *Top of the Pops* is used as an information service of the latest news on what records are available, it is a kind of shop window. The programme also sells fashion and hairstyles, much teenage fashion can be attributed to what is picked up from the programme . . . First of all we are given a run down on the most popular goods selling at the moment. Each record is given a number and space of time. This happens to the beat of a tune playing. We are greeted with 'Good evening Britain' by a Disc Jockey, a master of word and wit. He gives verbal details on the charts and we get down to business, a free sample of a cross section of best selling music.

Each group projects an image, the image of this group is that they are all friends, this groups seem to be factory workers with a uniform with the name of the company on the back, they treat their instruments like machines with great precision, but in fun. This is their gimmick. The camera swings around the group and cuts to close ups of the singer's face in unison with the song. The next item on the show is Peters and Lee 'singing' a song. For this a completely different treatment is given. The cameras glide around the singing couple and fade into close ups of the petite females face, as though the cameras were snooping into their love life.

The female is in passionate love and her delicate face smiles as she sings, her arm is around the man's protective body. Whilst I am sure that there is probably a deep affection between them, whenever I see it made public, I wonder how deep it goes, and if it is really only an act.

The song is not really worth listening to, because the picture tells the story, the song as seems often to be the case is about two lovers having to not be with each other.

On the whole the programme stands for everything that is up to date to teenagers. (Simon Byron)

2. Analysing title sequences

The introductory sequences to television programmes repay detailed study. Indeed they are very often more creative, interesting and enjoyable than the programmes which follow. ('It makes you think you're going to see something really interesting', as one pupil said of the dazzling new visual introduction to the old-hat *Tonight* series, 'but all you get are people sitting in a studio'.) Title sequences are highly compact, almost purely visual in their impact, and encapsulate both the content of the show to follow and the mythology it is attempting to project. Traditionally British television programmes have adopted low-key titling techniques in comparison with their slicker American counterparts, where the necessity of hooking the audience before the commercials which follow, and of giving some indication of the splendours to come have produced montage sequences of some interest in themselves. Along with ads, they are television's most visually interesting phenomenon, and are likely to remain so, particularly as in British television giving new title sequences to old shows has become one way of disguising the paucity of new material in the schedules.

In analysing and discussing television programmes pupils will need to pay particular attention to title sequences since the programmes' key elements can often be located within them. For this reason it is a valuable and stimulating exercise early in a television course to scrutinise a number of prerecorded introductory sequences. Run together they form a highly concentrated visual experience which should certainly stimulate some pupil responses.

Exercise
1. Prerecord eight title sequences.
2. Show the tape, without interruption, to the group.
3. Distribute eight pieces of paper to each pupil.

4. Re-show the tape, stopping after each sequence for a few minutes so that the group can respond in writing.
5. After each sequence and class analysis, show that sequence again.
6. After the showing of the final sequence gather together individual analyses of each sequence and hand them to a team pair (if there are 16 in the total group; a team of three if there are 24).
7. Each team pair must produce a final analysis of their sequence, based upon the evidence of the observations of the whole group.

3. Introducing genre

The concept of genre is a useful one to introduce to pupils early in their study of television since without it, it is difficult to bring any kind of order to the study of television programmes let alone make useful generalisations about them. Pupils will readily recognise that most television programmes fall easily into one of a number of possible categories, and a useful way of beginning to establish both the range of television genres, and the significance of iconography in identifying them is to use *Genre Recognition Extracts*. Collect together on one tape fifteen or twenty 5-second extracts from a random range of television programmes. Play the tape through two or three times to the group who must guess which kind of programme each extract is taken from. The exercise provides a means by which pupils can themselves begin to construct the principal television genres without the direct intervention of the teacher, and emphasises the extent to which genres can largely be identified by their iconography.

4. Television cartoons

The simplest of all of television's dramatic forms, television cartoons are particularly appropriate material for detailed study early in a television studies course. Through the medium of cartoons many pupils will be able to grasp quite difficult aesthetic concepts normally accessible in schools only through more complex material. Pupils can in fact be lead to consider, perhaps for the first time, questions about different kinds of narrative structure through the even simpler, more static medium of the comic strip.

a. Comic strips: narrative sequencing, narrative prediction and cloze exercises

Narrative sequencing   For each pupil cut up a short one-page comic strip into its individual pictures and shuffle them until they are well mixed. Pupils must put the strip into its original narrative sequence. When this has been done and the order noted, pupils should attempt to outline briefly the principles by which the plot develops. Pictures should then be reshuffled and handed on to the next pupil. Sequencing exercises force attention upon the larger organisational structures of the strip by asking pupils to recreate them; but they also demand an attention to detailed evidence from the text, for it is often minute details which provide the clues to correct sequencing patterns.

Narrative prediction Another method of focusing attention upon narrative conventions and of encouraging detailed observation is through the use of *prediction exercises* in which each pupil is given a whole page comic strip, complete apart from the final box. Pupils must draw what they believe to be the contents of the final box.

Cloze exercises One or two panels from a narrative are omitted, and have to be guessed on the basis of what leads up to and follows from the missing sections. This forms a third technique for sharpening detailed observation.

Individual or paired exercises should be given wherever possible, though at some stage the teacher may wish to examine one particular strip with his whole group via an overhead projector. In this context it ought to be possible to encourage comments on some of the following aspects of comic strips: (i) the techniques by which character is delineated; (ii) the overall visual impact and layout of the page; (iii) the use of simple montage techniques, and the creative role of the reader who fills in the gaps and relationships between the static panels of the comic.

b. 'The Flintstones' book

The group, by now quite used to discussing narrative structure, humour and character in comics, chose to look at an extract from *The Flintstones* for their first analysis of television cartoons. It was decided that the comments of everyone in the group would be gathered together, photographed, given a cover designed by one of the group and displayed in the youth wing of the school in which we were working. This was a procedure which we frequently followed and at the end of the course many books of analyses representing an impressive body of work had been produced and pinned to a television studies notice board. The eventual production of *The Flintstones Book* undoubtedly provided a major stimulus for the production of a large number of perceptive and well-written pieces. *All* pupils treated the work seriously and responded at some length. One girl, who had never shown much interest in school work, and who was later to run away from school altogether, produced an 800-word piece (itself something of an achievement on a 12-minute extract) of some originality which displayed both an enthusiasm and ability conspicuously lacking in every other aspect of her school work. Length precludes the inclusion here of the entire Flintstones book (the thirteen pupils in the group produced well over 5000 words between them); one short extract must suffice to give something of its flavour:

The Flintstones' life-style is modern-day, yet with certain attributes of the stone age, e.g. they have telephones, cameras, cars, buses etc., all recognizable by shape as their modern day counterparts, yet crudely made from wood, bone and rock.

The Flintstones, like most cartoons, uses mock violence to get laughs, e.g. people get thrown around, but never hurt (the best example of this is Tom and Jerry). The drawings are simple, but well done, in the distinctive style that the Hanna-Barbera studios had at that time. The background, scenery, and other non-essentials are always there, not skimped like many other cartoons. Like a lot of cartoons, the animals are given human attributes and intelligence. Another much-used technique is improbability, for instance, the baby of Barney Rubble, 'Bam-Bam' is strong enough to break a marble play-pen, and throw a man around.

The structure has to be different in a cartoon this length, as opposed to the five-minute length of usual cartoons. There are several climaxes, and these help to keep your attention rivetted on the screen.

Work on the Flintstones was followed by a session in which four short television cartoons were shown. After the showing of each one (seen twice) the group broke up into discussion groups so that every pupil had an opportunity to talk about what he had seen. A large number of issues were raised by these discussions, and by *The Flintstones Book*, so I undertook to bring our work on cartoons to a close by producing for our final session a summary sheet of the ground we had covered. The sheet represents a pulling together of ideas from the group's own analyses and should be read as a summary of what they now knew about the genre.

---

c. Television cartoons: hand out

We have spent the last two weeks viewing, discussing and analysing some typical television cartoon programmes. This has given us the opportunity of trying out some of the interpretive skills which were introduced last term upon material which is relatively simple and unambiguous; it has also been our first extended look at a particular television genre, a concept which we discussed earlier this term. Again, it is the comparative lack of complexity of the cartoon genre which makes it appropriate for study in this part of the course. Before we go on to the next part of the course, it may be worthwhile putting together a number of points about cartoons which emerged from *The Flintstones Book* and from our discussions over the last two weeks.

Narrative structure   Cartoons tend to have an easily discernible narrative structure. There will be an *exposition* in which a situation is given or a theme stated, a *development* ending in a climax or a series of climaxes, and a *resolution* in which conflicts are settled and problems finally solved.

Some narrative devices　The narrative may proceed as a number of variations upon a particular theme (*Tom and Jerry* Cartoons use this technique a lot, as in the one we saw about the dog's repeated and futile attempts to build his own ideal home). Or it may set up a problem, and work through a number of possible solutions until it is solved (as in the gopher cartoon). Within this structure there may be additional motifs – *chases*, swift changes of fortune, *reversals* of situations, and *retribution* which is invariably *physical, violent* and *impermanent* in its effects.

Morality　Like most plays, novels and poems, television cartoons tend to present us with situations in which there is a *moral* conflict. Good opposes evil, the weak are set against the strong, the clever against the stupid, the hunter against the hunted, the innocent against the unscrupulous. It is worth asking of any cartoon: 'What moral point is being made here?'

Anthropomorphism　A clumsy word but one worth learning because it's an important cartoon convention which many of you drew attention to in *The Flintstones*. It means literally 'in the form of man', and refers to the tendency of the animals in cartoons to talk and behave like human beings. (The word also has religious connotations which we have discussed.) The use of anthropomorphic animals is one of the principal sources of humour in television cartoons.

The cartoon image　Cartoons are rather like moving comics. The individual frames are quite lacking in the detail of photographs, and meanings are communicated by a kind of visual shorthand, which generally concentrates upon communicating one, and *only* one meaning at any particular time. Clarity of meaning is attained through the *exaggeration* of actions, emotions and physical features, and *stereotyping* is a stock technique. Whenever foreigners are introduced they must be instantly recognizable and even the animals themselves – cats, dogs and mice – are reducible to a few well-worn features and characteristics.

Though the cartoon image is highly stylised and oversimplified, it is worth noting that some images are more simplified than others. Many cartoons present no background detail at all, whereas from others (*Tom and Jerry* for example), it is possible to build up a picture of the house where the animals live, the furniture it contains, the temperament, footwear and even the social class of its owners.

Humour　Cartoons are undemanding fun, and the humour takes many forms. There is one repeated technique which is worth noting, however, and that is the visual or sound *analogy*, in which a sound or image is used in an unusual and surprising way to suggest something else. (Running animals screech to a halt like cars; bodies shred through fences like grated cheese; a flute becomes a baseball bat, etc.)

Political implications   Many of your analyses observed that in *The Flintstones* stone-age life was not portrayed realistically but as an extension of the American way of life. In American comics and cartoons different cultures, historical periods and ways of life are not often presented as being of some importance and interest in themselves but as either essentially the *same* as modern American society, or as so strange and odd as to be funny. This is true not only of cartoons but of Disney's nature films in which even the behaviour of animals is treated in terms of the life-style of an American suburban family. What is the purpose of presenting American values as normal and natural, and all others as unworthy of serious consideration?

Simplicity   Cartoons present us with a simple, instantly recognizable and uncomplicated world, in which all situations and characters can be instantly comprehended; they provide a refuge from a real world which is fraught with ambiguity and complexity. This is both the source of their appeal and their greatest limitation. It is appealing to enter a world of certainty, to 'escape' from reality, but ultimately unsatisfying, because so little of what is said to us by cartoons can help us to make sense of our own world and our own individual experience. And this, at best, is what books, films and television programmes can help us to do.

---

5. Establishing questions ('*Young Scientists of the Year*')

What questions may be asked of a particular television programme? Some indication of the ways in which questions can be grouped and classified, together with ways of handling 'questions about questions' has already been given in Chapter 1. The aim here is not to establish a particular methodology, nor to suggest that some questions are 'better' than others, but to take an objective look at the range of possibilities and to establish that the information which one wishes to extract from a piece of television will depend very much upon the questions one asks of it. The questions asked of the visual material in Chapter 3 were designed to elicit information about different aspects of its 'total communication'. But there are of course many other possible questions. It is important at an early stage in teleliteracy work to explore what these might be by examining a programme not for the *purpose of analysis* but in order to draw attention to the *pre-analytical* ability of separating out those areas and questions which might warrant further investigation. A *Young Scientists of the Year* programme (BBC 1) was shown to the group, who were then asked to make a list of those things in the show which could be made the subject of further investigation. Not surprisingly the lists tended to reflect the emphases of our previous work. Here are the responses to the assignment, the first operating at quite a low cognitive level, often vague, but nevertheless quite exhaustive; the second representing a level of conceptualisation which the first is edging towards:

Young Scientists of the Year

Possible Areas of Study
1. The way the individual projects are put forward.
2. The clothing the children wear. ⎱ Dress.
3. The clothing the scientists wear. ⎰
4. Equipment used in projects.
5. Personalities of scientists and the kids.
6. Audience.
7. Cuts, editing.
8. Music at beginning and end of programme.
9. Introduction put forward by the presenter. Credits.
10. Set out of the studio.
11. Questions put forward by scientists.
12. Tone.
13. Morality. What things they praise.
14. Idea of scoreboard. Points system.
15. Similarities to other programmes, e.g. *Top of the Form, University Challenge.*
16. Entertainment.
17. Structure.

You can look at, or analyse, any programme on a number of different levels, or headings. For this programme the headings could be:

1. *Genre*: This means the type or sort of programme, e.g. Comedy, Thriller, Documentary, Western, etc. *Young Scientists of the Year* was a competition/quiz with some documentary (film) parts.
2. *Tone*: Light, Serious, etc. *Young Scientists* was serious.
3. *Dress of characters*: this means just what it says; the people involved in *Young Scientists* were dressed formally, e.g. shirt and ties, school uniform, etc.
4. *Iconography*: ('objects and images seen'). In *Young Scientists* we saw scientific equipment, which shows obviously that it is about science, and we also saw chairs, audience, etc; which shows that it is in a studio.
5. *Surroundings*: *Young Scientists* was in a studio, showing that it was a quiz or 'staged' show, and that it was not an outside event.

6. *Narrative Method*: This is the way that the programme is put together, and gives its message. *Young Scientists* is mostly film of the experiments of the competition, interspersed with bits from the studio to give it excitement and entertainment value. Without the 'competition' aspect in it, it would lose its watchability and be no more than a pseudo-documentary. The kids are in it to make it watchable at that time of night (6.45) to families.

7. *Morality*: Morality means the setting of good against bad. Most programmes use morality by saying one set of values are bad, and another set are good. The morality in *Young Scientists* is that hard work is good, and the set of kids that have worked hardest are best. They are trying to convince you to work hard by setting an example.

8. *Audience*: This is the type of people who watch it, and is determined by not only the type of programme but also the time it is on. *Young Scientists* is on at 6.45 at night, and includes kids of about 14 or 15, the same age as the audience. The competitive element makes it watchable by that age of audience, and also makes it entertaining. This is underlined by the trophy.

The responses of the group were collated by a young teacher with whom I was working, Vale Humble, and formed the basis of a hand-out on *Young Scientists of the Year* which he wrote for distribution to the group the following period. His paper moves outwards from the particular observations of the group towards general questions which might be raised across a wide range of television material. It is also, incidentally, an interesting in-service education document since it was written by a teacher of no more than one year's teaching experience who was working in a field outside his subject specialism.

---

a. *'Young Scientists of the Year': hand out*

Last week you listed many questions which could have been asked of the television programme *Young Scientists of the Year*. Here are some subject areas and questions arising from your lists which might be applied to *many* different kinds of programme.

Introductory title sequence   What function does the title sequence serve? What image does it project of the programme to come? Examine the language of the title. Precisely what would we expect to find presented in a programme entitled *Young Scientists of the Year*. Take each word and explore its implications. Do the same with the following titles. What does each title lead us to believe about the nature of the programme to follow?

New Faces
Panorama
Dad's Army
Top of the Form
Play for Today

Music   What does it tell you about the programme? Does it help establish its tone and provide it with identity? In *Young Scientists*, the music was bouncy and quick moving, not the kind of sombre, stately or awe inspiring stuff one associates with programmes which treat science 'seriously' (cf. *The Sky at Night*). In fact John Rimmer suggested that the music reminded him of the kind used in *Sportsnight with Coleman*, simply because it was quick and sounded exciting and challenging. A useful comparison because this programme has a strong emphasis on taking part and challenging to win.

Compere   How is the show introduced? What techniques are used? Here Paddy Feeny, dressed in casual clothes and sporting a beard, introduces, interviews and talks with the contestants; he stands back when they are about to be judged by the 'experts' and then announces the winners. What differences exist between this role and that of Bruce Forsyth or Hughie Green or Nicholas Parsons in their quiz show programmes?

The indications are that this is more of a 'show' than a programme about 'science'. Paddy Feeny has been a questionmaster in *Top of the Form* and we associate him with education, questions, competitions, winners, trophies and school children. We are led to expect that the programme will contain some of these elements and Feeny's established image – rather earnest and 'square', but not too serious – can allow us to make assumptions about the tone and nature of the programme.

Format and structure
1. How does the programme develop? What is its fundamental structure?
2. Does it contain any conventions which are standard features of this kind of programme?
3. Note that there are a variety of techniques designed to hold the attention and ensure against flagging of interest. What are these?

Morality   Are there any moral assumptions? What is seen to be admired, praised, condemned or discouraged by the programme?

Mediation   What differences exist between the programme and the reality it is supposed to be depicting? Does it give an accurate picture of school science lessons, school pupils and university science professors?

Television tends to package everything – a general election, the daily news, football – as a show or spectacle.

All of these aspects of life exist outside television in very different forms from the way they are presented to us by television. *Young Scientists* packages science and presents it to us as a spectacle. As a result the programme tends to be like many other television programmes, and its avowed content (scientific enquiry) is swamped by all the paraphernalia of 'teams', scoreboards, trophies, supporters with mascots and panels of experts. It needs to be emphasized that all of this packaging has nothing to do with science, or with the real process of scientific enquiry (which tends to be slow, painstaking and largely 'unexciting' in television terms).

Language   Examine the language used in the show. What are its characteristics? How does the language in *Young Scientists of the Year* differ from the language of other shows?

Non-verbal communication patterns   Look at the dress, appearance, gestures, positions, movements, etc. of all the participants. Is there any stereotyping?

Iconography   What is distinctive about the *objects* you see in the show?

Genre   What *type* of programme is *Young Scientists*? Name some of the conventions operating in it.

Education   Young Scientists is in many ways an 'educational' programme, and it projects to us a number of ideas of what education is (or ought to be) about. Here are some assumptions which the programme seems to make about learning:

Learning thrives through competition.
The main pleasure to be derived from learning is in triumphing over others.
The results of learning can be measured pretty accurately.
Learning involves being judged by others.
The rewards of learning are extrinsic to it.
Science is too complex for ordinary people and is best left to earnest school
    children and eccentric experts.

In many ways *you* are experts on education (having received it for about ten years now). Do you agree with these assumptions about the nature of learning?
    Work out for yourself other possible assumptions upon which one might base a good education. (Vale Humble)

5

Television News

1. Why teach about television news?

Teaching about television news poses an immediate problem for the teacher; on the one hand many pupils are likely to respond negatively to the notion of studying television news – to many of them it will be 'boring', and the least appetising part of their television diet. On the other hand the teacher needs to be aware of the fact, familiar to audience researchers, that with increasing maturity there is a marked increase in interest in news programmes. Half of the United Kingdom's adult population watches at least one television news bulletin each day, and 95 per cent of all adult viewers claim to be at least interested in news. The audience for television news is not only massive, but is characterised by great faith. BBC television news is considered by 86 per cent of viewers to be 'always trustworthy' or 'trustworthy most of the time'; 'only' 78 per cent responded to ITN in this way – an interesting anomaly which I suspect has no logical basis but reflects attitudes towards the BBC and IBA as institutions, and perhaps even towards their different 'styles' of news presentation.[1]

Children on the whole consider television news to be as trustworthy as adults do. This faith is based upon two feelings. The first is that, in the words of one sixth former, 'television news items are delivered to the public by a neutral observer who passes on the news items with no factual distortion at all'. This belief is buttressed by comparison with newspapers, which as most children leaving school now know, are all 'biased', and generally confuse fact and opinion. The second feeling, which appears to have almost universal credence amongst school pupils, is that visual evidence is more reliable than print: 'You can see what is happening for yourself, and so make up your own mind about it.'[2] The fact that the overwhelming majority even of our most highly educated school students have not yet become aware of the fact that any piece of film or video *inevitably* offers a selective view of experience is a startling indictment of the level of visual literacy which exists in schools at the present moment. There is an imperative need to demonstrate to pupils the ways in which selection is integral not only to any form of news, but to most forms of visual communication. However nowhere does that great illusion of television as a presenter of unmediated reality have greater general credibility than in news presentations. Nor in any other field of television is the illusion quite so sedulously fostered by the broadcasting organisations. In no other area of television education therefore is it quite so incumbent upon the teacher to demonstrate to his students the constructed nature of what they see. The teacher's task then is both vitally important and long term. The real measure of his success will lie in the effect he will have upon his pupils when they become part of that mass adult audience which regularly consumes television news broadcasts.

2. News simulations

Any initial resistance there may be in the classroom to the idea of studying news is more than counterbalanced by the abundance of materials already available for studying news, by the comparative ease of preparing one's own original material and by the relative simplicity of involving pupils in practical activities which will illuminate the processes of news selection and presentation.

a. 'Front Page' and 'Radio Covingham'

Front Page and *Radio Covingham* are two carefully written simulations by Kenneth Jones which make excellent resource material for use with pupils in the middle and higher age ranges of secondary school. *Front Page*, in which pupils do the job of a subeditor on a local newspaper, is an appropriate introduction to the study of televised news since it provides pupils with the opportunity to evaluate and select news material within a simple, yet realistic organisational framework. Although the subject matter is journalistic what is really being learned, because it is being acted out, is that news is necessarily the end product of a selection and shaping process, an understanding which as we shall see can be consolidated and deepened in later work. The simplicity of *Front Page*'s framework is also of some importance in that for most pupils this will be very much an initiatory exercise – a suitable introduction both to the study of news and to a new way of working, for the simulation demands the use of basic social and co-operative skills on the part of pupils, who are required to make effective group decisions under the pressure of a time deadline.

Pupils who have cut their teeth on *Front Page* will possess many of the organisational and communication skills necessary to undertake a more complex simulation like *Radio Covingham*. This simulation involves pupils in producing a 'live' local radio news magazine programme using fictional material. The programme must last ten minutes, and since its title is *News and Views at 7*, it has to incorporate interviews as well as news items. The simulation does therefore assume the existence of some interviewing skills on the part of pupils, and teachers may wish to give pupils practice in interviewing techniques (see Chapter 9) before they attempt this simulation. Finally mention should be made of a most imaginative recent simulation, *Choosing the News* by Andrew Bethell and Michael Simons, in which pupils are required to cut out stories and 'crop' photographs in order to (literally) compose the front page of an imaginary local newspaper.[3]

b. 'Television News': an original simulation

Introduction *Television News* is an original simulation, based upon real events and their presentation in a regional television news programme. The simulation can be as simple or as sophisticated as the equipment you have at your disposal. It can be shot with a Portapack, or with two or three cameras and inserted pre-filmed material if you have the time and equipment to do it. *Television News* does make two assumptions about pupil capability. First, it assumes that the group will have had some practice and experience in operating television cameras and videotape equipment; secondly, that pupils will possess social and organisational skills of the kind developed by simulations like *Front Page* and *Radio Covingham*. *Television News* is intended to extend the skills of selecting and presenting news into the medium of television, to begin the process of demystifying both television and news by providing opportunities to work creatively in the medium with news material and to introduce the group at first hand to some of the specific problems relating to television news presentation.

Organisation The teacher will need to split his class into groups of between seven and ten pupils. If there is more than one camera available, the group will need to have cameramen and a producer in addition to the programme participants. He will tell each group that they will be required to produce a ten-minute long television news programme from news material which will be distributed to them throughout the simulation. The programme should be as interesting and varied as possible and include interviews and expert comment as well as straight presentation. It will be televised live, so time for rehearsals and dummy runs should be made before the programme goes out. The time deadline for live presentation should be given (about one hour hence), the importance of making the programme last for *precisely* ten minutes stressed and the programme controller's memo (see below) and a small number of news stories should be distributed. These, it should be explained, are stories which are already on the news desk when the team begins its work. Other stories will be placed on the desk as they come in. Any of these stories may be edited or re-written. At least fifteen minutes should be allowed for the group to read and sift the materials, assign roles and begin organising its work before any additional news stories are fed in. They should then be placed on the table, either individually or in small batches at intervals during the time remaining before the programme goes on the air.

How to produce materials for television news   There are a number of possible ways of producing materials for this simulation; the method chosen will depend upon the time available and the sophistication of the equipment available.

1. Make a videotape recording of one edition of your local television news programme, and write down the details of the stories reported on the programme, using a separate sheet of paper for each story. Add to these stories other news items not reported on the programme but appearing in the local press. Present the stories to pupils in such a way that some will require re-writing to be suitable for television presentation. When the simulation has been completed and the pupils' programmes played back and discussed, the original local news programme may be shown, together with a copy of the local newspaper, so that detailed comparisons in coverage and emphasis can be made.
2. Prepare material which is right up to the minute by tape-recording two or three hourly news bulletins from radio just before the simulation. Write or type out the details of each story on a separate piece of paper. Continue to monitor radio news bulletins while the simulation is in progress and feed this material into the groups. If this simulation is played in the morning, early television news programmes can be watched at around 1.00 p.m. for the purposes of comparison.
3. If you have editing equipment available, provide video stories taken from local television news to supplement the written material. You will need to provide for each group (a) a description of each video story, its precise length and whether commentary is provided; and (b) the facilities to view the videotaped stories.

Whichever method is used, any materials fed in to groups should be prefaced by this programme controller's memorandum:

Television News

MEMO

From: Programme Controller
To: Production staff, regional television news programme

I was very concerned yesterday about the weak linkage between your regional news programme and *Nationwide* which immediately follows it. May I stress once more the absolute necessity of finishing on time. If you over-run, you will simply be cut off in mid-sentence as you were yesterday. Under-running is less serious but, even so, you should try not to under-run by more than half a minute. Please pay the utmost attention to this. Yesterday's bad timing almost ruined a very enjoyable programme and all of your hard work.

Ed Morrison (signed)

c. The value of simulation: some notes

Simulation is a technique still comparatively little used in the classroom, although it is an enormously valuable and involving technique, experience of which every fully trained teacher should certainly have at his fingertips. Nevertheless the 'play' element in simulations, the high degree of often unorthodox pupil involvement, the openness of their structures, the break they make with more formal classroom organisations, and even the very newness of the technique will still be enough to cause suspicion and even hostility amongst many colleagues. It is essential therefore for the teacher to be aware of precisely what his pupils are likely to learn through participating in a simulation like *Television News*. The following notes are intended to assist in that task.

Social learning   In *Television News* what is most effectively learned arises from the social dynamics of the situation, from the experience's 'hidden curriculum', rather than from its nominal content. This manifest content – the selection, packaging and presentation of news material – takes place within a social context which necessarily involves teamwork, the give and take of ideas and the acceptance of personal responsibility and decision-making within a group context. The motivational thrust for this kind of activity comes not from the acquisition of personal kudos, but from having contributed towards the successful completion of a joint enterprise.

The development of self-criticism   A further fundamental learning arises from the character of the videotape recording equipment (VTR) itself as an educational tool. VTR provides for pupils such an immediate feedback of their own efforts that the development of personal and group self-criticism – the dissatisfaction with first efforts and the desire to polish and improve work without teacher insistence – could be said to be almost endemic to the medium. The educational 'message' probably most effectively communicated by the medium is, therefore, the very opposite of that implicitly passed on by most schools; that success and disappointment, far from resting upon the personal and often arbitrary judgements of teachers are, in actuality, an organic part of any learning process.

Communication abilities   These are generally classifiable under the following headings: (i) speaking – in both private and public contexts; (ii) communicating through the medium of television, either as 'subjects', presenters, cameramen or producers; (iii) written skills – re-writing material to make it appropriate to the visual medium; (iv) practice in interviewing and being interviewed.

Personal abilities   One of the advantages of simulation is that it not only gives the individual practice in abilities predetermined by the teacher, but allows him to utilise any additional skills he possesses which are appropriate to the situation. Many of the aptitudes displayed during the course of *Television News* were of a kind which a teacher could not have known about beforehand and to which schools normally attach little importance. Nevertheless, they were performed well and with pleasure. The fact that pupils were allowed to demonstrate them at all was of critical importance. Many of the group grew almost visibly as people during the experience, becoming more self-confident and, therefore, more self-critical and more openly accepting of others. Some of the skills displayed were:

guitar-playing (for a signature tune)
the accurate impersonation of a regional accent
encouraging and bringing out a shy group-member
giving a straight story a humorous slant
creative production skills
timing a joke
sensitivity in role-play
ability to improvise and hold the fort on camera when disasters occurred
'instant' lettering and artwork for credits and captions.

Motivation   At a time when the net result of a good deal of teaching is to turn pupils off school subjects for life, it is probably worth commenting upon the high degree of motivation which classroom simulations generally manage to stimulate in pupils. In so far as it is possible to isolate the factors which generated this kind of commitment in the simulations described, they seemed to be:

the emphasis upon activity-based learning, demanding a creative input from pupils

the opportunity for pupils to show what they were capable of doing, rather than having exposed what they couldn't self-evaluation, not in terms of marks but of the effectiveness of the product of their work

a pupil–teacher relationship in which the teacher facilitates rather than judges. Teacher intervention should rarely be necessary in simulations; when it occurs it should ideally be in role or through memoranda. In this situation, the role of teacher as critic and judge withers away.

Television Finally, what had been learned about television and about television news in particular?

In *general* terms, opening up the medium and giving pupils the opportunity to use it as a means of expression demystifies the medium in a way which nothing else can, for the mystification of the broadcasting media so assiduously cultivated by those who control them is nothing more than a function of their limited accessibility.

Other important learnings are suggested by Paul Willis's analysis of the ways in which news may be perceived:

> News seems to arise naturally out of the world. It is almost as if most people still regard the content of news reaching them as the whole news, the only news; a direct relay somehow of the real world. It is very easy to overlook the fact that any news presentation is a tiny fraction of all the news carried by the communications systems. There is also a feeling that if this news, the only possible news, were distorted or biased it would be obvious to the receiver – the belief that bias and distortion are an addition to the truth and are therefore identifiable and separable from the truth. A very wide perspective is needed to understand that bias and distortion are closely interwoven with so-called facts from the stage of selection right through to the presentation of news, and indeed that the notion of truth and objectivity is an abstraction. Once an item of news has been selected for transmission to the public there is already bias, some selective principle, some value, quite apart from the way it is presented.[4]

The feeling that 'news seems to arise naturally out of the world' is probably one which most pupils have, though the detection and discussion of bias in newspapers is now something of a standard procedure in schools. Willis's distinction between bias as something *integral* to news, rather than as something *added* to it, is however a crucial one. It is difficult to see how this distinction can be learned (as opposed to being simply received as information) except by some kind of simulation technique. Certainly it is this very distinction which *Television News*, with its emphasis upon the first-hand experience of selecting and packaging news from a wide variety of possible alternatives, encourages pupils to make. And to engage in a process whereby news is recognised as being *necessarily* the end product of a selection process inevitably subjective in nature is to undermine radically the pervasive myth of news as being generally objective and impartial reporting, in which any bias which does appear can be screened out by the perceptive viewer.

The *specific* points about television news presentation which the simulation raises will differ each time it is played. In spring 1976, one version of *Television News* was played by a group of undergraduates at Liverpool University as part of their degree course in media studies. A description and analysis of that occasion is given below to indicate the range of issues raised by the simulation and to illustrate the way in which practical television work can relate to the analysis of actual television programmes.

d. Case study: 'Television News' simulation played at Liverpool University, February 1976

Student notes　These notes were handed out:

> For the purpose of this exercise you will be expected to act out the various roles of the staff of a typical television news magazine programme. These roles represent the way in which a local television newsroom operates. Such a programme depends on team work, each member making a contribution to the programme, with someone to lead the team and decide on programme content and running order.
>
> A TV magazine programme consists of both news items and items of general interest. The latter, known as features, need not be topical items but may also be follow-ups of news stories, perhaps adding the human interest aspect to a news report. In a newsroom team we have a Programme Editor who is responsible for the overall programme and a News Editor who is responsible for the news report section of the programme. These roles may overlap; thus we may have a big story that breaks in the region such as a steelworks closing down. The News Editor will be interested in reporting on the immediate facts of the situation whereas the Programme Editor will be interested in other aspects resulting from the closure. In fact the Programme Editor may decide to devote the whole programme to the topic, for the amount of time devoted to any news report is decided by him. The News Editor has to work within this time limit.

Student roles　The roles undertaken were:

Programme Editor　　　　Decides on overall programme content and time devoted to the news report section of the programme. He decides on the programme order and writes the links to the various items.

News Editor	Receives raw news reports, selects items and decides on the news order. He passes some of the stories to the Subeditor for 'subbing' and does some subediting himself.
Subeditor	Subedits the raw news reports to make them suitable for television. (For the purpose of this exercise he may double the role of news reader.)
3 Reporters	Each reporter reports on a topic decided by News Editor or Programme Editor. (Writes own scripts/sound tracks/conducts interviews/presents in studio or on location.)
Link Person or Anchor Person	Presents the programme to camera, reading links to the various items.
Graphic Artist	Prepares last-minute captions using Letraset or free hand drawings.

Technical roles   The roles of producer, floor manager and cameramen were undertaken by the staff of the course.

Materials   Material used was:

Materials provided	Five copies of the *Liverpool Echo*. Seven stories from previous evening's *Look North* (regional television programme). Film material for some of the stories.
Materials fed in	Twelve stories from *Look North*, some with film material, fed in intermittently throughout the simulation. Three or four fabricated and trivial 'dummy' stories. A very late story on a jet crash, fed in when the programme's organisation was almost complete.

Post-play analysis   This fell into four divisions:

(i) News values: One of the first things which needs to be established in a post-play discussion are the criteria used by the group for the selection and placing of their news items. Why were some stories selected and not others? How was a story's importance evaluated? The group is unlikely to have been consciously aware that it was establishing its own news values during the course of the simulation, and the teacher's task here will be made easier if he has eavesdropped on discussions from time to time during the simulation, and

can draw attention to those points in the discussion when news values were implicitly if not overtly established. It is worth stressing that the possibility of news values being brought out into open discussion during the simulation is extremely slight. The Liverpool undergraduates were a highly sophisticated group of media students. Yet faced with the concrete task of sifting through the stories and producing a coherent programme within a strict time deadline, their response of immersing themselves in the task at hand so that criteria for selecting stories never became obviously explicit, and therefore never became the basis for discussion, was entirely typical. Nevertheless some characteristics were articulated as giving value to a piece of news, though they were neither coherently argued for, challenged or even discussed but simply 'appealed' to:

1. '*Relevance*': often used as a criterion of value for a piece of news ('Is it particularly relevant though?', 'I think this is relevant') but never challenged or thought through. The implication of a notional audience to whom material might or might not be relevant was never established. Perhaps what was meant was not 'Relevant to whom?', but 'Relevant to what?' – to a preconceived notion of what constitutes news perhaps?
2. *Availability of film material*: ('We have film for that') – a criterion which finally emerged as possibly the most potent value of all. The final decision on the order, and therefore the priority of news items was based on the 'aesthetic' grounds of presenting features to a film/report/film/report formula. This is probably an accurate reflection of current television practice. One suspects that the inclusion and even primacy of many news stories are determined by the availability and impact of filmed illustrative footage. And *within* a story it is also clearly likely that the 'angle' of the coverage will be determined by the footage available. It is the close link with film material which tends to make television news even more *event*- and *person-orientated* and even more likely to ignore the underlying structural content of a situation (through what Stuart Hall has termed a picture's 'personalizing transformation'[5]) than conventional newspaper coverage.

The importance of the visual material in shaping news scripts has been well illustrated by Nigel Ryan, who was an editor at ITN:

> I found that the script I originally had in mind gradually disintegrated as the film progressed. I realised that I was not going to be able to talk about death because I had not got pictures to cover it, and I was not going to be able to talk about what the Opposition man said because he was out of focus, and I was not going to be able to talk about some other matter which I thought was of enormous importance because I had not filmed it properly.[6]

The primary significance of film material indeed imposes constraints upon the content of television news which are purely technical. Factors irrelevant to the status of the story can come to be primary determinants of whether it will be screened. The state of the light for instance becomes a prime consideration for the coverage of out-of-doors newsworthy events. As John Whale has observed:

> This is why there was a slightly disproportionate emphasis on fires in the television coverage of such disturbances as the one at Cleveland in July 1968. Besides being a powerful symbol of pillage and ruin, a fire is its own source of light.[7]

Further technical constraints upon the content of news stories have been elaborated by Tom Burns:

> A camera crew and a reporter have to get to the scene, the equipment has to be set up, the story photographed; afterwards, the film has to be sent to the studios, processed and edited to 'fit the story line', and made ready for narration before transmission. All this takes time. Ordinarily, therefore, it is only possible to film a news event if it leaves photographable debris or survivors – or if it is known about some hours beforehand . . . The most common use of film is of meetings, demonstrations and public ceremonies . . . conferences and conventions have become as indispensable to television as they are to political parties.[8]

3. *Balance between serious and light items*: ('All of these items are so serious; why can't we end on a light note?'). The feeling that a balance should be achieved between 'serious' and 'light' material had the effect of pushing to the forefront stories which the group unanimously considered trivial or unimportant (an item on a charm school for instance). This desire for balance may have been based upon an attempt simply to imitate the practice of actual television news programmes – the feeling that the programme should 'end on a light note' certainly seems to be derived from this source. But the group also clearly felt that they wanted to put on a viewable show and that their programme should make an explicit attempt to keep the viewer entertained as well as informed. The insistence upon a 'mustn't-bore' formula and a happy ending point up the *reassurance* function of news broadcasts which is discussed later (4d: *News as reassurance*).

4. *Copying the 'real' news*: The tendency of students and pupils to imitate on video what they see on BBC or ITV operates here as an equation of news with what appears on television news programmes and works against an understanding of, say, BBC News as one version amongst many possibilities. So, when one of the Liverpool students said 'I think that the item on technology ought to come first' she *may* have been telling us something

about her own values. More likely however she was appealing to a generalised notion of what news *ought* to be about built up from her previous experience of the content of news broadcasts. If this is so, she is both internalising and acting upon implicit news values which may be very different from her own values, interests and priorities. The question which needs asking here is 'What and whose values and priorities are being internalised?'

(ii) Work parameters: The 'meet-the-deadline' atmosphere generated by the simulation is a bustling, busy, working, somewhat *non-reflective* one, presumably quite close to the kind of atmosphere within which newspaper and broadcasting journalists actually work.[9] This in itself determines some of the qualities of news programmes – their breathlessness, their absorption with up-to-the-minute surface events, and the implicit nature of most of the value judgements made – and indicates the extent to which these qualities are endemic both to the journalistic professions and to news agencies as institutions.

To an overwhelming extent BBC News, like any daily newspaper, will look much the same irrespective of the individuals who are staffing it. News is an institutional product and will reflect institutional and vocational norms. These are partly determined by time parameters but even more significantly by the authority structures of the institution. As we have seen, commercial television, like the national newspapers, is linked to big business either directly or through major shareholders. The BBC through its Chairman, Governors, Director-General and Board of Management is locked into a vast range of established social and political institutions. The ways in which these connections work as constraints upon the activities of individual journalists and broadcasters is difficult for the outsider to establish with any precision. It is not of course, simply a question of the Director-General telling news editors (who in turn order reporters) what to do, any more than within a school teachers are necessarily overtly constrained by their head (which is not to say that this does not sometimes happen). There are enough screening devices surrounding institutions and professions to ensure that those whose 'attitudes' are undesirable are unlikely to join them, while once within most institutions or professions the way to the top lies largely in possessing the ability to please one's superiors. Eamonn McCann has graphically described some of the processes involved in establishing authority and control within a newspaper:

In the first place the editorship of a national newspaper is a responsible position and 'responsibility', as understood by the owners of newspapers, would be incompatible with the belief, say, that private ownership of industry is a bad thing. One of the qualifications for editorship is, naturally, a general acceptance of the owners' attitudes.

This is reflected in the editorial 'line' of every paper and it filters through to reporters, sub-editors etc. A journalist who has covered Northern Ireland for a British daily paper explains

You must remember that every journalist wants what he writes to appear, and in practice all journalists know pretty well what their paper's line is, what is expected of them. There is a fair amount of self-censorship. This happens without thinking. No journalist I have met writes what he knows will be cut. What would be the point? If he has a story which he knows will cause controversy back at the newsdesk he will water it down to make it acceptable.

Even if a reporter does send through copy which is critical of the establishment and its representatives (e.g. the army) it is at the mercy of the news editor and the sub-editors. These are likely to be the most conservative of all the journalistic staff, with years of grinding practice in what is acceptable to the editor and the management. The average senior sub-editor will, as a reflex action, strike out any sentence which jars his sense of propriety.

Reporters who know what is expected of them; news editors and sub-editors trained to recognize and eliminate 'unhelpful' references; editors appointed with 'sound' attitudes; boards of management composed of substantial businessmen: the whole sprawling machinery of news gathering and publication automatically filters, refines and packages the information fed in and works to ensure that the news, as printed, is fit to print. The general picture is enlivened by occasional bursts of maverick radicalism. A 'fearless expose' every now and then helps to maintain the official myth of the independent press (and can be good for circulation) but does not alter significantly the pattern which emerges.[10]

As we begin to learn more about what happens within our broadcasting institutions, the patterns of control seem remarkably similar to those described by McCann. Anthony Smith writes from his experience as a BBC producer that 'there is a system of referral upwards of difficult decisions . . . and there is a system of meetings at various levels at which judgements are formed and shared. There is seldom any doubt about what the man above you thinks on any important issue. You can therefore avoid referring upwards by deciding them in a way which you know he would approve of',[11] while Tom Burns' major study of the BBC confirms that 'the selection of broadcasting staff and their promotion is also a sanctioning process which reinforces the standards and requirements which the organisation implicitly, as well as explicitly, wants observed. Again, whatever sanctions there might in principle be, they are hardly ever invoked; operationally, they are incorporated in the career system.'[12]

All of this takes us a long way from the experience of the simulation in which time and the availability of material form the most pressing parameters. Nevertheless time should certainly be spent in discussing with students some of the additional professional constraints faced by broadcasters.

(iii) Juxtaposing news items: As students of montage will recognise, when two stories or pieces of film are juxtaposed, new and independent meanings can often be unexpectedly generated. In fact on television news programmes the meaning of a particular story or image is often quite radically affected by the context within which it is presented. In the Liverpool simulation the students juxtaposed two 'medical' items: (i) an official protest by angry medical consultants against the government's proposal to phase out private pay beds; and (ii) the death of an old aged pensioner through hyperthermia. The effect of placing these two unconnected stories side by side was to suggest that there may have been a connection between them; that somehow this old aged pensioner might not have died through neglect had the consultants not been protesting. The connection is an emotional rather than a logical one, but it brings into sharp focus two particular aspects of the medical consultant's action: the 'concern' it expresses for the well-heeled rather than the poor, and the fact that time and effort are devoted by a powerful professional 'caring' group to a cause affecting their own financial and professional status while desperate problems of social health go unattended. Raymond Williams has even suggested[13] that there is a deliberate perversity in our *refusal* to make precisely this kind of connection between disparate news items, and certainly the attempt to establish such patterns of meaning across news items would make an interesting media exercise. Nevertheless there was no evidence in the simulation that the meanings generated here were consciously intended or that the students had been aware of the dangers or possibilities of juxtaposed news items.

(iv) Televisual codings: It is likely that the most important meanings of television news programmes are communicated to us in ways which we do not yet fully understand, for the study of the predominant televisual codings within news broadcasts has only just begun. Yet it seems likely that the way in which we perceive a particular news story will be fundamentally affected by such considerations as framing, camera placement, editing and the presentation technique employed (filmed interview, expert correspondent, etc.). Are there for example any *integral* differences in meaning between a story covered by a piece of video with voice over, and one presented as a series of interviews?

This precise question was raised during the Liverpool simulation when the 'programme editor' suggested covering a story about school vandalism with a piece of recorded video material with voice over. This decision was made because the story carried great visual impact. The damage done to the school was horrific and spectacular: windows smashed, the head's study door kicked in, equipment ruined. The visual evidence was so striking that no self-respecting newsman could possibly have passed it up. What impression did this coding convey? Unequivocally the visual material with commentary simply describing what had happened carried with it the message that there was no controversy here, simply a senseless act defying any logical or causal explanation. The visual material, presented as 'unmediated' data, was assumed largely to *speak for itself*.

What impression might have been conveyed had the story been covered by two or three interviews? The different coding immediately suggests that there may be more than one possible reaction to the phenomenon of vandalism. Interviews with *particular* people suggest particular social contexts within which the problem may be rooted; interviews with local youths or an employment officer suggest one such context, with the headmaster and pupils of the school another. What needs to be stressed is that a decision to employ the interviewing rather than filmic code for this story would have been to opt for a view of vandalism as explicable event rooted within a social context, rather than senseless event 'caused' by individual or group fecklessness. This primary decision is the determinant of the story's most significant meanings because the coding used *prestructures* the possible responses which the viewer may bring to the story.

3. Analysing televised news in the classroom: comprehensive school pupils' responses

What kind of response to an unseen news programme will comprehensive school pupils make, having worked through the exercises described in Chapters 3 and 4? Here are two analyses from fourteen-year-old pupils:

Extract: The Nine O'Clock News
An interesting thing that I noticed while watching the excerpt was the resemblance of the programme to a visit to a bank. First, there is the hierarchy of an old-established and respected firm, which is apparent in the structure of the programme. The lowest rung of the ladder is the post of 'Reporter'. These are the equivalent of local bank staff – they use local accents, are not seen on film, and they are the ones who do the hard work collecting reports and sending them to the 'Head Office' – like all good firms, the Head Office is in the City.

The 'Chairmen of the Board' are the newsreaders. They positively exude impartiality and their age gives them status, dignity, and authority. They are dressed soberly but smartly, and to heighten the feeling that they are advising you, there is a plate with their name on it on the desk in front of them – and facing you.

The desk heightens still more their impartiality, by separating you from them. They appear to be looking at things from a distance as it were, and to be collating all the information and giving it to you as an adviser.

Their 'aides' at Head Office are the correspondents, who are slightly younger (though older than the reporters) than the newsreaders. They are experts in their own particular field, but they are not treated as being quite as venerable as the newsreaders.

In short, the news is treated as though it were information about an account of yours, at the bank. Some information is received by a local branch manager, and it is shown to you by the manager at Head Office, who refers you to the expert on this sort of matter, and finally back to himself, to say 'It is your decision', from all his impartiality. (Chris Maillard)

Extract: The Nine O'Clock News
This programme starts off its credit sequence with a picture of the world and the logo on it and the music is a fanfare of trumpets which suggest the herald of news in medeval times by messinger. This music then sounds repeative like a typewriter printing its news as it comes in and suggesting the news is "hot from the presses" and new in. The picture of the world is faded out in a circle to show the studio through a fish eye lens with all the people cameramen, reporters etc moving about giving a sense of movement and urgency.

The newsreader is then shown he is dressed in a smart jacket and flashy tye to appear frendly to the majority of the audience who would dress like him. He is shown face on to the camera and his eyes are looking straight at yours and making eye contact so that the television set makes him appear to be talking directly to you and appearing frendly and pleasant, this would be to take the shock and horror out of some of the news storys like when a frend tells you some bad news.

Differant newsreaders report on differant subjects ie a political editor, sports etc this gives change and contrast to the programme instead of getting boared with the same face all the time: The film in between liven up the programme as they show a view of the world outside the studio.

At the beginning of the show the newsreader reads out what the main items of news are rather like the bill on a variety show starting with the most shocking awful and disastrous and ending with good and plesent.

The main thing the news is about is people. It shows films of people, the newsreaders are people, it is people that make the news. They relie a lot on peoples opinions in interviews and quotes. The people on the films and in the studio are different. In the films reality is shown, the people dress ordinarily the scenes are dirty and grubby but in the studio every thing is bright and clean and nice and it gives the impression that the studio is the real world and the people in it, and the film clips are a long way away from us and dont really affect us. After each film strip people who dislike it because it shows them some disaster or catastfie always see the familiar face of the newsreader which reassures them as they know he will always be there arid is more real to them than the news items. (Jeremy Guy)

The layout of the studio, details of the introductory sequence and dress of the newsreader were features which were commented upon by almost *all* pupils. What is interesting is that a concentration upon these features – which are actually some of the most significant iconographic features of news broadcasts – emerges organically from the kind of exercises described in Chapter 3.

It was especially significant that by employing almost purely *descriptive* methods, pupils were able to progress much further 'in' to the various myths surrounding the presentation of news, its professionalism, integrity and objectivity, and to see that these qualities are adduced from class-based codes of dress and speech. The movement from description to analysis is imperceptible, yet inevitable for the very act of consciously observing such features as the hair, clothing, speech and manner of newscasters and reporters is to reveal them, perhaps for the first time, as having meanings.

Of particular interest in Chris's piece is the way in which the extended analogy is made to yield insights of its own. Chris sees that the signification of television news codings stretches across other professions, but more originally that the illusion of impartiality, a commonplace in news broadcasting, also operates (equally spuriously, the tone suggests) across a much wider professional spectrum. There are the beginnings of a recognition here that *myth* and *mystification* are integral to a whole social *system* of which the mass media are only a part.

Jeremy's piece is remarkable for the way in which description is related to possible meanings at every point. Earlier work on connotations has clearly been of benefit here (see the first paragraph for example). Something ought to be said on the quality of Jeremy's English. Clearly some remedial guidance is necessary, particularly on spelling, but Jeremy is able to handle quite sophisticated ideas with both enthusiasm and insight – indeed his spelling is not uniformly weak, and there is some evidence that many of his mistakes are caused by his primary concern with ideas and his desire to get them down on paper as quickly as possible. The interest in and the ability to handle television material evidenced here are future growth points and they (rather than formal exercises) ought to provide the context for any remedial action.

It is worth observing that Jeremy raises in his own language all of the issues (and more) on the reassurance function of news articulated by professional critics (see 4*d.* below). He also makes explicit some features of this function which are quite original, in particular the hygienic nature of the studio in comparison with the contaminated nature of the world outside, and the greater sense of *reality* of the studio world as opposed to the world of the film clips. He also observes, most significantly and originally of all, the difference between 'studio people' and 'film people' – a point raised only recently in the literature (and since Jeremy wrote his piece) by Tom Burns:

'Them' and 'us' had also taken on a new dimension. The former now made their appearance as the leading figures in a prearranged, often rehearsed and certainly staged performance. As against this, we were presented with the disordered, or embarrassed, or distraught, or – often enough – disfigured appearances of those of 'us' whom disaster, rioting, bombing or the pavement interviewer in search of 'vox pop' thrust, unprepared, distracted or dismembered in front of a random camera.[14]

4. Analysing television news: other possibilities

In spite of the paramount importance of pupils' building upon their own aptitudes and abilities in their analyses of news programmes, it must be said that there now exists a substantial literature on the topic of news of which teachers will need to be aware if they are to take advantage of the range of possibilities available to them in discussing news broadcasts with their classes. The following section attempts to indicate this range, providing references to texts which give more detailed consideration to the various points which are raised. The section is perhaps best regarded as a guide for teachers to the literature relating either directly or indirectly to television news. The points which a teacher will wish to raise with his class will, of course, be largely dependent upon the particular news broadcast being analysed.

a. News selection and values

A most important area of discussion since the questions 'What is selected as news?' and 'Why are some stories selected and not others?' are properly applicable to *all* televised news. The classic text here is by Galtung and Ruge[15] who raise a large number of criteria for the selection of news, amongst which may be mentioned the following six:

Frequency 'The more similar the frequency of the event is to the frequency of the news medium, the more probable that it will be recorded as news by that news medium.'[16] Television news will give preference to stories which occur within a daily period of time. Only the vital or climactic points of longer events will be covered. And as a result of the frequency factor it is events that will be concentrated upon rather than processes. There will be what Galtung and Ruge call 'an under-reporting of trends' (cf. Ben Hecht's comment that 'trying to determine what is going on in the world by reading the newspaper is like trying to tell the time by watching the second-hand of a clock').

Ethnocentricity Ethnocentric items – those having a 'cultural proximity' to the viewer – are favoured in news broadcasts. Or as one pupil expressed it: 'In the credit sequence *Nine O'Clock News* is printed on a picture of the world. This symbolises that the news is world wide, but as far as I can see it is mainly about politics from this country.' The further away an event is from the experience of the viewer the more cataclysmic it must be to become news. There is almost a kind of gruesome mathematics to the formula as a journalist in one of Michael Frayn's novels suggests:

> A rail crash on the Continent made the grade provided there were at least five dead. If it was in the United States the minimum number of dead rose to twenty; in South America 100; in Africa 200; in China 500.[17]

And who could forget Claud Cockburn's headline expressly designed to be as unsensational as possible: 'Small Earthquake in Chile: Not Many Dead'.[18]

Foreign news stories will have an ethnocentric angle whenever possible, a tendency which can produce some surprisingly distorted priorities. In October 1976, for example, the story of a one day general strike in France in which hundreds of thousands of workers marched through the streets of Paris, and the Secretary General of the TUC in France declared the government's austerity policy to be 'a declaration of war against the workers' was given this headline coverage on BBC News:

> In France a 24-hour strike was called today by the main unions. There was widespread disruption and cross-channel ferry services were affected.

The inheritance factor Some stories are selected not for their intrinsic importance, but because of their connection with a news story of the previous day. This can give rise to 'stories' in which literally nothing has happened.

> The hunt for the lioness believed to have been seen yesterday in Nottinghamshire continued today with no further sightings. Bruce Miles reports . .

Or take the following non-story in which a different kind of inheritance factor is in operation. Here, the pre-definition of a story as newsworthy and the despatching of a reporter to some far-flung spot to cover it operate as potent news values even when nothing has actually happened:

> The start of the Orkneys' seal cull has been delayed again. The Norwegian vessel carrying the marksmen, who have been engaged to kill the seals, put back into Kirkwall this morning. For the latest news here's Sue Lloyd Roberts who is on board the trawler *Rainbow Warrior*.[19]

As Galtung and Ruge suggest, 'Once something has hit the headlines and been defined as "news", then it will *continue* to be defined as news for some time even if the amplitude is drastically reduced. The channel has been opened and stays partly open to justify its being opened in the first place, partly because of inertia in the system, and partly because what was unexpected has now also become familiar.'[20]

A further form of news 'inheritance' arises from the tendency noted by Rock and others for news agencies to feed off one another:

> Once some newspaper ratifies an event as news, others may accept that ratification and treat the event as independently newsworthy. Journalists religiously read their own and other newspapers; they consult one another; and look for continuities in the emerging world which their reporting has constructed.[21]

Graham Murdock has demonstrated how this process worked in the newspaper coverage of an anti-Vietnam War demonstration:

> The fact that newspapers are increasingly in competition for an overlapping audience tends to increase the similarities in their reporting. The development of the Demonstration Story, for example, shows a clear pattern in which one paper followed another by carrying the latter's story either in its own late editions or on the following day. There is an almost obsessive concern with being scooped . . . This element of competition means that newspapers will print a story while it is still 'soft' i.e. still at the stage of rumour and probability rather than 'hard fact'. Having once appeared in print however, both the basic themes of the story and the context within which it is interpreted become 'set' and subsequent coverage is obliged to work within this framework. In this process newspapers become locked in a cycle of self-infatuation which takes them further and further from the underlying reality of the situation.[22]

Television news is itself locked into this same cycle, though exactly how great the influence of this form of inheritance is upon a particular news programme can only be assessed by comparing individual stories, and the 'angle' of their television coverage, with the choice and treatment of stories by newspapers and radio. In the study of news magazine programmes such as *Nationwide* the inheritance factor is likely to be of particular significance in determining the selection and construction of items.[23]

News is elite-centred   The hierarchy of stories within a television news programme will tend to be determined by the relative social or political status of the actors in each item. 'Thus a hierarchy of newsworthiness is established in which the actions of members of the legitimated political elites have the highest rank.'[24] An item on the monthly unemployment figures has pride of place because the prime minister, trade union leaders and CBI representatives have commented upon them. A story about rabies is *by definition* less important since it is being handled at local authority level. This of course is to say nothing about the *actual* relative importance of those unemployment figures or that rabies scare.

Rules about 'royals' are less clear. Twenty years ago, if a royal story were included it would always lead. Now this seems to be true only of conspicuously important occasions such as the opening of Parliament or once-in-a-lifetime – though cumulatively frequent – royal events such as births, marriages, Jubilees and deaths.

An important aspect of the elite-centred nature of news is that it applies as rigidly to nations as it does to individuals. Foreign news coverage is dominated by the United States and Western European countries, and the whole question of the uneven international flow of news, discussed by Groombridge, Nordenstreng and Varis[25] and others needs to be brought to the attention of pupils.

News is person-centred Television news's emphasis upon film material tends to make the medium even more person- and event-orientated than newspapers. Pupils have no difficulty in observing this, as Jeremy Guy's analysis illustrates but its significance will need to be brought out by the teacher. In that events are seen, often literally, as the consequence of the actions of individuals or groups rather than as related to deeper societal structures or more abstract social forces, television news presents us with an a-historical view of the world.[26] The visual evidence continually leads us away from its wider political implications towards the specificity of *that* person doing *that* thing. It is perhaps worth adding that even when television does attempt 'wider' explanations of the events it depicts it does so in a safe and thoroughly predictable way, as Dennis Potter has pointed out:

Saturday nights are never a good time for a sermon, but this week Jimmy Hill tried his hand at a bit of random moralising in such a determined manner that one can only suppose that he had been deeply affected by the accident in the schedules which allowed viewers to switch from the end of *Edward Gibbon: the Decline and Fall of the Roman Empire* on BBC-2, almost straight into the carnage on the terraces of decadent Chelsea in *Match of the Day* on BBC-1. Pulling his toga around him and glowering straight into the autocue, the bearded emperor was so upset by a Kung Fu kick delivered by a Chelsea fan upon a Crystal Palace supporter (or vice versa) that he signalled the action replay of Gibbon's long-running spectacle, the collapse of a civilisation. 'Such violence is a disease of society,' he said in those tones of awe normally reserved for talking about Don Revie or the future of Stan Bowles. 'Its roots are in the homes and in the schools,' he continued, with an expression above the chin that told us he was saying something particularly significant. I wish he would confine himself to sliding tackles and disputed penalties. Imagine, though, the terrible consequences if Jimmy Hill had announced that the degradations on this and many another football ground might have just a little to do with the gross inequalities of our society and the deliberately stunted horizons of those young men whom – to quote Ludovic Kennedy on Monday's *Newsday* (BBC-2) – 'we used to call the lower classes'. *Match of the Day* would then have been denounced by the Football League, the BBC governors, the *Daily Telegraph*, Mrs Thatcher and the National Viewers and Listeners Association. It's a thought – and one which helps put in perspective so much of the 'straight talking' which increasingly passes for genuine outspokenness on television.[27]

Negativity of news values   This is nothing more than the trite point that negative news tends to be preferred to positive. Exactly *why* this should be the case however is less obvious. Among the factors cited by Galtung and Ruge perhaps the most illuminating is that negative events satisfy the frequency criterion discussed on p. 94.

There is a *basic asymmetry* in life between the positive, which is difficult and takes time, and the negative, which is much easier and takes less time – compare the amount of time needed to bring up and socialize an adult person and the amount of time needed to kill him in an accident: the amount of time needed to build a house and to destroy it in a fire, to make an aeroplane and to crash it, and so on. The positive cannot be too easy, for then it would have low scarcity value. Thus, a negative event can more easily unfold itself completely between two issues of a newspaper and two newscast transmissions – for a positive event this is more difficult and specific.[28]

b. Bias and balance in news programmes

Questions about bias and balance will inevitably be raised whenever news programmes are discussed, so deeply are attitudes towards these notions embedded both within the official philosophies of broadcasting institutions, and the arguments of their critics. Nine possible areas for discussion about bias and balance are suggested below:

Manipulation and rigging   To what extent are events within news programmes manipulated and even rigged to give a biased and distorted impression of reality? The first thing that ought to be stressed here is that the presentation of events through the media of film and television necessarily involves the manipulation of material. Hans Magnus Enzensberger:

Every use of the media presupposes manipulation. The most elementary processes in media production, from the choice of the medium itself, to shooting, cutting, synchronization, dubbing, right up to distribution, are all operations carried out on the raw material. There is no such thing as unmanipulated writing, filming or broadcasting.[29]

In an interview with Nicholas Garnham, former television producer, Philip Whitehead goes even further:

Garnham: The average audiences are simply not aware to what extent things inevitably have to be rigged and so on. Does that worry you?

Whitehead: Yes, it does. Television is the only profession in which the word 'cheat' is an inseparable part of the vocabulary. I think it's alarming that so often, in order to preserve a smooth visual flow and in order to re-create an assumed sequence of events . . . you do dishonest things.[30]

There is no doubt that the existence and even necessity of this kind of rigging ought to be more widely understood than it is. But these routine professional practices are often inevitable and certainly seem acceptable within limits since their intention, presumably, is to *clarify* events for the viewing public. Whitehead's use of 'cheat' and 'dishonest' seems to go beyond this to suggest a widespread intention to deceive through conscious and deliberate distortion. This, on the face of it, seems unlikely. Hood, who has written one of the best general accounts of the problems of balance, objectivity and neutrality as they confront the professional broadcaster concludes that deliberate dishonesty would be very difficult to get away with:

More important are . . . allegations that the editing of film can lead to distortion of what a speaker has said. Distortion by manipulation might — like the manipulation of tape in radio — take various forms. In the worst case, it is possible to imagine the essence of a speaker's argument being discarded and only peripheral remarks retained. This is an unlikely contingency. Alternatively, it might be made — by collocation with other statements — to appear to have a different meaning from that intended. This would be editorial dishonesty of the most reprehensible kind. It is unlikely that any reputable organisation would countenance the practice; cynicism suggests that they would not easily get away with it.[31]

Nevertheless, as we have already seen, bias as a function of selection is something integral to news presentation. The news stories, films and pictures appearing on the screen are but a minute proportion of the total number of stories, films and pictures available to the news editor. And each one of *these* stories, films and pictures is itself the final result of a selection process carried out by journalists, photographers and cameramen. For simply to point the camera is to select. The material we see and hear in television news appears to be bias-free because both the many acts of selection and the criteria used for selecting are hidden from the public. News is bound to be slanted in some way or other, but we have no way of knowing how since we do not know what the rejected stories and films were.

Bias in interpretation of visual material   Does the visual material really make the point suggested by the commentary? The classic background text here is the film *Protest for Peace* (see Chapter 9), in which the disparity between film and commentary reaches comic proportions.[32] Work on captions and *Teachers' Protest* described in Chapter 9 will here prove to be of considerable help to pupils.

Bias through placement   Within a news bulletin the importance of a story may be inflated by being made the lead or principal story or diminished by being placed towards the end of the programme. The spatial characteristics of newspapers obviously lend themselves to greater subtleties in the employment of this technique, but it remains of some significance in television news particularly in stories dealing with controversial social issues where television can be extremely influential in either playing down, exaggerating or even creating the significance of an issue.

Do the balanced interests have real equality?   Collins draws attention to the sleight of hand which every day makes equivalent the interests of elites or small groups, and the interests of the vast majority of people. 'The formulation "between management and men" makes equivalent the majority who sell their labour and the minority who employ labour.'[33]

Bias in language   Does the newsreader or reporter convey an attitude to the news story through his language or tone of voice? The adjectives in expressions such as 'alleged injustices' or 'the so-called "Vietnam Moratorium Committee"' can betray unconscious attitudes in what purport to be factual news stories. As Stuart Hall remarked: 'I await without much confidence the day when *The World at One* will refer to "the so-called Confederation of British Industries" or the so-called Trades Union Congress or even the so-called Central Intelligence Agency.'[34]

Some writers have argued that the language habitually used in news coverage of strikes betrays the same kind of unwitting bias (for example, 'As a result of the dispute 8000 men are *idle*'), a belief confirmed by a recent Glasgow study of the treatment of industrial relations in television news programmes. The study points up a number of normative assumptions made about industrial disputes by television:

industrial action is somehow reprehensible.
unions (rather than disagreements between unions and management) are responsible for stoppages.
reasons for stoppages are less important than their *effects*.

trade unionists (of which there are some 10 million in Britain) are a 'marginal' minority group with too much power for the country's good.

It is worth drawing attention to the widespread concern which exists within trade unions towards their coverage by the media. Indeed the ACTT (Association of Cinematographic and Television Technicians), a union closely concerned with television, submitted this resolution to the 1975 Annual Conference of the TUC, which was overwhelmingly carried:

Countering Anti-Trade Union Bias in the Media

Recognising the over-simplification and distortion which characterises the manner in which the majority of the media discuss and report economic issues, and aware that this over-simplification and distortion frequently expresses itself in savage attacks on the objectives and methods of trade unions engaged in free collective bargaining, Congress calls on the General Council to instigate the production on a regular and ongoing basis of a counter critique, deliberately written to correct and counteract the distortions of the media and to provide for shop floor trade unionists a straightforward and effective refutation of anti-trade union propaganda.[35]

Bias in interviewing What is the attitude of the interviewer to his subject? Richard Collins suggests three styles.

The three basic styles of neutral, gladiatorial and devil's advocate are applied to structure the content of an interview situation from an anterior conception of that situation and to make the situation conform to an anterior notion of what balance will look like. Thus the gladiatorial style is characteristically used with deviants; 'extremists', students, workers engaged in industrial action, the IRA (if they get on the screen); the deferential/neutral with consensus politicians; and the devil's advocate when it's necessary to cast doubt on the credentials and propositions of the interviewee in the interests of balance. For example the treatment of the doubly deviant (being a woman and working for a foreign television system) British sound recordist working for Swedish Broadcasting who advanced the clearly suspect notion that Eritrean guerillas enjoyed popular support, and who was given the devil's advocate style.

In other words it is an implicit working assumption that some material, some phenomena in the world, are inherently 'unbalanced' and need redress through the intervention of an appropriate interviewing style, other phenomena or processes do not and can be allowed to speak for themselves.[36]

Hall relates different interviewing techniques to areas of consensus, toleration and conflict. 'Areas of consensus cover the central issues of politics and power, the fundamental sanctions of society and sacred British values. To this area belong the accredited witnesses – politicians of both parties, local councillors, experts, institutional spokesmen.'[37] Here the interviewing technique tends to be soft[38] (though this can be masked by a 'hard' and aggressive style) in that the probing 'does not penetrate to underlying assumptions':

> Areas of toleration cover what might be called 'Home Office issues' – social questions, prisoners who can't get employment after discharge, little men or women against the bureaucrats, unmarried mothers, and so on. The more maverick witnesses who turn up in this group get, on the whole, an off-beat but sympathetic 'human interest' – even at times a crusading – kind of treatment. Guidelines in this sector are less clear-cut. When such topics edge over into the 'permissive' category, they can arouse strong sectional disapproval. But here even the scrupulously objective news editor can presume (again, a matter of negotiation and judgment, not of objective fact) on a greater background of public sympathy, more room for manoeuvre.
>
> Areas of conflict have their un-accredited cast of witnesses too: protesters of all varieties; shop stewards, especially if militant, more especially if on unofficial strike; squatters; civil rights activists; hippies; students; hijackers; Stop the Seventy Tour-ers; and so on. In dealing with these issues and actors, interviewers are noticeably sharper, touchier, defending their flanks against any predisposition to softness.[39]

Consensual bias   A number of writers have drawn attention to the fact that balance within news broadcasts only takes place within a consensual framework.[40] Crudely, middle-class minority perspectives are projected as universal by the news, and achieve physical expression through the speech, dress and bearing of the newsreaders themselves. Tom Burns, interviewing a BBC newsman, has come closest to discovering the source of these assumptions and attitudes and to exposing the dislocation between them, and the attitudes of the audience:

Burns: I think there is a sense in which the BBC is still very much a private world.

BBC newsman: Yes, I agree. This does sometimes strike us in the newsroom. The terms in which we would put it are these – we would say that we've been broadcasting to the people along the corridor [that is, to editorial and managerial superiors] not to the people who are listening. You know, one has followed their policy, done the sort of thing that we know will please them, and we haven't really thought about the listener, about what is the best way to tell the listener.

Burns: But how can you, if you don't really know the listener? Have you any information about the listener?

BBC newsman: Quite. Yes, this is true. I haven't talked much about it, but it would be nice to know more about the sort of people who are listening . . .

Burns: . . . With the BBC, it seems to me, there is a certain set of conventions which are visibly present . . . in programmes from news to comedies. These can't be conventions developed between the audience and the people doing the programmes. So there is a natural inference that they all developed within the BBC. What I'm interested in is how they've developed . . .

BBC newsman: I believe it's partly a product of the sort of people who work here, and it's their collective background that is one of the largest factors in [determining] the type and quality of programmes which are produced.[41]

If we were to eavesdrop; as one of the writers of a recent research report did, upon a typical top-level weekly meeting at the BBC between the editor of television news and his editorial team, the nature of the prevailing assumptions would become quite clear:

> The whole meeting had the atmosphere of head boys, and prefects or regimental pow-wow (re-emphasised by the fact it is an all-male assembly), which was most clearly expressed in the kind of humour employed.
>
> One item, a festival of art and music in West Yorkshire to be attended by the Prime Minister, was dismissed as a 'fish and chip' festival (laughter and applause). The launch of the Fiat economy car was greeted with 'made with slave labour in Yugoslavia' (cheerful assent). The Conference of National Federation of Business and Professional Women's Clubs caused quite a lot of sexist comment — 'we can't get that many trendy bottoms in' and so on.[42]

In the coverage of political events, the consensualist framework is provided by parliamentary democracy. In the words of Sir Charles Curran: 'One of my senior editors said recently in a phrase which I treasure: "Yes, we are biased — biased in favour of parliamentary democracy". I agree with him. It is our business to contribute to a debate by making available to the widest general public the opinions of those who are directly engaged in it. It is not our business to shape the end of the debate. That is for the electorate, guided by the politician.'[43]

If the broadcasting institutions share the same basic assumptions as Parliament, however, their ability to place the activities of politicians into any kind of critical perspective is severely limited, as John Dearlove elaborates:

> The BBC is caught up with the dignified side of British politics. Coverage is anchored around Parliament and the speeches of the established party politicians. Studio discussions replicate parliamentary debates, and impartiality is seen as secured if balance is maintained between the two major parties: the BBC grew up with the two-party system and it cannot think of politics outside of the terms of reference which the acceptance of such a system provides. There is the assumption that every problem has two sides

and that political conflict is manageable, since the scope of politics is regarded as contained within the two-party system where differences can be both revealed and transcended in ordered debate. The BBC bridges the gaps and cements us into one nation. Politics is seen as a rational problem-solving exercise; it is seen as about means and not ends, and the body politic is regarded as one 'vast seminar'.

But the truth of the matter is that, as Harrison says 'we still leave vast areas of the British political process under explored by the medium'. The BBC fails to stand back from the established system of government and because of this it tends to present the myths as to how the system should operate as the concrete reality of how it actually does operate. The BBC may be neutral and it may be objective, but only within the context of the liberal consensus and of established authority. This being the case, party politicians are presented to us as they themselves want to be presented – within the context of an unquestioning acceptance and defence of a two-party system of parliamentary democracy. To a very considerable extent senior figures within the BBC and established party politicians share a similar view as to the educative role which the BBC should assume in our polity. Charles Curran's statement that he wishes he could 'contribute to the public respect for Parliament which ought to exist by being able to televise its proceedings' makes clear the extent to which the concern is to use the media to educate the public *into an acceptance of, and a respect for, the established system of parliamentary government irrespective of the capacity of that system to advance the interests of the mass of the people.* Individual politicians and systems of rule should not expect to be given respect and legitimacy as of right: it should be earned, it should be won, and this demands that we receive a critical and sceptical perspective on our politics and politicians which we are not getting from the BBC.[44] (italics added)

The balance sustained in news broadcasting then is between the major parties and not between say parliamentary and non-parliamentary groups. What is significant about this is that increasingly the *content* of news broadcasts concerns the activities of groups who do not share the assumptions of either the politicians or the broadcasting institutions and who therefore find themselves without any legitimate means of expression. The serious consequences of this combination of unrestricted coverage and restricted access within the mass media have been demonstrated by the well-known case study of Halloran, Murdock and Elliott,[45] who point out that if blacks, students, squatters, militant trade unionists and fringe political movements continue to be alienated from and frustrated by conventional democratic channels of expression, then violence will increasingly come to be seen by them as their only alternative.

Stuart Hall has taken the argument a stage further by suggesting that the consensual framework habitually adopted within broadcasting is useless as an explanatory or evaluative tool for helping us to make sense of real events in the real world:

> The groups and events upon which, increasingly, the media are required to comment and report, are the groups in conflict with this consensual style of politics. But these are precisely the forms of political and civil action which the media, by virtue of their submission to the consensus, are consistently unable to deal with, comprehend or interpret. The nervousness one has observed in the treatment of these issues reflects the basic contradiction between the manifestations which the media are called on to explain and interpret, and the conceptual/evaluative/interpretative framework which they have available to them.[46]

Consequently the media, far from clarifying our understanding of significant events, mystify us about them, feeding 'our general sense of a meaningless explosion of meaningless and violent acts – "out there" somewhere, in an unintelligible world where "no legitimate means" have been devised "for the pursuance of interests without resort to open conflict" '.[47]

But 'out there' exist not only unintelligible places like Notting Hill or unintelligible people like the South Yorkshire miners, but whole unintelligible areas of the globe – Africa, the Middle East, Latin America, China, indeed most of the rest of the world – which simply cannot be comprehended within current consensual models. Why then do consensual models persist as interpretative tools? Simply because they support and share the assumptions of the powerful political, economic and social institutions of our society.[48] As such they serve an important ideological function, and do so all the more powerfully for parading as objective sets of professional routines.

'Framework' theories   Consensual bias is a particular example of the general media principle that the meaning and significance of a particular event will be prestructured for the audience by the interpretative framework within which it is placed. In Halloran, Murdock and Elliott's case study a preconceived formula of 'expected violence' provided the framework for the media's coverage of an anti-Vietnam War demonstration. When the 'violent' protest turned out to be peaceful, emphasis was placed upon those violent elements present and there was even reference to 'buildings which were *not* attacked'. An extract from the television news commentary illustrates the nature of the interpretative framework: 'The police were taking care today that the violence of last March would not be repeated. Occasional searches on roads into London produced little result, itself encouraging. The demonstrators continued at least without obvious weapons.'[49]

The framework here not only structures and carries the meaning of the event, it excludes, of course, other possible frameworks. It would have been quite possible to have seen the demonstration, as Halloran, Murdock and

Elliott point out, as the way in which many thousands of morally right young people were protesting against a barbaric and unjust war in Vietnam.

Framework theories have come to be seen over the past few years as having an important contribution to make to the 'effects' debate:

> It may be that the media have little immediate impact on attitudes as commonly assessed by social scientists, but it seems likely that they have other important effects. In particular they would seem to play a major part in defining for people what the important issues are and the terms in which they should be discussed . . . 'Media influence' is seen as operating on interpretive frameworks – the categories people use when thinking about matters – rather than on attitudes directly.[50]

The writers here, Hartmann and Husband, are primarily concerned with the significance of the media's interpretative frameworks on racial issues, and their essay ought to be consulted in detail whenever racial issues are in the news. They note the ways in which race-related material, as handled by the media, 'serves both to perpetuate negative perceptions of blacks and to define the situation as one of intergroup conflict . . . Events that carry or can be given connotations of conflict or threat are more newsworthy than others', a news value which is disastrous in terms of race relations.

It is the extreme social segregation which exists between groups in urban society which makes the media's anterior frames of reference of such significance. It is because the media and particularly television are the major and often the *only* source of many people's information and ideas about a whole range of social problems, groups and phenomena, that a scrutiny of the assumptions and preconceived formulae of news stories is such an urgent educational task.

Institutional bias   News sources tend to be permanent and reliable institutions. Parliament, the trade unions, Law Courts, football clubs, etc. are all regular suppliers of news, produce events, and have their own press releases and often press officers. 'The ambiguity of events is considerably dispelled by trapping the activities of reliable and permanent organisations. News is less likely to be made by ephemeral groups of people, by ill-structured groups or by groups whose behaviour does not appear on a suitable schedule.'[51] Newsgetting then is not a random search but takes positive forms. The institutional bias of news is of course inextricably bound up with the monopoly of consensus models, and the predominance within the news of predictable rather than unexpected events.

c. The news as show

It is perhaps not unfair to say that television news is less concerned to provide information as *authentically* as possible than to provide it as *attractively* as possible without jettisoning its reputation for reliability, responsibility and probity. Authentic and important information may be 'dull', factual, difficult to summarise, undramatic and with little immediate appeal, and there will be an understandable desire to 'spice' it, and to package it as attractively and entertainingly as possible. This process has two dimensions. On the level of *content* it may take the form of an emphasis upon dramatic 'clashes' and bizarre or spectacular events. *Stylistically* it will tend to make news programmes look very much like other television programmes which also have as one of their chief functions the attraction of viewers:

> Stylistic links may be identified with on the one hand documentary programmes and on the other variety and chat shows. The similarity and connection between news and documentary/current affairs programmes are unsurprising; both programme categories have as their concern reportage; the mediation of information and understanding of the world, attention to social and political affairs and they share rhetorical features, film or video inserts, vox pops, and other interview strategies, location shooting, 'here-and-now-ness'. Shared with variety/chat shows is the succession of items or turns, a number of discrete spots orchestrated to display a variety of treatments, live action, in-shot narrator, the role of the star personality (whether it be Michael Parkinson or Robert Dougall) to organise the montage of attractions into a coherent dramatic structure of prologue, star turns, humorous or spectacular ending.[52]

d. News as reassurance

The raw content of news programmes depicts a world of constant flux, crises, unexplained events, contradictions, conflicts and violence. The encapsulation of these diverse and disturbing events within the narrative structure of the news (with happy ending), the familiar personality of the newsreader, the rhetoric of reliability and expertise which runs as a continuing thread through each news story, 'the production of news at a regular time, of constant format, length, and dramatic structure',[53] and, as Jeremy Guy noted earlier, the hygienic, rational, well-ordered realness of the television studio all contribute to what is perhaps the most pervasive of all of the messages conveyed by the news – that the world is ultimately a reassuring one of order, continuity and stability.

e. Visual codings

Finally it is necessary to draw attention to an aspect of television news which is likely to receive increasing attention from analysts in the immediate future – its visual codings. Given the development of the appropriate analytical skills it is a field in which students are themselves capable of original findings.[54] Some attention has already been devoted to some of the operative visual codings within news broadcasts. What other codings might we pay attention to? Stuart Hood:

> There are codes of geography within the studio indicating to the audience who is who and what their respective functions are – who are the experts and who the public. There are codes of interviewing which are related to what the Americans call proxemics, the rules governing the physical relationship of one person to another; thus ordinary people are interviewed jostling in the street; more important people across the interval of a desk.[55]

The point is confirmed and elaborated by the Glasgow study which paid a great deal of attention to the dominant codings in news coverage of industrial relations:

> Working people come onto the news in a very limited range of circumstances which will be familiar. As a result all those things which enhance a speaker's status and authority are denied to the mass of working people. This means that the quiet of studios, the plain backing, the full use of name and status are often absent. The people who transcribed our material here pointed out to us that the only time they had difficulty making out what was said was in interviews with working people. Not because of 'accent', but because they were often shot in group situations, outside, and thus any individual response was difficult to hear. The danger here is that news coverage is often offering up what amounts to stereotypical images of working people.[56]

The task of the television teacher here is not simply to draw attention to the existence of these findings but to encourage the development of those abilities which will enable pupils to decode for themselves in a conscious way such latently transmitted ideological messages as these.

5. Conclusion

The two most important determinants of a teaching strategy for helping pupils understand more about television news are the nature and interests of the pupil group itself, and the issues raised by the particular broadcast under analysis. This chapter has attempted to draw together and indicate a range of activities and analytical approaches relating to news broadcasts which are available to the teacher and his class. The possibilities for news analysis are vast. The references in this chapter indicate the range of sources available for more detailed exploration; in the last resort it is the teacher and his pupils themselves who must choose which areas they wish to examine in depth.

6

Football on Television

1. Introduction

The British Film Institute monograph, *Football on Television*,[1] is a breakthrough, the first serious study of televised sport published in this country, and in concentrating upon the crucial problem of mediation – whether television 'records' or 'constructs' events – it makes an important contribution to a contemporary media debate. For sport, of all televisual events, appears to come to us 'raw', in the form of natural events which the television camera is fortunate enough to catch and record. It is this myth which *Football on Television* conclusively demolishes, demonstrating how a multitude of mediating influences act to shape our responses to a game often before a ball has been kicked. The monograph is of immediate relevance to the teacher in the classroom for it shows how 'popular' material can be used in a serious and educative way. And although it examines the television coverage of a specific event – the 1974 World Cup – the monograph both suggests a large number of approaches relevant to the study of televised sport in general, and has an obvious application to the study of domestic football coverage. I wish in this chapter however to focus attention upon the problems of *teaching* about televised football. What precisely are the difficulties of introducing the study of televised football into the classroom? How transferable are the approaches suggested in the monograph to the presentation of *domestic* soccer events of the kind habitually watched by many pupils? And are there any serious differences between the World Cup and domestic presentations which make necessary other approaches to those suggested by the monograph? The conclusions reached here are based upon a study of the 1976 Cup Final between Manchester United and Southampton undertaken with fifth form comprehensive school pupils.

2. Teaching about televised football: some difficulties

a. The reactions of other teachers

There are serious professional difficulties associated with the teaching of televised sport. The attitude of teachers to the mass media has been well summarised by Murdock and Phelps:

> Negativeness was perhaps the most important characteristic of the overwhelming proportion of teachers' responses to the question of the effects of mass-media on pupils' behaviour . . . Although the views expressed by the majority of teachers who answered our question could not be described as extreme, they were nevertheless almost always distrustful, and frequently hostile, towards the mass-media.[2]

Most teachers respond to television negatively; the few who might argue for its greater intrusion into the classroom would do so according to Murdock and Phelps on the grounds of its increasing pupils' 'awareness of social and political issues'. One can safely conclude that *almost all* teachers would consider the study of televised football unworthy of serious consideration within the classroom. The real significance of this lies in its effect upon those few teachers who might consider such an activity worthwhile. For, as David Hargreaves has shown,[3] teachers, particularly young teachers, tend to be dependent upon the understanding and commendation of their headteacher and colleagues in measuring their own pedagogic competence, and in legitimising what they are doing in the classroom. Professional peers, in other words, are a major source of the teacher's own self-evaluation, and the young teacher is likely to use the attitudes of his colleagues towards him as a measure of his worth as a teacher. The relevance of this to televised football needs no stressing. Unless the intellectual climate of the school is favourable a teacher is unlikely to incur the disapproval of his colleagues by pursuing an activity simply because *he* thinks it is worthwhile. This is why the real significance of the BFI monograph lies in its very existence rather than in its content. Important as *Football on Television* is in providing a number of intellectual frameworks for the study of televised sport, its real significance lies in the status and authority it gives to the study of televised sport in the classroom. Its intellectual value to the teacher, while considerable, is, in the short term at least, likely to be outweighed by the support it will give to his confidence and morale.

b. Organising and planning

The study of televised football is likely to lead to at least two possible organisational problems of which the teacher needs to be aware before he begins his work.

The necessity of individualised learning techniques   Sport is by no means of universal interest, and particular sports may be anathema to large numbers of pupils. For this reason the teacher should attempt to make the study of televised sport optional and provide alternative work for those who wish to study something else. To do otherwise is to invite disaster. My own experience has been that an active enthusiasm on the part of many boys – often those who enthuse over very little else in school – to 'do' football, has been matched by an equal hostility amongst many of the girls. Of course the teacher can argue that – like it or not – everyone must study the same topic, and he will have some grounds for arguing this: what is being studied will go beyond football; looking closely at the transmission of the Cup Final is a means to an end, a way of understanding a concept such as mediation, which is crucial to an understanding of the medium as a totality. It is not difficult, however, to stand this argument on its head: if the concepts are important rather than the content, there is no necessity for the group to study the same material. Both boys and girls can arrive at a comparable intellectual understanding through autonomous routes, and the teacher will be wise to be guided by pupil response and devise materials and exercises which everyone finds relevant and congenial. In effect this means that class teaching must go. The study by one group of the Cup Final went on alongside the study by other groups of other things, and there was a corresponding emphasis upon individualised learning techniques with worksheets and exercises linked to videotapes and pre-publicity material.

The constraints of topicality   There is another reason for stressing the teacher's effective organisation of his material. The study of televised sport is likely to be linked to an event of great topical interest such as a Cup Final, the Olympic Games or the Grand National. Part of the art of good television teaching lies in this ability to make the most of topical events – to use the enthusiasm and interest generated by the mass media, ride upon their massive resources as they take up the story, and finally to harness the wealth of available materials for the purpose of real and significant learning. This is the excitement of teaching about television, but it does constitute a great challenge to the teacher not only in terms of creativity and the ability to seize the moment, but also through the sheer hard work involved, for materials must be collected and organised for class use within a matter of a day or two. Such material, however, will yield an interest, motivation and level of cognitive understanding in his pupils which conventional school subjects will be quite unable to match. Time is of the essence, however. Last week's event is cold. It won't sell newspapers and it will have limited impact within the classroom.

3. The Cup Final: suggested approaches

The monograph suggests a number of possible approaches to the teaching of televised sport. These are outlined below (with monograph page references in parentheses), and comments are added on the relevance of each approach to the study of a domestic football event – the FA Cup Final.

a. Pre-publicity material (pp. 8–15)

Pre-publicity coverage of the Cup Final in *Radio Times* and *TV Times* yielded a rich harvest. The magazines set the scene for the viewer in more than a descriptive way, inviting him, as we shall see, to set the event within any one of a number of different perspectives. Studying the magazine material also provided a stimulus to viewing the event itself and gave to pupils a quite complex analytical framework within which to work. Asking the question: 'How are we being encouraged to view the game?' before it had been seen seemed to produce a distancing or alienation from the event and a sharpening of awareness during viewing which was a new experience for many pupils and which some of the group actually commented upon ('I didn't just slump down in the chair and look at it. I actually watched it'). *Radio Times* and *TV Times* are normally not available until Thursday of each week so that only one evening was available to examine the material, organise it and type up assignments before the group met on Friday – the day before the match. If the assignments and questions appear unduly directive – as I think they are – this is because it seemed important to draw pupils' attention to as many features of the coverage as possible in the limited time available – about one hour.

ITV Schedule (Plate 3, between pp. 112 and 113)
1. Look at the layout of the whole page. What general meanings are being communicated by it?
2. Comment upon the graphic design at the bottom of the panel. What meanings does it suggest?
3. Manchester United v. Southampton. We are invited to view the match as being more than a mere contest between two teams. What connotations are the teams given which widen the significance of their 'tussle'?
4. 'Football on TV has more in common with other TV programmes than it has with a real football match.' What methods of presentation are used here which suggest other television programmes?
5. Can you discern any constant 'themes' running through ITV coverage? Do any words or ideas occur again and again?
6. Why do you think Cup Final coverage begins so early?
7. In three hours there are twenty-two separate items or features in ITV's coverage (and this includes the two halves of the match lasting forty-five minutes each). Why are there so many items?

continued on p. 114

Plate 1 (see pp. 59-60)

Plate 2 (see p. 114)

12.5 AT THE TEAM HOTELS

Up-to-the-minute news on the fitness, mood and morale of the finalists, from team managers **Tommy Docherty** (Manchester Utd.) and **Lawrie McMenemy** (Southampton). They have a last opportunity to talk before they meet on the turf at Wembley.

12.10 MAN IN THE CROWD

ITV's roving reporter, Fred Dinenage, has his first meeting with the fans, characters and personalities who make this day so colourful.

12.15 SUPERGOALS AND SUPERSTARS

Manchester Utd.
The road to Wembley is both long and arduous. Ultimate success depends on goal-power and flair. We retrace United's path to the Final and through **Lou Macari** meet the players who have put United so triumphantly back on the map.

Southampton
Remember how Second Division Sunderland beat First Division Leeds in 1973? Well, Southampton have shown that they must not be taken lightly either. Relive their moments of Cup success and meet those super Saints with England star striker, **Mike Channon**.

12.50 AUSTRALIAN POOLS CHECK

12.55 NEWS FROM ITN

1.0 THE TEAMS LEAVE

ITV cameras bring live pictures of the teams as they leave their hotels on the final leg of their journey to Wembley.

1.5 FOOTBALL CRAZY

Ed 'Stewpot' Stewart goes to local schools in Manchester and Southampton with captains **Martin Buchan** and **Peter Rodrigues** to meet their young fans who make up the army of partisan supporters cheering them on at Wembley.

1.15 'BE A SOCCER COMMENTATOR'

Brian Moore talks to the winner of a brand new national competition designed to find an under-16 year old who will surely never forget *his* Wembley debut.

1.25 MAN IN THE CROWD

Fred Dinenage finds more personalities in the crowd who now await the teams' arrival.

1.30 THE TEAMS ARRIVE

That emotional moment as the Manchester Utd. and Southampton coaches bring the players down Wembley Way.

1.40 ON THE PITCH

Interviews with the players as they taste the Wembley atmosphere and inspect the pitch, shortly before they disappear to the dressing rooms.

♟ CUP FINAL SPECIAL

MANCHESTER UNITED v. SOUTHAMPTON

Introduced by DICKIE DAVIES
from Wembley Stadium at 12.0

Dickie Davies sets the scene as tension mounts for English soccer's greatest occasion as First Division Manchester United take on Second Division Southampton in a North versus South tussle for football's most coveted trophy—the F.A. Cup. Leading ITV's team for uninterrupted live coverage of the big day is top commentator BRIAN MOORE, with expert analysis and comment from England team manager DON REVIE, current England captain KEVIN KEEGAN and JACK CHARLTON, manager of Middlesbrough. My View by Jack Charlton: see page 26.

2.0 CUP FINAL PREDICTION

Georges Bode, famous Dutch astrologer who predicted the World Cup Finalists and result, and picked today's finalists, now predicts the winner and score of this afternoon's match.

WORLD OF SPORT

Compiled for Independent Television by London Weekend Television

---

2.10 FINAL COMMENT

Brian Moore, Kevin Keegan, Don Revie and Jack Charlton offer their expert analysis, last-minute comment and match forecasts.

2.25 THE WEMBLEY SCENE

Brian Moore takes us up to the kick-off as we enjoy the huge, electric atmosphere, the songs of a hundred thousand singers, and the music of the Massed Band of the Brigade of Guards.

2.50 THE PRESENTATION

The teams are presented to the Duke of Edinburgh.

3.0 THE KICK-OFF

Live, uninterrupted coverage of the first half, with Brian Moore, and comments from Jack Charlton.

3.45 HALF-TIME

Expert assessment of the first half with action highlights. Action, too, from the Scottish Cup Final.

3.55 THE SECOND HALF

The whole of the second half live with Brian Moore and Jack Charlton.

4.40 THE FINAL WHISTLE

The moment of triumph followed by the presentation of the F.A. Cup.

4.45 THE TEAMS TALK

Spontaneous comments and reactions from the players and managers with action highlights to relive the moments that turned the game.

4.55 FINAL ROUND UP

Final expert comment from the ITV team, plus news and action highlights from the Scottish Cup Final.

GRAPHIC DESIGNER AL HORTON: PRODUCTION TEAM MICHAEL ARCHER, JEFF FOULSER, MARTIN TYLER, RICHARD RUSSELL, ANDREW FRANKLIN, TONY MCCARTHY, KEITH NIEMEYER, CHRIS HAYDON, RICHARD WORTH: EDITOR STUART MCCONACHIE: EXECUTIVE PRODUCER JOHN BROMLEY: O.B. DIRECTORS JOHN P. HAMILTON, JOHN SCRIMINGER: STUDIO DIRECTOR DAVID SCOTT: WEMBLEY DIRECTOR BOB GARDAM

⬤ Times are subject to change.

Plate 3 (see p. 112)

BBC1

11.15
Cup Final Grandstand
direct from the Empire Stadium,
Wembley
with **David Coleman**
Frank Bough, Jimmy Hill

The 1976 FA Cup Final
Manchester United v Southampton
BBC outside broadcast
cameras bring you the
whole of this Royal
occasion, with slow-
motion replays of the
game's outstanding moments, and
interviews with the players.
Commentator DAVID COLEMAN
Comment by JIMMY HILL, BOBBY
CHARLTON and FRANK MCLINTOCK

11.15 Cup Final Morning
FRANK BOUGH introduces *Grandstand* from Wembley. BARRY DAVIES
and JOHN MOTSON talk to the players of both teams at their Cup
Final hotels.
TONY GUBBA meets the supporters
on their way to Wembley.

11.50 A Cure for the Doc
A report on the turbulent career
of Manchester United Manager
Tommy Docherty, who, after managing Chelsea, Rotherham, QPR
(for 28 days), Aston Villa, Portu-
guese club Oporto and Scotland,
is enjoying success at one of
England's greatest clubs.

12.0
The Women's
FA Cup Final
Southampton v QPR
Highlights of the Women's Football Association match of the year,
for the Mitre Trophy, played at
Bedford Town FC. Southampton,
the holders, have won the Cup
four times out of the five previous
competitions.
Commentator JOHN MOTSON

12.20 pm
Cup Final Knockout
The excitement of *It's a Knockout*
as teams fom the supporters' clubs
of Manchester United and Southampton compete in this special
contest for Cup Final Day. Among
the personalities joining in are
present and past players, and
celebrity supporters.
Introduced by EDDIE WARING and
STUART HALL
Referee ARTHUR ELLIS

1.5 The Cup Final Managers
Tommy Docherty (Manchester United) and **Lawrie McMenemy** (Southampton) talk to DAVID COLEMAN

1.10
Racing from Ascot
1.15 Top Rank Club Victoria Cup
(Handicap) (7 furlongs)
The season's most coveted 7-fur-
long handicap has attracted some
of the top horses in training over
the distance.
Commentators PETER O'SULLEVAN
and JULIAN WILSON

1.20
Boxing
*The World Heavyweight
Championship*
Muhammad Ali v Jimmy Young
(Champion)   (USA)
This morning's title fight in Balti-
more, USA – Ali's sixth defence
since he regained the title in 1974.
Young, who stopped Richard
Dunn two years ago, is unbeaten
for three years.
Commentator HARRY CARPENTER

1.45
Inside Wembley
The Cup Final atmosphere mounts
as the teams arrive to inspect the
Wembley turf.
Goal of the Season
See the winning goals, and find
out who has won the £200 of
Premium Bonds in this popular
annual competition.
Action Highlights of the road to
Wembley.
Meet the Teams
Action profiles of the players.
The Final Word
from JIMMY HILL, BOBBY CHARLTON
FRANK MCLINTOCK

2.45 Abide with Me
The return of the Cup Final hymn.
2.50 Presentation of the Teams
to HRH The Duke of Edinburgh

3.0
The FA Cup Final
Manchester United v Southampton
3.45 Half-time marching display
by the MASSED BANDS OF THE
GUARDS DIVISION. Director of Music
MAJOR E. G. HORABIN
3.55 The FA Cup Final
Second half
**4.45 Presentation of the Cup and
Medals by HM The Queen**
4.50 Meet the Winners
The outstanding players of the
match talk to BARRY DAVIES, with
action of the outstanding moments.
5.5 Final Score
Including news of the Scottish
Cup Final at Hampden Park between Hearts and Rangers.

Television presentation:
FA Cup Final ALEC WEEKS
Women's Cup Final JOHN SHREWSBURY
Cup Final Knockout CECIL KORER
and GEOFF WILSON
Grandstand presented by
BRIAN VENNER and
RICHARD TILLING
Editor ALAN HART
(Cup Final Match of
the Day: 10.25 pm)

FEATURE P58

Plate 4 (see p. 114)

Plate 5 (see opposite and p. 152)

Plate 6 (see opposite and p. 152)

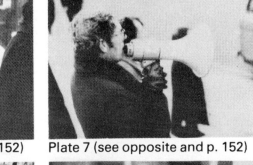

Plate 7 (see opposite and p. 152)

Plate 8 (see opposite and p. 152)

Plate 9 (see opposite and p. 152)

Caption exercises sharpen awareness of the relationship between words and pictures and demonstrate the ambiguous nature of much visual evidence – see text on p. 152.

Plate 5
(a) As our picture shows, the tall commanding Madeley (white shirt) completely dominated Cruyff (dark shirt), who spent most of the game anxiously looking over his shoulder
(b) Our picture embodies the gulf between the two players. Look at their faces: Cruyff's (dark shirt) aware, urgent, looking to create; Madeley (white shirt) gaunt and stressed, being hauled he knows not where

Plate 6
(a) The vast majority were socialist sympathisers
(b) A friendly marcher selling papers to inform the teachers
(c) People seemed uninterested in the marchers' propaganda

Plate 7
(a) The demonstration was well organised and went peacefully according to plan
(b) Militants shouted at the police and incited the crowd. One onlooker called them 'rabble-rousers'
(c) Teacher-leaders got their point across
(d) A young Marxist provokes violence . . .

Plate 8
(a) A teacher finds time to help children across the road
(b) The public managed to stay cool
(c) Onlookers watched the demonstration with interest
(d) Support for the march grows
(e) The people on the streets laughed at the demonstrators
(f) Children came along to support their teacher

Plate 9
(a) The police showed their contempt for the marchers
(b) No police control was necessary
(c) A policeman jokes with some of the teachers
(d) A policeman asked kindly if they would put their placards away
(e) Policemen warned demonstrators about their language

BBC Schedule (Plate 4, between pp. 112 and 113)
1. Why does BBC coverage begin earlier than ITV's? And why begin so early anyway?
2. What differences are there in *overall format* between BBC and ITV coverage?
3. BBC coverage stresses that this is a 'Royal Occasion' and that the Cup and Medals will be presented by the Queen. ITV doesn't mention this. Why is this?
4. Plan your own likely viewing schedule of the Cup Final, saying when you will be switching on and why, and explaining whenever you think you may change channels.
5. Look closely at and analyse the front cover of *Radio Times* (Plate 2, opposite p. 112). (You may quickly read the relevant article inside if you wish. You may also wish to compare it with the photograph on page 13 in *Football on TV*). Is it an appropriate picture for the occasion?

b. Introductory or credit sequences (pp. 16–34)

The introductory sequences to the Cup Final programmes themselves were not studied, but along with all of the pre-publicity material there was included a videotaped introduction to *Match of the Day* – the extract included everything in the programme up to the point at which the first match kicked off. Pupils were asked to note the different ways in which viewers were invited to look at the matches.[4] In this way it was possible to widen and make more coherent the notion of mediation introduced through the study of the pre-publicity material.

c. Cultural codes (pp. 3–5; 16–24)

In international events such as the World Cup or the Olympic Games the ways in which the images and sounds are given particular connotations and inflections for the British audience is obviously of major importance. In a domestic event such as the Cup Final they are of less significance; nevertheless, there was an attempt to invest the Cup Final with wider cultural overlays both in respect of the teams ('First Division Manchester United take on Second Division Southampton in a North versus South tussle . . .'), and in the treatment of particular individuals (notably Peter Rodrigues, the Southampton captain who was quite unable to escape the 'veteran'/dream-come-true/Third-Division-reject-to-Cup-Final-captain/treatment whenever he happened to kick or mis-kick the ball).

d. Stereotyping of teams and players (pp. 11–14; 60–5)

As Andrew Tudor remarks in the monograph, 'The general ethnic/cultural stereotype remains *the* interpretive tool of international sports coverage',[5] and this applies as much to pre-publicity material and the opinions of 'experts' as it does to visual presentations and the meanings imposed upon them by commentators. The study of stereotypes then ought to play a major role in the examination of any international sporting event. As with cultural coding – of which stereotyping is a form – it is of less significance in the presentation of domestic events. Nevertheless, stereotyping of the teams (United as 'fast', 'open', 'refreshing' and 'attacking'; Southampton as 'dour', 'hard', 'uncompromising', 'experienced', etc.), and of individuals ('booky' Thomas, the referee, or Gordon Hill, 'the bargain-buy-match-winner', for example), remains of some importance in providing for the viewer frames of reference within which he is invited to see the game. Almost inevitably it is difficult to think of a single stereotype which was in any way supported by what happened during the game itself.

e. Football and the star system (pp. 2; 9–11; 54–60)

The title sequence of *Match of the Day* suggests that the two most positively endorsed features of televised football are goals and immediately recognisable 'star' players. The show packages both for our consumption and is introduced by star/expert Jimmy Hill in whose personality the worlds of football and showbiz coalesce. The television magazines also orientate their presentation of football around stars. As Colin McArthur makes clear, *Radio Times* and *TV Times* treat almost the entire output of television as a set of 'star vehicles', and adapt any event they are covering to their on-going identities as 'fan' magazines.[6] Television, however, is unable to gorge football stars whole. Their personalities off the field are very often somewhat underdeveloped, and this makes them notoriously unreliable vehicles for the 'television star' treatment. Better to feed off their activities and dispense with them as quickly as is decently possible. And in its Cup Final edition *Radio Times* managed to do just this, ignoring the footballers almost completely, and leaving the field clear for stories and pictures of showbiz stars who support the game. This is in itself a significant development, part of what in 1974 was certainly a trend, but which is now becoming a dominant tendency in television coverage of football: to attach as much, if not greater importance to mediators and the process of mediation itself as to the event ostensibly being transmitted. Whereas in 1974 the stars of the World Cup were players like Cruyff or Bremner, by 1976 star status legitimised by television itself was accorded almost exclusively to the tele-experts, and to a lesser degree – since both possessed personalities amenable to showbiz packaging – to the two managers, Tommy Docherty and Lawrie McMenemy (himself a tele-expert in 1974).

There is an insidious media hubris at work here, which Raymond Williams noted some years ago, a tendency to make 'the ante-room the arena, the reaction the event, and the commentators the real agents'.[7] A more detailed analysis of this phenomenon is offered below (4a.), but certainly it is now an area of central importance in current television coverage of sport.

f. Visual style (pp. 35–53)

The visual style of football matches presented on television is the subject of two essays in the monograph.[8] It is important to be reminded that televised football does not have a uniform style, and that the coverage of different matches can serve quite different functions.[9] To see the relationship between style and function however, requires painstaking comparative analysis of a kind which is difficult to achieve when attention is being focused upon a single event. Further, for many teachers and pupils, analysing the patterning of shots and images during a game may well seem an esoteric activity better suited to more advanced media work in colleges and universities than to introductory work in schools. For these reasons a consideration of visual style played no part in our study of the Cup Final.

g. Soccer experts and panels (pp. 54–65)

'Panels' are a well-worn television convention. Panels of experts commenting upon football matches were, however, an innovation when introduced by ITV during the World Cup of 1970. By 1974 they had become, in Andrew Tudor's words, 'An over-fed albatross'. Today one can observe that the bird remains plump and voracious. The notion of a 'panel of experts' draws together two quite distinct television traditions. In television terms panels have traditionally been games players, and their games are played for 'fun' rather than as serious competitive or intellectual exercises. They are the province of 'personalities' such as Lady Barnet or Patrick Campbell, rather than experts, and belong to the world of light entertainment rather than news or current affairs programmes, where the expert tends to find his natural habitat. A panel of experts then draws together and blurs the distinction between the three classic functions of television – to inform, to instruct and to entertain. A panel expert derives his status as much from showbiz values as from his specialist knowledge.

Andrew Tudor rightly draws attention to the significance of television experts quite outside of the context of football.

Tele experts are a powerful family of whom the football fraternity are only the infants . . . Both experts and audience may fall prey to the very image of omniscience that television confers, seeing limited television discussion and analysis as both exhaustive and representative of the capacities of the medium and our more general culture. One can see that now in current affairs coverage where the old guard especially (for example, Ludovic Kennedy) seem to see their own views with much the same certainty espoused by the politicians they interview. Their world is cast in absolutes of both style and content, and they no longer recognise many of their own limitations: that would not be 'good television'.[10]

   The ease and frequency with which television is able to dub people as experts make it essential for the teacher to expose the concept's ideological basis. To name someone an expert is a way of both endorsing and depoliticising what he says. It is to erect the purest of myths. For out of the mouths of experts come bias-free truths, from a world of knowledge unsullied by interests and existing outside of any political or personal framework.

   What is really fascinating about this area, however, is that effective teaching and learning must inevitably reverberate into classroom practice. For tele-experts themselves are merely one-dimensional reflections of a whole mythology of expertise and professionalism – the class appropriation of knowledge – which is one of the cornerstones of our society. And the place where pupils and teachers witness that mythology's most concrete manifestations – its rituals, contradictions and moment-to-moment nuances – is, as I have discussed in Chapter 2, in the classroom. It is unlikely that pupils will gain any insights into the nature of expertise until the teacher's own supposed expertise and his pupils' supposed lack of it are themselves investigated. This will form part of that investigation of the system within which pupils and teachers are both operating, which, I argued earlier, should accompany any study of the media. Given this kind of investigation, pupils will have at their disposal an instrument which can cut right to the heart not only of football panels, not only of programmes such as *Mastermind*, *University Challenge* or *Young Scientists of the Year*, not only of such diverse tele-experts as Jimmy Hill, Magnus Pyke or James Burke, but of all those 'official spokesmen' and experts on foreign affairs, economics or whatever who habitually people the television screen.

4. The Cup Final: other approaches

As I have suggested, there are some aspects of televised football which receive little attention in the monograph, partly because they have become a more significant part of football coverage since 1974 and partly because they relate more directly to the coverage of domestic games than to international events. Of central significance to any analysis of an event like the Cup Final are the ways in which the event is appropriated and ritualised by television and the mushroom proliferation of programmes around the central event.

a. *Appropriation and ritualisation*

Cup Final day represents a supreme example of the way in which an event is appropriated and ritualised by television. It's what one might call the Christmas-with-Kojak syndrome, a blurring of the distinctions between the real event and its media presentation. The interest and enthusiasm aroused by the event are deflected away from it and turned towards the television companies themselves. Brian Moore and Jimmy Hill habitually talk about their programmes 'bringing you all the excitement, the atmosphere and the action of the big occasion' as though these things were the *creation* of television, rather than existing quite independently of it. To those who do create the event – the players and crowd – television coverage is quite incidental and the television representation one-dimensional, partial and altogether lacking the richness of texture of the actual occasion. A football match is in this respect quite different from an event like *It's a Knock-Out* which has no independent life of its own, exists only for the purpose of being televised, and in which the 'stars' are not the participants but the television personalities who frame the programme. Television people cannot manage to divest themselves of the illusion that at a football match, similarly, it is the presence of the medium itself which is of central importance. The point was strikingly illustrated during a recent *Pebble Mill* interview with ex-World Cup referee, Jack Taylor. A piece of videotape was shown in which Taylor was severely reprimanding a player. 'You show your experience there', commented an ingenuous Donnie McLeod, 'in turning your back to the camera so that no one could see what you were saying to him.' 'Not so clever really', replied Taylor, 'I didn't realise the cameras were there.' Of course, on Cup Final day everyone realises the cameras are there, but it is evident that to the players, appearing on television is a small and peripheral part of playing in the Cup Final. Indeed, it has nothing to do with playing the game itself. This of course is not the television professional's view of it. Interviewing the players before the game, televising the match, and then going down to the dressing-rooms to get reactions is seen as a continuous and organic process, but the Cup Final on television very strikingly demonstrated that to the players themselves playing the game and appearing on television are two disparate and only marginally related activities. In the Southampton dressing-room after the game, Bobby Stokes looked into the camera and shouted 'Hello, Mum'. He was now 'on television' and acted accordingly. But to his interviewer he had been on television for the past six hours.

Donnie McLeod's revealing assumption that at a football match the presence of the camera is of great significance stems from the fact that in sports *programmes* such as *Match of the Day* or *Cup Final Grandstand* the players are merely actors, strictly under the control of the television professionals who select, mediate and frame what we see. It is but a short step from here to assuming that within the *events* themselves the presence of the television cameras and commentators play an equally significant part. As we have noted one sometimes gets the impression that what the media men really yearn for is an ideal closed televisual world from which fumbling inarticulate sportsmen have disappeared altogether leaving the stage free for a few television and showbiz personalities.

Nor is this mere fancy. A glance at the front cover of the Cup Final edition of *Radio Times* (see Plate 2) reveals a striking dramatisation of this ideal world. Here is an analysis of the picture offered by a sixteen-year-old pupil, Chris Maillard:

> The picture is, at first sight, quite appropriate to the week of the FA Cup Final and the European Cup Winners' Cup Final. It shows four people grouped as if on the terrace, with football scarves on, and shouting. The photograph however, is at closer inspection obviously a grouped, posed studio shot because of the uniform blue background (not to mention the four different club scarves). The blurb, in the clear space at top right of the picture, begins with the big headline 'Anyone for football?' This is significant, as the four 'fans' on the photo are all media personalities. The 'Anyone' of the caption is slanted to make them seem ordinary, in fact just like 'anyone' else who watches football. The main connotation of the photograph and the blurb is that these media personalities watch football just like any 'ordinary' person. They are 'plugging' football as a spectator sport for everyone, and saying that these 'stars' are passionate about football, and that therefore if they like it, you should too. (Chris Maillard)

The picture's overt text outlined here is that football is an exciting game whose fans include famous personalities. There is more to be said however. Hill links the other three figures and is the picture's focal point, his face revealing his own awareness that it is he who is the real centre of attention and not the imaginary football match upon which their eyes are supposedly fixed. The picture's overt text is subverted by its subtext: 'Football is made important by the media personalities who grace it.' The picture is important for the glimpse it gives us of a world without any inner life or purpose of its own. It is the world of showbiz ritual in which rhetoric has become divorced from purpose. The figures touch but have no real relationship to each other. They exist without function, dependent for meaning upon the presence of the camera and made significant only through their association with the game they feed upon.

b. The nature and function of support programmes

Support programmes accounted for 30 per cent of World Cup coverage – a high figure indeed, but less than the 73 per cent occupied by support material on Cup Final day. One of the most remarkable features of current Cup Final presentations is the extent to which the game itself is now almost incidental. What is being sold to the audience isn't a ninety-minute game but a six-hour occasion, for that audience consists of millions of people whose interest in football is peripheral. A glance at the ITV schedule (Plate 3) reveals some of the techniques used to hook this audience – most specifically the stimulus–response technique, which demands a change of topic and scene every ten minutes or so, and the emphasis on the slow build up of emotion and excitement climaxing in our enjoyment of 'the huge, electric atmosphere'. Because ITV and BBC are competing hard for the massive Cup Final audience, and because they are both transmitting the same event, a comparison of the two programme-planning techniques adopted is especially revealing. Briefly, each seeks to outdo the other with better 'inheritance'. The 'inheritance factor' is a kind of apathy principle, an expression of the fact that viewers, having watched a programme they want to see, will watch the next programme, as Nicholas Garnham says 'not out of choice but of inertia'.[11] Most viewers will watch the game on the channel they happen to have switched on when it begins. And the vast majority will continue to watch the whole game on that channel. Here is former BBC executive Paul Fox: 'The inheritance factor is the key thing. Take things like the Cup Final. I think that one will make an effort to provide a good lead into that programme and, therefore, hope that the audience will come with one to the main event.'[12]

To explain the tremendous proliferation of pre-Cup Final paraphernalia, however, another factor needs to be taken into consideration: the phenomenon of pre-scheduling (see Chapter 7).

The BBC is able to plan its programmes against the known schedules of ITV, which because of its more complex networking system must plan ahead of the BBC. The most important reason why BBC's *Cup Final Grandstand* began at 11.15 a.m. is that ITV's Cup Final Special *World of Sport* began at 12.05 p.m. Presumably if ITV Cup Final transmission had begun at 11.00 a.m. the BBC would have felt compelled to open up at around 10.30 a.m. This is why the situation is totally unreal and why pre-match programmes are literally mere time fillers.

5. Conventional football coverage

Very little has been said so far of 'bread-and-butter' coverage of football of the kind most frequently served up on television. Though a domestic event, the Cup Final is nevertheless 'special' and as such a-typical. What approaches can the teacher make towards the study of more conventional football coverage?

One of the major differences between 'special' and typical televised football events is that typical events tend to be both recorded and compressed or edited after the event. The reasons why 'live' football coverage is so rare will need to be discussed by the class, but of greater significance to an understanding of conventional football coverage is the extent to which the time gap between the pro-filmic event (the match itself) and its television presentation affects the nature of the programme we are offered. The guiding principle here seems to be this: the longer the gap between pro-filmic event and presentation, the greater the necessity for presenting the event within the framework of a 'show'. Mid-week matches, for example, presented only an hour or two after the event have a strong enough appeal to stand on their own. It is even possible to reproduce in viewers the curiosity and excitement felt by the match crowd by keeping from them details of the score of the televised game. *Match of the Day* transmitted some six hours after the final whistle when the result is no longer news cannot do this and must be content to mull over points of controversy and reproduce the goals and principal incidents. In this sense the programme performs a similar function to a Saturday night pub inquest.

There is a high risk factor involved in Sunday afternoon football coverage which may radically affect the kind of programme we are shown. Each region pre-commits itself to major coverage of a particular match. The problem facing the regional producers is that if their game turns out to be dull, uninteresting or lacking in goals most viewers will already know this and have little incentive to switch on. Some of the regions have responded ingeniously to this difficulty by concocting a programme around the featured game which may include competitions, favourite goals from the past, discussions and interviews. The emphasis upon controversy and larger-than-life personalities make the programme *predictably* worth watching, and cushion it against the possibility of a dull featured game. This strategy for loosening dependency upon the quality of a game has been most effectively employed by LWT's *The Big Match* whose success owes a great deal to the authority of its hard-worked anchor-man Brian Moore (who as previewer, commentator and post-match coroner does the work of three BBC men). The other regions are markedly less successful and inventive. They range from the honest endeavour of Yorkshire's *Football Special*, whose match is cocooned in rather dull studio interviews and stale snippets of news, through ATV's *Star Soccer*, which suffers from being entirely an outside broadcast with weak continuity between items, to the abysmal *Shoot!* (Tyne-Tees) which offers only the game and the egregious Wolstenholme as a guide to it.

7

Television Specificity and Programme Planning: Two Participatory Exercises

1. Television specificity

Inevitably at some early point in the study of television the teacher will wish his pupils to consider the defining characteristics of the medium which they are studying. In what precise ways are the television message and the conditions of its reception different from those of other media? What is it which constitutes television's uniqueness? These questions can be handled in the classroom through discussion, but this has never seemed to me to work satisfactorily. The topic isn't *inherently* interesting to most pupils, and since the teacher knows most of the answers anyway, there can be a deadening quality about the proceedings. It is a necessary chore to be accomplished and disposed of as quickly as possible. The exercise below attempts to overcome some of these difficulties by placing the discussion of television specificity within a game format.

What is it which makes television so very different from other forms of communication such as plays, novels, poetry, newspapers, films, posters, records, radio, or the telephone?
What qualities does it have which the rest lack?
Below are listed thirteen characteristics of television. Rank them in order of their importance to the uniqueness of television as a medium of communication. Place the most important quality as number 1 and the least important as No. 13:

1. Television is a domestic medium whose messages are received in the home.
2. Television is a continuous medium available 'on tap' most hours of the day.
3. Television viewing is most often a group experience.
4. Most television is easily understood by most people.
5. The cost of watching television is relatively low.

6. Television is an electronic medium relaying things to you as they happen.
7. Television can reach large numbers of people.
8. Television provides choice of programmes.
9. Television provides a combination of sound and moving visual images.
10. Television is controlled by large institutions.
11. Television can be watched while you do other things.
12. The same programme can be seen simultaneously in different parts of the country, and even in different parts of the world.
13. Television presents 'real' rather than 'interpreted' events.

Before proceeding further, the reader may like to spend ten or fifteen minutes working out a ranking order of his or her own.

There are some conceptual difficulties involved in this exercise (the uniqueness of the medium for example might arise from a *combination* of characteristics no one of which is itself unique; there may be difficulties in placing characteristics seen as unique but as not especially important, or conversely, as extremely important though not unique. Some of the characteristics enumerated apply to the technical nature of the medium, others to the conditions of its reception or the characteristics of its audience. How can these very different factors be assigned values on the same scale?). In spite of these possible confusions the teacher should encourage his pupils to make their best way through the maze, and complete their individual rankings as efficiently as possible. Rank numbers should be placed in a column alongside the given list.

Next, pupils should be placed into groups of four or five and asked to decide upon a *unanimously agreed* group list. When completed, this group ranking list should be placed alongside each individual's original list. The process of compiling the group list is the most valuable part of the exercise. The teacher who tapes or overhears the ensuing discussion will discover that pupils at this juncture begin to make most of the points he would have wanted to raise himself. The 'winner' of the game is the pupil whose original list is closest to the final group list. This can be *scored* by subtracting the smaller from the larger number placed against each item giving a score for each item. (If characteristic 1 were placed eighth by the individual and either fourth or twelfth by the group, the individual would score 4 on that item.) Each individual should add up his total score; lowest score wins (the perfect score in which the individual and group lists are identical is 0).

Finally each group may compare its list with the 'experts' list' below, compiled by Stuart Hood, Professor of Film and Television at the Royal College of Art, Manuel Alvarado of the Society for Education in Film and Television, and Ed Buscombe of the British Film Institute, who kindly agreed to play the game, so that it could be given a final twist in the classroom. This is their group list arrived at unanimously but not without a good deal of controversy and hard bargaining. Brief notes are provided in order to give some indication of the panel's reasoning, though they scarcely do justice to the fullness of their discussion.

Ranking	Character-istic number	Comments
6	1	Domestic availability is a characteristic of many of the media mentioned. And the point was made that television viewing is primarily an external and communal experience rather than a domestic one in many European and African countries. However, taken in conjunction with characteristic 9, television's domesticity is of some significance. It is the only 'moving-image' medium widely available in most homes.
3	2	Apart from radio other media are not 'on tap' in the same way as television. Books and records need to be constantly changed by the individual, while the telephone is not available at all in most homes.
7	3	Not necessarily true. Television is widely acknowledged to alleviate loneliness and very large numbers of people watch television in isolation.
11	4	A proposition greeted with a good deal of scepticism by the panel, who felt that lack of attention and misinterpretation probably resulted in a quite widespread lack of comprehension of television messages.
9	5	Television was felt to be more expensive than radio and (given widespread public library facilities) books. In terms of 'entertainment or instructional time bought' paperback books are probably no more expensive than television for which there is, even in its cheapest form, a considerable capital outlay.
4	6	Potentially potent, but rather infrequently realised. Most television does not consist of live events.
1	7	All of the mass media have, by definition, a mass audience, but none can match the sheer magnitude of the television viewing audience. The sheer size of the audience, it was felt, was what primarily made television such a potent and unique medium.
10	8	Choice was not felt to be as wide as that offered by other media.
5	9	Not unique in isolation, but taken together with its domestic availability, this contributes a great deal to the medium's unique appeal.
12	10	True of all the mass media.
8	11	Both 'watched' and 'other things' are open to interpretation here. What degree of attention is implied by 'watched'? The panel doubted that very much *direct* attention would be paid to television if one were engaged in other activities. On the other hand the medium *is* frequently on and glanced at while one is doing something else. Other media — radio or records in particular — probably serve this function as much as television, however, while those occasions on which 'other things' do not claim a great deal of direct attention — while eating a meal, for

Ranking	Character-istic number	Comments
		example – could equally well be used to attend to a newspaper or book as to television.
2	12	Follows on from 7. It is the *simultaneity* of this mass viewing experience which makes the medium so unique.
13	13	Not even true, it was felt, of television at all.

Your own list may differ widely from this 'master' list, but this is not, in itself, of great importance; the individual lists of the panel members actually differed quite markedly from the finally agreed list. Had *you* been a member of the panel, the list would not have been very different. Your thinking would have been influenced by others and vice versa, and the final outcome would have been minor rather than radical alterations to the list as it now stands.

The master list does not have the status of a 'right' answer, but should be of some interest in reflecting the thinking of three men all professionally involved with television. It is worth pointing out to pupils that though these men are all in different ways television 'experts', their list is not an objective one. Experts do not produce unsullied bias-free facts. They have their own perspectives, ideological convictions and professional concerns. So, to take an example from the list, to the man professionally interested in television, whether he be producing material for it, or examining its effects, the sheer magnitude of the television audience possesses a significance it quite lacks for the individual child watching at home with his family. It is a significance which pupils should understand, but it goes without saying that the master list ought not to be used as an instrument for undermining the validity of the pupils' own perspectives. However, the master list does not incorporate any obvious factual oversights or errors in the way that an individual pupil's list might, and to this extent it may be used to demonstrate the effectiveness of group discussion in generating answers which are based upon more accurate evidence than those produced by independent thought, as the following final twist to the game demonstrates: (i) compare the master list with the original list of each individual student (students should add up their own scores in the way already demonstrated); and (ii) compare the master list with the list formulated by each group (so that a group score can be arrived at). Which are lower (that is, closer to the master list), group or individual scores? The most frequent result of this exercise is that group scores are lower than the scores of any individual within that group, demonstrating the effectiveness of group discussion in generating answers from which individual oversights and errors have been eliminated.

On some occasions individuals may achieve lower scores than the group of which they are a part, that is, individuals may do better on their own. The reasons for this phenomenon will need to be discussed. It suggests that there have been blockages to effective group decision-making. It is likely that either

(i) a very dominant group member over-rode the evidence presented by others or (ii) one or more group members made little contribution to group discussion and so did not help to fashion the group's list.

2. Programme planning: a simulation

Because the processes by which television schedules are planned and ordered remain hidden and somewhat mysterious, that a particular programme should appear at a particular time on a specific day is as natural to most pupils as the forms of the programmes themselves. Of course many pupils will have some knowledge of very basic aspects of programme scheduling and the teacher might well begin his work on this topic by eliciting some of these from his group. Pupils are likely to recognise that programmes aimed at specific groups will be shown when those groups can watch (school and women's programmes during the day; children's programmes early in the evening, etc.) and that violent, provocative or minority programmes will be shown late at night. But they are unlikely to be familiar with some of the more intricate techniques forced upon programme planners by the exigencies of competition, or of the ways in which the schedules of BBC 1, BBC 2 and ITV relate to one another. These issues can best be raised by engaging pupils in a simulation which will demonstrate that programme schedules do not simply emerge from a vacuum but are the result of specific human choices based on fairly hard and fast criteria. The simulation method also enables the teacher to introduce a good deal of factual information about programme planning techniques in such a way that it becomes immediately useful in the service of a highly practical activity.

Introduction

The simulation is divided into two parts. The first part is designed to illuminate the relationship between the schedules of BBC 1 and ITV; the second to show the relationship of BBC 2 schedules to the overall pattern. Each part gives students the opportunity to practise some programme scheduling at their own level of sophistication.

a. Part one

Each student is given the task of producing a BBC 1 programme schedule for Wednesday 24 March. The ITV schedule comes out first, because of the more complex organisational problems associated with its planning, and it is against this known rival schedule that the student must plan. The teacher should stress that this particular evening is a very strong one for ITV (here PP1 should be handed out for detailed scrutiny) beginning with three guaranteed audience-pullers, moving on through two immensely popular comedy shows and exclusive soccer coverage, and ending with a royal gala night. The strength of this line-up is worth some elaboration: *The Benny Hill Show* (though not on this specific night) attained third place in the TAM ratings for the whole of the year in question. Of all television series *This is Your Life* and *Man About the House* pulled in the highest number of viewers for particular programmes in that year.

Next, documents PP2 and PP3 should be handed out, and time should be allowed for a careful reading of each one. Finally the nine Programme Cards for BBC 1 should be distributed to each student. The student's task is to fill out the BBC 1 column of his Programming Master Plan using the programmes available to him on his cards. He must begin his schedule at 6.45 when *Nationwide* ends, and end it between 10.45 and 11.00 in time for *Tonight*. The *Nine O'Clock News* is a fixed point which must be planned around.

PP1   *Programming master-plan, Wednesday 24 March*

	BBC 1		ITV
5.45	News and Weather		
6.00	Nationwide		
		6.35	Crossroads
6.45			
		7.00	This is Your Life. Eamonn Andrews springs a surprise on a special guest
		7.30	Coronation Street. Wendy wants to be less involved with Ken
		8.00	Man About the House. Chrissy and Jo meet a man with bionic legs
		8.30	The Benny Hill Show. Benny Hill returns – along with McCloud, Ironside, Cannon, Poirot and Kojak!
9.00	News		
9.25			
		9.30	News
		10.00	Wales v. England. Exclusive recording of today's international football match
10.45 to 11.00	Tonight	10.50	The Royal Film Performance 1976. The film industry's gala night of the year

Notes

Reasons for choices

PP2

You are Bill Watkins, Controller of Programmes for BBC 1. Your task is to plan the BBC 1 programme schedule for Wednesday, 24 March. The commercial television network, because of its more complex organisation, has had to plan its own schedule well in advance, and their schedule for the evening can be seen on the Programming Master Plan (PP1). You should plan BBC 1's schedule bearing the strengths and weaknesses of the commercial network's schedule in mind. Refer also to *Programme Planning Notes* PP3 to help guide you. Your aim is to pull in as large an audience for the evening's viewing as you possibly can, given the programmes at your disposal. The programme alternatives you have are limited, and can be seen on the programme cards.

PP3   *Programme planning: some techniques*

1. *CHANNEL LOYALTY*: The audience tends to watch one or other channel all evening. The object, therefore, is to encourage them to watch yours all evening. The crucial moment is when people switch on for the evening. If they switch on to your channel to begin with, they are likely to stay with you for the rest of the evening. (Peak viewing period is from 7.00 p.m. – 10.00 p.m.)

2. *INHERITANCE FACTOR*: Following a very popular show, a high proportion of the audience will stay to watch the next show, not out of choice, but simply because it is on. A very 'strong' show, attracting a large audience can, therefore, 'carry' or support a programme of minority appeal which follows it.

3. *PRE-ECHO*: Related to the inheritance factor – an audience will tend to watch part of a programme on the same channel *preceding* the main programme they wish to see that evening. They are prepared to suffer a certain amount in the preceding programme to make sure that they don't miss any of the programme they really wish to see. Pre-echo is dependent upon having a clear and assured popular hit.

4. *PRE-SCHEDULING*: If both channels are showing a feature film and one starts theirs ten minutes before the other, the earlier starter will, regardless of quality, tend to gain a bigger audience. A common tactic, therefore, is to attempt to schedule a big audience puller a few minutes earlier than the opposition.

BBC 1 programme cards

> #### Sportsnight
>
> The Greyhound Television Trophy Final
> Save of the Season
> David Wilkie in Florida
>
> Time: 45–60 minutes
>
> (There is room for manoeuvre here. The David Wilkie film could be cut saving 15 mins if necessary)

Omnibus in Hollywood

Cuckoo – The story of Laurel and Hardy,
narrated by Eric Morecambe and Ernie Wise.
(Repeat of programme shown earlier this year)
Time: 65 minutes

Harry O

American detective series starring David Janssen.
Not scheduled regularly
Time: 1 hour 30 minutes

World Champions on Ice

A gala performance at Richmond Ice Rink.
Including John Curry and Vladimir Kovalev
Time: 30 minutes

Disney Time

Roy Castle introduces a selection from Walt
Disney films
Time: 50 minutes

Santiago

Alan Ladd in 1956 film: en route to Tampa,
Florida gun-runner Cash Adams is contacted by
Cuban agents anxious to buy his valuable cargo
Time: 90 minutes

The Morecambe and Wise Show

Eric and Ernie in BBC's top-rated comedy
show

Time: 45 minutes

Documentary Special

A film from the USA about the history
and culture of the Hopi Indians

Time: 70 minutes

Cartoons

Three short cartoon films are available.
You may use any number of them, or none at
all if you wish

1. Tom and Jerry – The Three Mouskateers
   – 5 mins
2. Deputy Dawg – 5 mins
3. Polish Prize-winning cartoon – 15 mins

When students have understood their task, assimilated their material, and begun to work, the teacher should at some stage draw attention again to PP3, a document which can considerably assist them in their task. When the assignment has been completed students should be encouraged to give some indication of the thinking behind their choices in the *Notes* section of PP1. In post-play discussion, class or group agreements need to be established, and conflicts clarified. The teacher may if he wishes introduce Document PP4 at this point in order to examine the solution reached by the BBC 1 programme planner for that particular evening.

This document will repay detailed study by the group. It should not be regarded in any sense as a 'right' answer against which pupils should judge their own, but as one solution meriting close scrutiny since it has been arrived at by a professional. The group should attempt to follow the line of thinking implicit in the BBC 1 schedule, even if they finally disagree with it, since it exemplifies some of the techniques outlined in PP3.

PP4   *Programming master plan Wednesday 24 March*

BBC 1	ITV
5.45 News and **Weather**	
6.00 **Nationwide**	
	6.35 **Crossroads**
6.45 **Santiago**. Film starring Alan Ladd	
	7.00 **This is Your Life**. Eamonn Andrews springs a surprise on a special guest
	7.30 **Coronation Street**. Wendy wants to be less involved with Ken
	8.00 **Man About the House**. Chrissy and Jo meet a man with bionic legs
8.15 **The Morecambe and Wise Show**	
	8.30 **The Benny Hill Show**. Benny Hill returns – along with McCloud, Ironside, Cannon, Poirot and Kojak!
9.00 **News**	
9.25 **World Champions on Ice**	
	9.30 **News**
9.55 **Sportsnight**. Including The Greyhound TV Trophy, David Wilkie in Florida and the Save of the Season	
	10.00 **Wales v. England**. Exclusive recording of today's international football match
10.45 **Tonight**	
	10.50 **The Royal Film Performance 1976**. The film industry's gala night of the year

Analysis   The BBC 1 ace card, *The Morecambe and Wise Show*, is played with great skill here both *before* and against the ITV ace, *The Benny Hill Show*. When it begins it is placed directly against the *commercial break* for *Man About the House*, and this theoretically represents a major switching over point. The 'weak' news slot is cushioned by the inherited audience from *The Morecambe and Wise Show*, and by the fact that no new ITV alternative appears at 9.00 p.m. To switch over to ITV here would be to join a show halfway through. *Santiago* represents a 'strong' film attempt to break through the early evening ITV stranglehold and is pre-scheduled against ITV's principal initial hook for the evening's viewing, *This is Your Life*. The length of *Santiago* however precludes a major pre-echo boost from *The Morecambe and Wise Show* of the kind which might have been enjoyed by a shorter preceding programme, and the BBC 1 schedule caters weakly for viewers

switching on between 7.15 and 8.00. Pre-scheduling is the order of the day
after the *Nine O'Clock News*, and students should note that 10.45 is the ideal
time for scheduling *Tonight*.

b. Part two

The second part of the simulation explores the relationship between BBC 2
schedules, and those of BBC 1 and ITV. The techniques employed are the
same as in Part One of the simulation, though this exercise should be shorter,
since pupils should now be considerably more adept in applying their skills.
Pupils should be given copies of PP3, PP5, PP6 and a pack of BBC 2
programme cards. The first programme must begin at 7.30 p.m. *Newsnight*,
the late night BBC 2 news, must be scheduled at some time between 11.00 and
11.20.

PP5

BBC 2		BBC 1	ITV	
	5.45	News and Weather		
	6.00	Nationwide		
			6.35	Crossroads
	6.45	Santiago. Film		
			7.00	This is Your Life
7.30			7.30	Coronation Street
			8.00	Man About the House
	8.15	The Morecambe and Wise Show		
			8.30	The Benny Hill Show
	9.00	News		
	9.25	World Champions on Ice		
			9.30	News
	9.55	Sportsnight		
			10.00	Wales v. England
	10.45	Tonight		
			10.50	The Royal Film Performance 1976
Newsnight				

Notes

Reasons for choices

PP6

You are Jeremy Wheatley, Programme Controller for BBC 2, and your task is to plan
the BBC 2 programme schedule for Wednesday, 24 March. You are required to
provide alternative and complementary programming to BBC 1 – offering the viewer

a genuine choice. You should not, therefore, schedule a film or a light entertainment programme at the same time as a similar offering on BBC 1. *You must ignore the commercial network's schedule in your planning.* What they show does not affect you at all. You simply have two aims: (1) *To achieve a good 'vertical' pattern of programming*, an interesting and well-balanced evening's viewing on your own channel; and (2) *To observe the 'horizontal' alternative requirements* – i.e. to present a genuine alternative to those programmes already scheduled for BBC 1.

The BBC 1 schedule has just been decided upon, and after carefully examining this and the programmes you have at your disposal (see programme cards for BBC 2) you may begin.

BBC 2 programme cards

Oneupmanship

Comedy sketches, based on book by Stephen Potter

Time: 30 minutes

Third of six programmes

Gardeners' World

Percy Thrower prunes roses and shrubs

Time: 25 minutes

Regular Wednesday series

The Health Show

New series on fitness and diet, introduced by Terry Wogan

Time: 25 minutes

Network (Documentary)

Vivian Whiteley – On Her Own

A widow talks about how she has coped with her 34-year-old husband's death. Follow up to a film transmitted last year in which Mr Whiteley spoke about himself as a victim of cancer

Time: 30 minutes

Playhouse

Practical Experience: A comedy play with
Barry Foster as an architect having staff
problems

Time: 55 minutes

Nana Mouskouri

Nana stars in her own show.
Guest: Keith Michell

Time: 45 minutes

Worldwide (documentary)

KOJAK and Co.: A look at America's commercial
television

Time: 50 minutes

Newsday

News followed by interview with a personality
who has been in the news today

Time: 15–30 minutes

Regular weekday programme

Arena: Art and Design

This programme looks at the new realism
painting

Time: 35 minutes

Regular Wednesday series

Time	BBC 2	Time	BBC 1	Time	ATV	Time	ATV (contd.)
5.25	Open University. Water for Oxford; 5.50 Dial-a-Bus; 6.15 Resources in Sound; 6.40 The Language of Poetry	4.00	Play School	3.55	General Hospital	10.50	The Royal Film Performance 1976. Join Chris Kelly and Judith Chalmers for the film industry's gala night of the year — The Royal Film Performance at the Odeon Cinema, Leicester Square
7.05	Closedown	4.25	Deputy Dawg	4.25	How. With Fred Dinenage, Bunty James, Jon Miller, Jack Hargreaves	11.30	Wrestling
7.29	Weather	4.30	Jackanory	4.50	The Molly Wopsies	12.00	Closedown
7.30	Newsday	4.45	Country Search	5.20	ATV Today—I. Junior Police Five		
8.00	Gardeners' World. Percy Thrower prunes roses, shrubs and the large flowered clematis	5.05	John Craven's Newsround	5.50	News		
8.25	Arena: Art and Design looks at the new realism painting	5.15	Rocky O'Rourke. 4: Joey O'Rourke is in trouble	6.00	ATV Today—II		
9.00	Nana Mouskouri stars in a series presenting her own special kind of music. Guests, Keith Michell and Swingle II	5.40	Captain Pugwash	6.35	Crossroads. The gossip about Lia may be bad, but for David the truth is worse		
9.45	Oneupmanship. The third of six programmes based on Stephen Potter's "Gamesmanship, Lifemanship and Oneupmanship"	5.45	News, weather	7.00	This is Your Life. Eamonn Andrews springs a surprise on a special guest		
10.15	Microbes and Men. Men of Little Faith, third of a six-part series	6.00	Nationwide. Midlands news and topics, including Consumer Unit	7.30	Coronation Street. Wendy wants to be less involved with Ken		
11.10	Newsnight, weather	6.45	Santiago. Alan Ladd, Lloyd Nolan, Chill Wills in 1956 film based on Martin Rackin's novel. En route to Tampa, Florida, gun-runner Cash Adams is contacted by Cuban agents anxious to buy his valuable cargo	8.00	Man About the House. In "Mum Always Liked You Best" Chrissy and Jo meet a man with bionic legs who can win prizes for sitting down . . . Robin's elder brother		
11.25	Closedown.	8.15	The Morecambe and Wise Show	8.30	The Benny Hill Show. Benny Hill returns — along with McCloud, Ironside, Cannon, Poirot and Kojak!		
11.30	Close	9.00	News, weather	9.30	News		
		9.25	World Champions on ice. A gala performance at Richmond Ice Rink including John Curry, Vladimir Kovalev.	10.00	International Soccer. Wales v England from the Racecourse Ground, Wrexham		
		9.55	Sportsnight. The Greyhound Television Trophy Final; David Wilkie in Florida; Save of the Season				
		10.45	Tonight				
		11.20	Weather, Midlands News				

Microbes and Man

Third of a six-part science series.
The previous two parts were broadcast on
the two preceding Wednesdays from 10.15–11.10

Time: 55 minutes

Conclusion   The BBC 2 schedule actually transmitted is shown in PP7. The common denominator in the BBC 2 schedule is the specialist, and in some cases even esoteric appeal of the programmes, compared with the very wide *general* appeal of most of BBC 1's offerings. The audience hypothesised for each programme, apart from *Nana Mouskouri*, is a small but more than averagely-interested and committed one. A striking feature of the schedule, the presence of only one programme junction with BBC 1 compared with the normal three or four, suggests that the audience sought is one which will be less fickle than the mass audience – they won't switch over before the end of the programme – and that there will be less chance than usual of picking up 'casual' rather than deliberate viewers. The exception to this is at 9.00, BBC 1's most vulnerable spot, and the point at which the only junction of the evening occurs between the BBC schedules. The opportunity of picking up chance switchovers from BBC 1 is extremely good, and BBC 2 offers here its most popular and widely-appealing (though still slightly off-beat) show, *Nana Mouskouri*.

*   *   *

Having participated in these two programme planning simulations, students should now be in a position to analyse programme planning techniques employed within the schedules for any particular evening.

8

Practical Television Work

The central paradox of practical television work in education today rests in the shadow which has fallen between the apparent potentialities of the medium and the thin, insubstantial results achieved by groups of pupils or students working with video equipment. The advantages and purposes of video work have been widely heralded by many teachers; they can be briefly elaborated. Here is a teachers' centre warden attempting to motivate local teachers to use his centre's video equipment:

> It is a unique educational tool. First you get *instant replay*, unlike movie film. While some machines are more instant than others, none involves the elaborate and time-consuming loading, unloading and processing procedures of film. Next, it's a personal medium — that is it places immense power in the hands of the people, *any* people, who are pressing the buttons. The power to recreate and order experience, to amuse, terrify, impress, convince – all are available not just to specially trained and approved media people, but to you and the children you teach [1]

The limitations of that 'power' are only now coming to be recognised by teachers. The most important reasons put forward by teachers for using video equipment rest upon assumptions which are taken to be so self-evidently true that they require no detailed justification.

> The passivity of the uncritical viewer can be undermined by putting him or her in a practical relationship with the means of TV production.[2]

> For most people television has taken over as the major medium of communication and it is therefore only sensible to give children some insight into what goes on behind the screen.[3]

But precisely *what* insights are yielded when pupils play about with video equipment apart from the banal ones that the pictures are produced by cameras and changed by vision mixers? And surely some evidence is needed to support the assumption of both writers that practical work illuminates television *viewing*. Theoretical formulations in this area are invariably imprecise and most writers hurry on to elaborate other pay-offs and educative by-products of video work:

> First, working informally with small groups has benefits in terms of personal relationships. Each group has to function as a team . . . In addition self-discipline comes from coping with the frustrations of television . . . Pupils can gain experience in group leadership, etc.[4]

Some writers have seen in video work a way of improving the pupil's self-image:

> . . . video can help towards a more relaxed and objective understanding of who you are . . .[5]

> Working as a director or appearing in front of the camera are useful exercises in developing pupils' self-confidence.[6]

I have been surprised over the past year by the number of teachers who even see practical work in television leading to particular career opportunities within the television industry, particularly, one suspects, as cameramen or technicians:

> Though the courses do not aim to train children directly for jobs in television production, several now want to make television their career.[7]

In suggesting that the conventional justifications outlined above form a less than adequate theoretical basis for video work, I do not mean any criticism of the writers I have quoted. They are 'progressive' teachers who have taken the plunge and attempted to do something constructive with television equipment often in the face of institutional hostility and scathing comments from 'academic' colleagues. Nevertheless most of the justifications offered for practical work are clearly spin-offs rather than primary objectives. If we were really concerned to develop group work or work experience then having pupils prepare videotapes would seem a rather curious and, as it is generally described, a somewhat piecemeal way of going about it.

But if such justifications for video work as these are of peripheral significance, as they surely are, wherein lie its central hopes and aspirations? They can, I believe, no longer be articulated without some embarrassment, so tenuous is their relationship with work actually carried out within schools and colleges. It is the non-achievement of these central objectives which have made teachers run so readily to less lofty but ultimately less defensible rationales. If these aspirations were to be articulated they would perhaps be expressed something like this:

By using video equipment students can present subject-matter which is much closer, more relevant and more particular both to them and to their audiences than professional broadcasters ever could. And they may even bring a freshness of vision to the medium, and begin to use it in genuinely new and even creative ways so that alternatives to the assumptions and conventions of professional broadcasting might become apparent. Their own practice, that is, might constitute a critique of professional practice.

Such sentiments now have a somewhat nostalgic ring. They can, perhaps, be traced back to those days in the early 1970s when video (like cable) seemed an alternative full of democratic promise and it was thought enough to unlock the cupboards and place the Portapacks at the disposal of individuals for that promise to be fulfilled. Have these hopes proved to be hopelessly Utopian? And if so, can more realistic ones be formulated? Edmund Carpenter, who has spent a great deal of time putting cameras into a variety of hands, was compelled to reach these depressing conclusions based on his work with villagers in New Guinea:

Western audiences delight in stories about natives who use modern media in curious ways, their errors being both humorous and profound, suddenly illuminating the very nature of the media themselves. Even when these stories are true, I think their importance is exaggerated. Surely the significant point is that media permit little experimentation and only a person of enormous power and sophistication is capable of escaping their binding power. A very naive person may stumble across some interesting technique, though I think such stories are told more frequently than documented. The trend is otherwise.[8]

Augustin Girard[9] reaches equally pessimistic conclusions about cable television claiming that the quality of the images is so inferior that, in spite of all the claims to the contrary, after a while nobody watches. In Quebec, for example, the original aspirations of community television were eroded until, ironically, self-preservation compelled the increasing use of commercial and foreign material. The story in Britain is even blacker. Of five cable stations licensed to operate in 1972, three had closed down within two years.[10]

The disappointments of cable television have their parallels in student video. What happens when cameras are placed in student hands? To begin with there is 'that strange mixture of embarrassment and excitement which everyone feels when he sees himself on the screen for the first time'.[11] Equally predictably there is the fascination of tinkering with the cameras, vision mixers and special effects, a necessary 'play' stage which will eventually be superseded by the desire to 'do' something, to perform or put on a show. Dancing, singing, conducting interviews, devising 'pop' or quiz shows or attempting some vestigial 'drama' are all likely activities at this stage. One of the difficulties which arises with early video work is that pupils are expected to perform in front of the cameras as well as behind them. Embarrassment in front of the cameras can be overcome by devising tasks for 'performers' which will be absorbing enough to deflect attention away from the cameras. I have found the setting up and playing out of simulations, such as the widely known American *Starpower*, or *Television News* described in Chapter 5 extremely useful in creating a classroom event which half of the group can become involved in, whilst the other half cover it with television cameras. But beyond these elementary stages, what? In my experience an endless wilderness of dreary third-rate imitative 'pop'-shows, embarrassing video dramas, and derivative documentaries courageously condemning war or poverty, much of it condoned by teachers to whom technique is all and the medium the only message. Hans Magnus Enzensberger summarises:

> It has long been clear from apparatus like miniature and 8 mm cine cameras, as well as the tape recorder, which are in actual fact already in the hands of the masses, that the individual, so long as he remains isolated, can become with their help at best an amateur but not a producer . . . The programmes which the isolated amateur mounts are always only bad, outdated copies of what he in any case receives. The poor, feeble and frequently humiliating results of this licensed activity are often referred to with contempt by the professional media producers. On top of the damage suffered by the masses comes triumphant mockery because they clearly do not know how to use the media properly.[12]

What can schools do to provide a context within which a more progressive video practice might develop? First of all video itself needs to be removed from the centre of the stage. We need to turn our attention to the encouragement of attributes and attitudes which might result in its effective use. Enzensberger's words suggest two ways in which this might be done. His stress upon the impotence of individuals working in isolation from one another brings into focus the necessity of teachers encouraging in their classes the development of a genuine group culture of the kind advocated throughout this book, and an awareness of the possibilities of group action. In a decade in which we are moving slowly but certainly towards increasing industrial democracy it is surely incumbent upon schools to encourage their pupils to agree upon their collective views, grievances and dissatisfactions and to express them through constructive and creative channels. Video work would clearly become a powerful cutting instrument for this kind of group expression.

Secondly Enzensberger's stress upon the limitations of emancipation by hardware should heighten our awareness of the fact that video's potential for liberation, like that of print, is predicated upon what Paulo Freire has called a process of 'conscientization'. Freire was able to teach peasants in north-east Brazil to read in thirty hours through the impetus of a pre-literacy process in which his students were encouraged to examine critically the realities of their lives, reach an understanding of the concepts which impinged upon them and express their real knowledge through group dialogue. It is a process through which a culture of silence — whether it be the Brazilian peasants', the New Guinea villagers' or working-class pupils' in our schools — may begin to find a genuinely authentic voice. Without undergoing such a process it seems unlikely that video work in schools and colleges will move beyond doing your own thing with a Portapack with the attendant production of alienated and humiliating tapes. The precondition of video work which is centred in the concrete reality of the pupils' world, which reflects their real concerns and problems, and which is derived from their language, activities and preoccupations is talk — dialogue if you like — about themselves, their culture, their background and their community, and it is this material which must form the field of the teacher's own research and further study. Only when pupils value their own language, background and personalities and are not demeaned by them, will they recover their eagerness for expression. And only when they are capable of harnessing group resources will that expression reach its fullest potency. Ironically, of course, the group may reach the conclusion that it does not wish to use video to express its concerns, and that other courses of action are more appropriate. It is not possible to *predetermine* the use of video; rather it should be seen as an available expressive tool, which is an integral part of a more total liberating education.

For this reason it is important that video equipment should be on hand as frequently as possible for use when the need arises. This applies equally to the use of video within the study of television itself. It is not always possible to foresee when video is likely to be needed, but the areas in which practical work may be introduced include the following.

Early exercises in non-verbal decoding Video is an excellent tool for increasing sensitivity and self-discovery in non-verbal communication. Recording a class discussion and then analysing the different kinds of non-verbal communication taking place forms an excellent introduction to the whole topic, and later work can bring under scrutiny particular aspects of non-verbal communication. Videos of busy street scenes are also useful stimuli to discussion in this area.

Interviewing (see Chapter 9) After early work both inside and outside of the classroom with tape recorders, street interviews with a Portapack should be attempted. Different interviewing styles (see Chapter 5) can be simulated within the classroom, and a sample of them shot on video for group discussion.

Video simulation The video simulation *Television News* is fully discussed in Chapter 5. Follow-up work to *Teachers' Protest* (see Chapter 9) might include making two simulated documentaries (perhaps on the school) one giving a favourable, the other an unfavourable view of its subject.

Sound/vision experiments   make anti-advertisements by: (i) dubbing your own sound on to well-known advertisements; or (ii) shooting your own visual material to accompany the soundtrack of an advertisement.

Project work   Encourage the use of video for project work both in television studies and in other school subjects. The whole range of possibilities for video within this area will need to be pointed out to students including: (i) the storage and retrieval of information, both from television and external sources; (ii) its value for presenting a case or argument; (iii) its appropriateness as a medium for the detailed study of particular topics (any aspect of non-verbal communication or the detailed study of a particular television genre for example). In other subjects, where students need to find out about people, they will find video an invaluable tool.

Code-breaking exercises   A recent classroom experience: in presenting a simulated news presentation, pupils unknowingly broke a number of established television codes. First of all the newscaster was held in much tighter close-up than normal, and secondly news stories were simply recounted by their principal actors (a shop steward, a housewife, a cabinet minister) rather than being 'mediated' by the comments of reporters or correspondents. The result was to draw attention to the existence of particular codings operating within television news broadcasts which had previously gone unexamined. But what meanings were carried by these codings? Two video experiments were set up: (i) a student reading news items was shot by two cameras, one using tight close-up, the other using a middle-distance shot; (ii) one student was interviewed by another about a street accident; then the interviewee gave her own account straight to camera. Each pair of tapes was then discussed. In the first case conventional codings for the framing of newsreaders were seen to convey 'naturalness', respectful distance, lack of threat; a tighter close-up, on the other hand, compelled the viewer to *interrogate* both the newsreader and the information he was giving. In the second case conventional codings suggested that truth is best served by those who lack either involvement or commitment in the events described.

Video is important for the study of televisual codings, since it allows individual conventions (of framing, camera-positioning, editing, etc.) to be isolated, experimented with and broken while variations in their meaning are explored.[13] The *systematic* and *detailed* study of codings is perhaps a little too abstract and specialised to be suitable for schools and may best be left to college and university students. In schools the study of codings is likely to be much more *incidental*, with video exercises springing from the observation by pupils of individual concrete codings as they arise in particular programmes.

Recording events Video equipment is frequently used in schools for the purpose of providing a permanent record of a special event within the school such as an open night, or a sports day. If there is a 'television group' within the school then requests to provide this kind of service are increasingly likely to be laid at its door. How should the television teacher respond to such requests? And how can this kind of activity be justified as contributing to the *study* of television? The answer to the first question is straightforward: since responsibility for undertaking this kind of assignment will fall upon the group rather than the teacher, the decision as to whether to go ahead with it or not should rest with the group.

The second question raises a more complex issue, since requests to 'record' events largely rest upon that very assumption of the medium's transparency which it is the purpose of television studies to challenge. The justification for recording events *within television studies* must be that in producing a tape the group will give some consideration to the principles of selection and the mediating frameworks it will have to adopt, and that these principles and frameworks should be the subject of subsequent analysis and discussion by the whole group. Under these circumstances the use of video for recording purposes will dovetail into the conceptual framework for television studies outlined in Chapter 1.

*   *   *

In this chapter I have described some of the ways in which practical television work can be integrated into a predominantly analytical television studies curriculum, examined the current theoretical bases of autonomous practical television practice, and suggested that viable video work in the future will need to grow out of a very different set of premises. These will involve, as Enzensberger has suggested, an acknowledgment of the limitations of individual work and an exploration of the potency of group projects, as they emerge from dialogue and a process of 'conscientization'. A delineation of the constituent elements of this process is an urgent task for the immediate future; ironically it may result in the ultimate rejection of video as the most appropriate medium for expressive action.

9

Aspects of Television

Because this book has been more concerned to clarify the processes rather than the explicit content of a television education, many important aspects of television have inevitably remained uncharted. This chapter attempts to fill some of the gaps by outlining possible teaching approaches to a number of aspects of television which have so far not been discussed:

1. The interview
2. Television documentary
3. Television comedy
4. Popular programmes of some 'educational' interest
5. 'Classic' serials

1. The interview

There are a number of pressing reasons why schools should encourage pupils to think about and practise the art of interviewing. It is the medium through which most people acquire their jobs, and it is becoming an increasingly important technique both at school and work for collecting information, discovering opinions and sounding out attitudes. But a television educator must pay special attention to the problems, techniques and codings involved in interviewing since it is *the* stock technique within broadcasting for eliciting first-hand information and opinions. Incidentally too, if we as members of the public are ever given access to the media it is as likely as not to be through the medium of the interview. For these reasons it seems important that pupils should practise at first hand the roles of interviewer and interviewee and should be encouraged to reflect upon the interview as an important cultural as well as media phenomenon.

a. 'Starters': simulating interviews

The teacher faces an initial problem: most of his pupils will possess neither the confidence, ability, nor motivation to carry off a successful interview with a total stranger. How can these attributes be developed in his pupils? First of all, motivation. Explain to the group the simple truth that the tasks they will be performing would tax the abilities of sixth-form students, and even mature and experienced adults. Treat the group, in other words, as though they were two or three years older than they really are, and explain carefully the general value to them of interviewing practice. The fact that the ability to interview well is less connected with academic prowess than with a whole range of oral and social skills, which 'unacademic' pupils often possess to a high degree, is a further motivating factor. Finally there is a personal challenge and responsibility in being 'out on your own' in a one-to-one relationship with a strange adult which most pupils will, with encouragement, rise to.

Given good motivation, confidence and ability in interviewing is something which will grow with practice. 'Safe' practice can be provided by the use of simulated interviews conducted within the confines of the classroom. To be really successful simulated interviews need to be more than dummy runs or practice interviews and ought ideally to generate a life and interest of their own. The teacher will need to think hard about providing a large number of simple but stimulating 'starters' to spark off successful encounters. One method of doing this is through the use of simple *story-cards*.

Divide the class into two groups, one group to be interviewers, the other to be role-players who will be interviewed. Each interviewer is handed a different story-card. This contains a short 'human-interest' story from a local newspaper and an instruction to interview a particular person connected with the story. Examples are shown in the three cards on p. 146.

Interviewers are told that they are reporters from a local radio station and their task is to follow up the newspaper story for their station. They are given three or four minutes to absorb the story and make a note of essential information. The cards are then taken from them and they are asked to prepare themselves for the interview which will take place in four minutes. Each card is then transferred to a different role-player who takes in the information and awaits the interview. After each interview new cards should be distributed and roles reversed so that each pupil has the opportunity both to interview and be interviewed. Three or four of the interviewers should use a tape recorder so that the whole class may hear the results. Playback of tapes will reveal that some interviews are more lively and stimulating than others, and that some have been recorded more effectively than others. Why is this? Precisely how can one judge the effectiveness of an interview or a recording? And what steps can you take to try and ensure that your next interview is more successful? In formulating answers to these questions the group should be able to make a list of tentative suggestions about what makes an interview interesting and successful. Armed with the pupils' list, the teacher can prepare and type up a more formalised sheet of suggestions for the group to work on and think about before they go out into the streets and confront the public.

Pistol is stolen

Police are searching for thieves who got into Bilborough College, probably by using a key, and stole a .22 calibre Webley and Scott starting pistol with a black and white plastic handle from the PE store.

They scattered papers on the floors of classrooms and the staff room.

Action: Interview Bill Noakes, the College Caretaker.

Complaint on poster

Vice Squad police in Nottingham have interviewed a Trent Polytechnic art student after a complaint about an allegedly indecent poster.

The poster – displayed in the city centre – is now being examined by officers.

A spokesman said the complaint from a member of the public was about the wording of the poster. The student declined to comment.

Action: Interview the member of the public who complained.

'Ideal motor' needed repair

Bus driver Reginald Kneen was told he was getting an 'ideal motor' when he bought a second-hand family car for £395.

But after driving it to his home in Chilton Way, Bestwood Park, he found 'vast' holes in the bodywork, he said at Nottingham County Court.

Mr Kneen, 36, was awarded £160.90 damages plus costs against Ashfield Autos Ltd of Radcliffe Road, West Bridgford, and an associated company Classbon Finance Ltd.

He said he bought the six-year-old Morris 1100 Traveller for family motoring.

Action: Interview a spokesman for Ashfield Autos Ltd.

b. Interviewing suggestions: hand out

Choosing a topic Choose something you are interested in, and would really like to have peoples' opinions on. Ask questions that you really wish to know the answers to.

Preparation How effectively are you prepared for your interview? Would you like to try out some questions first, or have one or two dummy runs with a few partners? Do you have all of the facts and information you may need at your fingertips without having to look at notes? Do you have some questions prepared? (Remember not to *over*-plan. Follow what your subject is saying and base your questions on this if possible, but it is as well to have some spare questions to hand in case the interview dries up.)

The illusion of the interview On tape, the illusion you might like to try to sustain as interviewer is that the person being interviewed is communicating directly to whoever is listening to your tape. This illusion will be broken if: (i) you talk too much or constantly interrupt the speaker; or (ii) you fall into the trap of interjecting encouraging remarks ('I see'; 'Ah, ah!', 'Yes', etc.).
   Two general rules follow from this:

1. The less you say the more successful the interview is likely to be.
2. Make as much use as you can of non-verbal signals – *nodding* approval or agreement, *smiling* broadly rather than laughing out loud, etc. – which will maintain communication with your subject but be undetectable on tape.

Fruitful questions Avoid questions which might be given a one-word answer. 'How?' 'What?' and 'Why?' questions are probably the most productive.

Language Use and trust your everyday way of talking – it's the liveliest language there is.
   Don't:

Read out your questions.
Use specialised, pompous or long-winded language.
Interview people who do talk in this way.

Listen critically to dummy runs Listen to all of the practice tapes you make of yourself. Are there any special mannerisms of which you were unaware, and which draw undue attention away from your subject?

Making people comfortable Most people are rather nervous about being interviewed, especially if they have to speak into a tape recorder. You can help put your subjects at their ease by becoming aware of and practising a whole range of non-verbal signals, of the kind discussed in Term One:

eye-contact – looking directly at the person you are addressing. Be confident and direct but not overbearing.

touch – touching the person while you are directing him will increase his confidence and willingness to co-operate ('Use the mike like this'; 'Stand about there', etc.).

tone of voice – informal, friendly, colloquial, joking. Don't read anything or refer to notes.

facial expression – smiling, communicating that it's not all that serious, a bit of fun, etc.

Interpreting non-verbal signals   You will not only need to communicate through the use of non-verbal signals, but also to *observe* and *interpret* such signalling in others, e.g.:

1. How is the person walking? If he's ambling he may have time to speak to you. If he looks as though he's in a hurry, don't bother him. Some people may even hang around and show an interest in what you are doing.

    Better to approach women with empty rather than full shopping baskets.

    Foreigners, tourists, etc. – will add variety to your tape, and they may well welcome being approached by a 'genuine' English person.

    Elderly people have a great deal to give you, but be very sensitive in approach. They may be much more nervous and apprehensive both of you and your machine, than you can imagine. If you get a rebuff, try to understand why, and critically examine the way you handled the situation.

2. Pick up as much information from clothes as you can before deciding to approach. Milkmen, shop assistants and others who are used to meeting and chatting with the public will tend to be willing subjects if they have the time. People dressed formally may take less kindly to being buttonholed than others.

Don't bully people into being interviewed; they are entitled to refuse.

Listening to your environment   If you are using a taperecorder, *before recording*, look and *listen* to your environment. Are there any obtrusive sounds? If you are interviewing in the street, move your subject into a shop doorway or any other place away from loud traffic noise. If you are indoors, think ahead for possible intrusions – unhook the telephone, place a notice on the door, anticipate any bells, etc.

Make an examination of the strengths and weaknesses of your sound environment. Which part of the house, which room in the building, which shop in the street, which street in the area will give you the best recording conditions?

In general, avoid heavy traffic and rooms with bare walls from which the sound will echo. An ordinary living room is quite a good recording place – the furniture absorbs the sound and creates a studio effect; it will help to draw any curtains. For the classroom a studio effect can be created by recording within a circle of fellow pupils, or inside a circle of outward facing chairs with jackets draped over the backs.

Background noises can be coped with by lowering the volume intake through the microphone and speaking closer to the mike.

Suitably prepared, pupils should now be ready to go out in pairs and using tape recorders and video equipment, collect a number of interviews on the topic of their choice. Pupils should then spend time listening to and viewing each other's tapes, and the teacher may wish to select specific interviews for detailed class comment. Ideally, pupils should be given the opportunity of editing audiotapes. Cassette recorders cannot be used for this purpose however, nor can most reel-to-reel recorders of the kind normally found in schools. The rewards of having access to a machine like a Ferrograph upon which editing is a comparatively quick and simple process are enormous, for students immediately learn what is so difficult to teach in any other way – that the production of a polished interview is a manipulative process. The more opportunities that pupils have for participating in this doctoring process the better, for the belief that interviews happen just the way that they are broadcast in the same logical and chronological sequence with everyone word perfect, never fluffing or suffering lapses of memory, is, I have found, extremely widespread amongst school pupils; one suspects that it is almost equally so amongst adults. This belief, duplicated in millions of individuals and continually reinforced by the broadcasting media, must contribute to a latently elitist, even fascist, mass psychology (often overtly expressed in quite different terms; we may desire 'socialist' leaders) in which rulers are seen as exercising a 'natural' right to lead through their possession of a 'manufactured' polish and even infallibility. To challenge this belief seems to me to be an important pedagogic task. Equally important is to challenge the official *raison d'être* of televised interviews – itself a significant component of the myth of the medium's transparency – that through them individuals are able to speak for themselves, putting their own point of view 'in their own words', and responding to questions which we would wish to (and, indeed, *can* through the mediation of the interviewer) ask them. This challenge necessitates an examination of the ways in which meanings are *constructed* within and through televised interviews. It is to a consideration of how this examination might take place in the classroom that we must now turn.

c. Analysing television interviews

Collect material for analysis by videotaping short interviews or extracts from longer ones, from a wide variety of genres (news and current affairs programmes, sports shows, documentaries, chat shows, etc.).

Turning down the sound, can students identify the genre from which the interview is taken by the visual conventions of the interview itself? Explore the variety of conventions which exist within the interview format along with their attendent meanings and overtones. (Pattern of editing, camera-positioning, proxemics, the setting of the interview and other visual codings are all likely to be of significance here.)

Replaying the interviews with sound, examine differences in the kinds of questions asked and answers given. Is the interviewee giving a personal opinion or an objective account? Does he talk about his ideas or his feelings?

What is the role and status of: (i) the interviewer, (ii) the interviewee? Is status related to the kind of questions asked, the kind of visual codings employed, the kind of settings used, the kind of editing and camera position adopted?

Do student findings confirm those of Brunsdon and Morley in their analyses of interviewing conventions on *Nationwide*:

> Participants of 'low' status will tend (a) to be questioned only about their 'feelings' and responses to issues whose terms have already been defined and (b) will tend also to be quickly cut short if they move 'off the point'. Those of 'higher' status will conversely tend to be (a) questioned about their 'ideas' rather than their 'feelings' and (b) will be allowed much more leeway to define issues in their own terms.
>
> This distinction is formally supported by the tendency to move in for bigger close-ups of subjects who are revealing their feelings, whereas the set-up for the 'expert' is usually the same as that for the interviewee – the breast pocket shot . . .
>
> Thus there is a clear differentiation . . . between those participants who appear principally as 'subjects' – something newsworthy has happened to them – and those who appear as 'expert' in some particular field. The distinction between the two types of participants is constructed through the interview questions.[1]

How are meanings constructed in the interviews? What mediating influences are there? e.g. How is the interview 'framed'? How is it introduced? Are there any concluding comments? Within the interview itself how is the interviewee introduced? How does he take his leave?[2]

What *style* is adopted by the interviewer? (See Chapter 5, 4*b*, pp. 98–106.) Is he aggressive towards, on equal terms with, or subservient towards the interviewee?

What meanings are suggested by the visual treatment (an area over which the interviewee has no control and where he is completely at the mercy of the producer)?

In recorded interviews, how frequently are 'cutaway' shots used to preserve continuity and disguise awkward cuts?[3]

Examine the mediating effects of the visual codings, conventions and settings mentioned earlier.

How far is the effect of the interviewee's words modified by reaction shots, follow-up questions, interruptions, etc.?

For the teacher who wishes to examine transcripts of television interviews with his group, good examples can be found in Pateman,[4] Hall, Connell and Curti,[5] and Heath and Skirrow.[6] The best available account of teaching about television interviews is by Gillian Dyer,[7] while many of the points raised in this chapter are applied to a *Nationwide* programme by Brunsdon and Morley.[8] Interviewing styles and forms have been discussed by Collins[9] and Hall,[10] whilst visual codings in news interviews are discussed by the Glasgow Media Group.[11]

2. Television documentary

a. Introducing documentary

There are many difficulties facing the teacher who wishes to conduct a serious investigation of television documentaries with his class. To begin with, no full-scale theoretical investigation of the genre has yet been attempted, and simply defining the area of study is a task bristling with problems and ambiguities. On the other hand no serious study of television is conceivable which does not directly confront documentary material at some stage, and the teacher is perhaps best occupied in deciding upon the qualities which he wishes his pupils to bring to the viewing of documentary material. My own best answer to the question is that pupils should possess:

1. Some knowledge and experience of how visual material can be selected, organised and treated to convey a particular point of view.
2. Some insight into the problematic nature of the relationship of sound track to visual image.
3. Viewing experience of some earlier television documentaries which have been of significance in the development of the genre.

Fortunately for teachers some excellent and by now quite widely-known material is available which is ideal for developing abilities and insights into the first two areas. *Teachers' Protest*[12] is a photoplay exercise which includes background information, press reports and packs of thirty photographs and slides which pupils have to manipulate and organise for presentation as documentary material within a number of possible formats. Teacher's notes accompany the pack and suggest many ways of using the material within the classroom. The exercises suggested ('Try telling the story in a deliberately biased way', 'make a police training film', 'make part of a textbook for television cameramen', etc.), are by no means unchallenging and assume some familiarity in handling visual material as well as a basic understanding of the nature and purpose of captions. I have used *Teachers' Protest* with most success when I have prepared the way for its use with one or two simpler caption exercises, which really do sharpen awareness of the relationship between words and pictures, and encourage close scrutiny of the visual evidence presented by pictures:

1. Prepare a set of cards, each consisting of one newspaper photograph and two captions, the real one, and one which is made up. The fictitious caption should give a completely different interpretation of the picture, but should still be quite appropriate to it. Students must choose the correct caption. (See Plate 5, opposite p. 113, and p. 113 itself.[13])
2. Prepare a set of cards each consisting of one newspaper photograph and two accompanying *headlines*, one, the headline actually attached to the photograph, the other, a headline which *might* have been attached to it but wasn't. Again, students must guess the correct headline.[14]

Follow-up work to *Teachers' Protest* might include a slide presentation, in which *different* captions which have been attached by the class to the *same* picture (see Plates 6, 7, 8, 9, opposite p. 113, and p. 113 itself) are collated by the teacher for class discussion. This exercise draws attention very clearly to the ambiguous nature of much visual evidence, and to the function of captions in anchoring meaning to visual material.

Finally the film *Protest for Peace*,[15] a compilation of old cinema newsreel extracts on protest marches, may be looked at to explore the relationship between image and sound commentary. The final extract, on an anti-Vietnam War march to Grosvenor Square, is worth playing silently two or three times so that students can write a commentary for it. The results can then be compared with the actual commentary in which British 'bobbies' are praised for their tolerance and moderation only moments after being shown kicking a prostrate protester.

b. Looking at documentaries

Preparatory work of the kind outlined above should enable pupils to frame many of the important questions which need to be asked of all documentaries: What point of view is being put forward? Does the argument develop out of the visual material or have the pictures been selected to illustrate a preformulated argument? Is the visual material ambiguous or does it really demonstrate what the commentary is saying?

Some notion of the tradition from which current documentaries spring may be gained by showing and discussing some of the most seminal television documentaries of which pupils may be unaware. Of all the films which I have shown to pupils the following five provided the most engaging and stimulating material:

Culloden (Concord)
The War Game (BFI)
Gale is Dead (Concord)
Cathy Come Home (Concord)
The Space Between Words: Education (BBC TV Enterprises)

The content of a number of these films is so disturbing that it would be perverse to discuss them in terms of documentary technique. Sometimes indeed it seemed best not to discuss the film at all, but to acknowledge the value of the experience of viewing it by allowing it to stand on its own without comment. There is great value in building up a large bank of common viewing experiences within a group, for without it it is difficult to establish common points of reference when more recent documentaries come to be discussed.

Teachers wishing to engage their group in a more comprehensive study of the television documentary will find appropriate source material within the catalogues of the following distributors:

British Film Institute Distribution Library, 81 Dean St, London W1
Concord Films Council, 201 Felixstowe Road, Ipswich, Suffolk
BBC TV Enterprises Film Hire, Woodston House, Oundle Road, Peterborough PE2 9P2
Granada TV Film Library, Manchester M60 9EA

Helpful literature on documentaries is somewhat thin. The best detailed analysis of a television documentary is Heath and Skirrow's discussion of one edition of *World in Action*,[16] the most useful account of teaching about documentaries is Susan Bennett's description of her course at the City University, London,[17] Bakewell and Garnham's *The New Priesthood*[18] contains interviews with ten documentary-makers and Vaughan's *Television Documentary Usage*, otherwise of marginal interest and value to teachers, contains a discussion of 'mannerism' – 'the attempt by film to approximate to the condition of verbal prose' – a useful conceptual tool in analysing documentaries.[19]

3. Some approaches to television comedy

a. Introduction

Teaching about television comedy will seem to many teachers to be, at best, a pleasant way of whiling away a wet Friday afternoon on the last week of a tiring summer term. Apart from the fact that much television comedy is trivial, ephemeral and doggedly unintellectual, humour is intensely personal, notoriously difficult to discuss, and can be murdered in the act of dissection. There are however a number of compelling reasons for seriously examining television comedy output in the classroom and it may be as well to clarify these from the outset.

A casual glance at the television schedules will reveal the importance of comedy programmes within them, both in terms of their quantity and placement. In the battle to attract viewers, successful comedy shows are very heavy weapons in any broadcasting company's armoury, often commanding larger audiences than 'exclusive' and expensive sporting events. Furthermore, in the brief history of television some comedy programmes have a particularly illustrious place and are widely regarded as examples of ways in which the medium has explored new forms and opened up new areas of entertainment. The study of television comedy then is integral to the study of the medium as an ever-evolving mode of communication. Studying television comedy is also important because it is simultaneously a significant part of the viewing experience of most pupils and an area in which they will have but a shadowy understanding of the development of the forms they observe. It is important to demonstrate to pupils that comedy shows, like all others, come not out of thin air, but belong to, or break away from, a particular kind of tradition. Some understanding of the various comic traditions which popular television shows draw upon is necessary for any insight into them. This is not to advocate the deadening, abstract, academic pursuit of 'tracing influences' but to emphasise that the way in which a particular programme grows out of, or perhaps simply reflects, an existing tradition will be important to any understanding of it.

Space does not permit a detailed account of the many approaches to the study of televised comedy which were tried out in the classroom.[20] Instead I shall try in this section to fulfil three principal objectives: (i) to show how the topic of televised comedy may be introduced in the classroom so as to suggest the breadth and variety of the field; (ii) to show how an understanding of the specific traditions of *surrealistic* and *realistic* comedy may be encouraged in the classroom; and (iii) through the study of stand-up comedians to draw attention to some larger questions about humour and jokes and to make students a little more aware of what makes them laugh and why.

b. Television comedy genres

One way of beginning work on comedy is to have pupils think about the total output of comedy on television and to categorise, draw comparisons and recognise distinctions within it. Each pupil will need to do this in his own way and at his own level.

> *ASSIGNMENT*: 'Write down the titles of as many television comedy shows as you can think of. Organise your list into subcategories of programmes which seem to have a good deal in common.'

Having compiled individual lists pupils may now work on a class 'master' list in the course of which some of the problems of classification inherent in their own lists will become explicit. It is impossible to foretell the kind of categorisation which the group will eventually come up with, but it will probably resemble this list finally produced by a group of fifteen-year-olds:

Types of Television Comedy
1. Situation comedies – British
2. Sitcoms – American
3. Surrealistic comedy
4. 'Star' variety shows, with sketches and music
5. Stand-up comedians within musical variety shows, or put together in shows like *The Comedians*

c. Resources

The next task is to have the class suggest, collect and bring in materials which relate to each of the above categories. Most pupils will in fact possess relevant records, tapes and books, and it ought to be possible to build up an impressive class library from which individuals can borrow to read or listen to at home. Some of the material will also be worked through in class. Here are the materials which we – a group of fifteen pupils and a teacher – managed to collect together within one week.

Situation comedies – British

Scripts	*Steptoe and Son*: Four television scripts by R. Galton and A. Simpson (Longman, 1971). Multiple copies available from school stock
	Hancock: Scripts by Galton and Simpson (Corgi, 1962)
	Porridge: Scripts by R. Clement and I. La Frenais (BBC, 1975)
	Whatever Happened to the Likely Lads: Scripts by Clement and La Frenais (BBC, 1974)

	Thoughts of Chairman Alf: Alf Garnett's Little Blue Book by J. Speight (Sphere, 1974)
	Script Conference: Peter Cook and Dudley Moore, *The Listener*, 12 March 1970 (script of sketch)
Records	Peter Cook and Dudley Moore
	Tony Hancock
	Stanley Holloway
	Forty Years of Television: *Comedy Spectacular* (BBC Records and Tapes)
Film	*The Blood Donor* (extract from a *Hancock's Half Hour* television programme) Available from British Film Institute
Sound Tapes	*ITMA*
	Take It From Here
Novels (all	*Billy Liar* by Keith Waterhouse (Penguin, 1970)
adapted for	*The Fall and Rise of Reginald Perrin* by David Nobbs
television	(Penguin, 1976) introduced later, but included here for
series)	reference
	A Touch of Daniel by Peter Tinniswood (Hodder, 1971)
	I Didn't Know You Cared by Peter Tinniswood (Pan, 1975)
Essay	*The Art of Donald McGill* by George Orwell in *Decline of The English Murder* (Penguin, 1965)
Videotape	*Porridge* extract from the series starring Ronnie Barker.

American sitcoms

Videotape	*Diana* (extract from ITV series starring Diana Rigg)
Autobiography	*You Can Get There From Here* by Shirley MacLaine (Corgi, 1976). Contains a blow-by-blow account of her disastrous television series

Surrealistic comedy

Scripts	*Goon Show* Scripts (Sphere, 1974)
	Monkey Business and *Duck Soup*: Scripts of Marx Bros films (Lorrimer, 1972)
Records	*The Goon Show* (Tales of Men's Shirts)
	Monty Python and *Beyond The Fringe* teams: *A Poke in the Eye* (Transatlantic)
Sound Tapes	*Round the Horne* (BBC)
	I'm Sorry I'll Read That Again (BBC)
Plays	*Rhinoceros, The Chairs, The Lesson* by E. Ionesco (Penguin, 1962)
	A Resounding Tinkle by N. F. Simpson in *Penguin Plays*, vol. 1 (Penguin, 1964)
	Revue Sketches by Harold Pinter in *A Slight Ache* (Methuen, 1966)

Books   *The Theatre of the Absurd* by Martin Esslin (Penguin, 1970)
             The Groucho Letters by Groucho Marx (Sphere, 1974)
             Monty Python's Big Red Book by G. Chapman *et al.* (Eyre
             Methuen, 1972)

Stand-up comedians
Book   *Funny Way to be a Hero* by John Fisher (Paladin, 1976). An
             indispensable study of the stand-up comic from Dan Leno to
             Ken Dodd. The book contains long extracts, quotations and
             descriptions from the music-hall acts of two generations of
             comedians, many of whom are now television personalities
Play   *Comedians* by Trevor Griffiths (script kindly lent by
             Nottingham Playhouse), published in 1976 by Faber &
             Faber

It would be quite wrong for the reader to imagine that the group who
collected together these resources were themselves particularly resourceful.
Television teaching is opportunistic; to a large degree any choice of topic will
be determined by the quality of the materials which are currently easily
available. We chose to examine comedy because at that time BBC Radio was
re-broadcasting some of its most famous comedy shows such as *ITMA*, *Take
It From Here* and *The Goons* as part of its semi-centennial celebrations, while
at the local theatre, the Nottingham Playhouse, the first production of Trevor
Griffiths' play *Comedians* provided the group with an opportunity to see a
work which specifically analysed comedy and stimulated a good deal of
discussion within the group about humour and jokes.

Once the materials have been gathered together a useful way of ordering
them and of imposing some kind of structure upon the 'bank' available for
pupil use is for the teacher or a small group of pupils to present to the rest of
the group an anthology of humour which will give a taste of what is available
for further exploration, and draw attention, without any insistence, to some of
the traditions which exist in British humour. Sometimes the group will wish to
discuss particular extracts, but for the most part the pieces should be left to
speak for themselves, and make their own connections with one another. Our
own anthology consisted of the following pieces and stretched over three
entertaining periods:

1. *Take It From Here* extract (The Glums) – sound tape
2. *Hancock's Half Hour* extract (The Wild Man of the Woods) – record
3. *Hancock's Half Hour* extract (The Blood Donor) – film
4. *Trouble in the Works* and *The Last To Go* – two sketches by Harold Pinter
5. *Steptoe and Son* extract (script)
6. *Whatever Happened to the Likely Lads* extract – script
7. *Porridge* extract – video

8. *ITMA* extract (sound tape)
9. *Duck Soup* extract (from script of Marx Bros film)
10. *The Goon Show* extract (Tales of Men's Shirts) – record
11. *Monty Python's Flying Circus* – extracts from *Monty Python's Big Red Book*

One more double period was allotted for the group to browse through, listen to or watch material from the resource bank, and the bank continued to be used for reading and playing material at home during the course of our study of comedy.

d. Surrealism and humour: some surrealist games

Many of the shows most widely enjoyed by pupils belong to a tradition of absurd humour which has been traced by Martin Esslin,[21] and has rich veins in the theatre, the music-hall, and children's stories and rhymes. The 'bank' materials reflect a number of facets of this tradition, but perhaps its most seminal manifestation as a philosophy and indeed way of life occurred in the 1920s with the burgeoning of surrealism. Some pupils will be familiar with surrealist paintings, reproductions of which can easily be made available for group perusal and discussion; a few early surrealist films such as Clair and Picabia's *Entr' Acte* (1924), and Bunuel and Dali's *Un Chien Andalou* (1928) are also easily obtainable, while less authentic but more modern and accessible surrealistic visions are presented by Roman Polanski most notably in *Two Men and A Wardrobe* and *Cul-de-Sac*.[22] But the movement's attack upon social conformity, its dedication to chance, its devaluation of language as a web of conformity, and its emphasis upon the power and significance of the unconscious are perhaps best illustrated by having pupils undertake some surrealistic activities of their own.

The exquisite corpse   The most famous of all surrealist games.
Sit five people around a table. Each one writes an adjective on a piece of paper without letting anyone else see. Each person folds the paper over to hide what he has written, passes this to the next person on his left and receives a similarly folded paper from the person on his right. It is now necessary for each player to add, to the adjective he cannot see, a noun. Follow the same procedure for a verb. Then for another adjective. And finally for another noun, the object of the sentence. Now each arbitrary sentence should be read out; they can be run together to form a surrealist poem. The first sentence ever obtained in this way, 'the exquisite corpse will drink the new wine', gave the game its name. The exercise is great fun and works well in the classroom.

Questions and answers   A similar game couples questions and answers formulated separately. Begin with simple examples, and have pupils pose questions using a 'What is an x' formula, followed by as accurate an answer as they can come up with. The following are some actual class examples:

1. What is a brick? A hard material used for building.
2. What is a stag? A male deer.
3. What is hunger? Lack of food.
4. What is beauty? Something you like looking at.
5. What is a hand? A human appendage with five fingers.

Now – for a surrealistic effect – place different questions and answers together in a random way.

Dice therapy   Dice therapy, fully described by Luke Rhinchart in his novel, *The Dice Man*,[23] is a recent phenomenon but is very much like the early surrealist attempts to make their lives open to chance or random factors. In dice therapy important decisions are determined by the throw of a dice. The activity is anarchic, liberating, destructive of order, logic and predictability, and potentially dangerous. I am not advocating that pupils should go very far along this trail, but it would do the teacher little harm to announce that for the next ten minutes of the lesson, activities will be determined by the throw of a dice. The group must decide upon six alternatives, one which they really want to do, one which is anathema to them, and four others representing neither extremely favourable nor extremely unfavourable choices. A number is assigned to each choice; the dice is thrown; the group must do the activity determined by the fall of the dice. The point of this activity is that it really does convey the flavour of surrealism, demonstrating that for its adherents it wasn't simply a curious aesthetic movement, but a whole way of life. In however diluted a form dice therapy can enable the group to feel something of the liberating and potentially destructive impulses which lie at the heart of the absurd tradition.

Such activities as these can now feed ideas back into discussion of surrealistic television material. Students should not only be able to pick out the surrealistic strands from such shows as *Fawlty Towers* and *Reginald Perrin*; they should have some understanding of the forces which give to such elements their meaning and life.

e. *Realism and social attitudes in situation comedies*

'Realistic' situation comedy represents a second significant strain within British television comedy. Discussion of programmes like *Porridge, Going Straight, The Good Life* and before them, *Steptoe and Son* and *The Likely Lads*, shows which seem to reflect life back to us with some degree of faithfulness, has tended in my experience to revolve around two issues: (i) the techniques used for signalling this 'realism'; and (ii) the limitations of such a realism, and an examination of the conventions which work against 'realistic' codes.

The question of which aspects of reality are expressed and which omitted in realistic comedy shows leads inevitably to a scrutiny of the social and political assumptions implicit in such inclusions and elisions. These issues can perhaps best be brought out by considering in some detail a rare attempt at analysis of the genre by Albert Hunt. Hunt's article, a comparison of the pictures of prison life presented by *Porridge* (BBC) and *Within These Walls* (ITV), relates the alternative pictures of prison life presented within the programmes to alternative approaches to acting, and ultimately to different social attitudes embedded within the two programmes:

Googie Withers, who plays the part of the prison governor in *Within These Walls* (ITV), belongs fairly and squarely inside the tradition of 'straight' British acting. She's a mistress of restraint, of understatement, of the slight, apparently natural – though carefully calculated – external gesture, which implies a scarcely controllable torrent of inner emotion.

In Googie Withers's case, the gesture . . . consists of taking off her glasses, staring with an earnest sincerity at the camera, then putting on her glasses and becoming businesslike again. But what depth of inner complexity that earnest stare conceals! Is she neglecting her family by caring so much for her prisoners? Is she making life too comfortable for those in her care? . . .

Ronnie Barker, who plays the old lag, Fletcher, in *Porridge* belongs to a different school of acting entirely. To begin with, he's a comic, and recognized as such – the presence of a studio audience tells us that 'them', the programme controllers, see this as 'comedy series' and not 'drama'. Secondly, he himself, in his performance, although he's called 'Fletcher', makes no attempt to disguise the fact that he's still Ronnie Barker, the bigger and more aggressive member of the Two Ronnies. All the same, the skills Ronnie Barker shows in *Porridge* do spring from a tradition of acting, and one that goes much further back in theatre history than that to which Googie Withers belongs. They're skills that have nothing to do with hidden emotion, but that relate to externals – to the deadpan way of delivering a line; to the precise timing of a single word. 'Are you awake, Fletcher?' asks a restless fellow prisoner in *A Night In*, and the reply, 'No', is comic in spite of the corniness of the gag and because of the exact rightness of the way Barker utters the monosyllable.

Barker's style is about self-evident comic skills; Googie Withers's style is about implying 'sincerity' and 'truth of feeling' behind a mask of restraint. What's interesting is the way, in these two series, that the different styles are directly related to conflicting political implications.

The part played by Googie Withers is, superficially, related to 'liberal' attitudes. The governor is not only a woman, but a progressive woman at that. She's always looking for ways of helping the prisoners under her control. All her problems spring from this. For example, she makes the Drug Unit such a happy place that a prisoner deliberately escapes in order to have her sentence extended.

But, in spite of the surface liberalism, the series is committed to an extremely hierarchical view of social relationships. *Within These Walls* is about the terrible problems people who choose to assume and exercise power over other people create for themselves. It would be possible to imagine Googie Withers playing the same part and going through the same gestures as the head of any other authoritarian establishment . . .

Ronnie Barker, on the other hand, plays the part of a man who uses his comic skills to undermine authority and to question the basic sanity of the prison institution itself. He even plays at being 'sincere'; at hiding a private emotion that is too deep to be revealed. After having advised all the other prisoners on how to deal with their absent wives, he finds, apparently, both his reputation with his fellow-prisoners and his marriage destroyed together when his daughter arrives to say his wife has gone off with another man. He stands in front of his own prison governor, the picture of inner hurt, and the governor gives him a weekend's parole. 'It worked again!', he shouts in delight, when a policeman finally leaves him alone at home with his wife: and he spends the weekend at the pub, the football match, and in bed – with his fat, sexy wife.

The style of *Within These Walls*, in spite of the programme's apparent liberalism, reflects an acceptance of the sanity of authoritarian institutions. *Porridge* demonstrates the basic insanity of authoritarians, whether liberal or not. And it does so, not by preaching or issuing manifestos, but by providing a vehicle for the comic skills of a big, apparently clumsy man, who knows how to time exactly the single word, 'No'.[24]

Porridge, and earlier shows like *Steptoe and Son* and *The Likely Lads*, represent an honourable strain within British television comedy. They attempt to explore and illuminate our experience through their humour, rooting believable and even complex characters within recognisable and authentic environments, and exploring relationships in a serious and often poignant way. But what is the nature of the reality which the programmes ask us to accept? And are the illuminations they offer us, as Hunt suggests, subversive?

The first thing which needs to be underlined about these shows is how heavily they are ostensibly committed to surface realism. The title sequence in *Porridge* for instance, is straight documentary in content and tone. The fact that the principal performers are (*pace* Hunt) actors rather than comedians and that they act 'naturally' and without any obvious technique, together with the attention paid to local detail in all of the programmes proclaim that they are about situations and people as they really are. Their commitment to authenticity has meant that the shows have flowered naturally in the medium: they are distinctive to television in a way that the other great comedy genre, the star-based show built around such personalities as Benny Hill, Tommy Cooper, Des O'Connor and Morecambe and Wise, is not. Here the music-hall tradition of sketches, singers and dancers has been grafted uneasily onto television's 'host and guests' formula, so that one inevitably gets the feeling that one is watching the death throes of a tradition which has its roots in another time and another place. This is emphatically not so with the realistic situation comedies. The life-blood of relevance flows through them and they properly take their place beside documentaries, current affairs and news programmes as being peculiarly appropriate to the medium.

It is central to an understanding of the political implications of these shows, however, to see how limited their realism is. It comes as something of a surprise to realise how little they give us insight into the social areas they are ostensibly exploring. We learn remarkably little about totting, prison and life in the north-east from *Steptoe and Son, Porridge* and *The Likely Lads*. Rather their settings tend to be colourful backdrops to what is really important, the interplay between the characters and the tightly constructed plots with their subtle reversals and neat endings. The series have in fact far more in common with each other than they have with the reality they depict. Even *The Likely Lads*, where the action seems rooted in the problems of living in a particular environment, has really very little interest in the authentic idioms, customs and attitudes of the north-east of England. What are served up are the signs of authenticity – references to drinking, football, nights out with the boys, and occasional scenes set in pubs. One has only to place these devices next to an actually subversive comedy-drama like Barry Hines' *Speech Day*, where the commitment to the people and their language is real, to discover how empty they are and to see that their function is to soften and process reality, not for our illumination, but for our consumption.

Perhaps the most significant feature of these series, however, is that they present to us worlds in which all the dramas are personalised and scaled down in significance, and in which characters and action are almost perversely divorced from their social determinants. They are worlds which have been scrupulously depoliticised, so much so that any attempt by the characters to draw attention to the system within which they live is in itself comic, and invariably a rationalisation of questionable personal motives, as when Harold Steptoe tries to put Albert into a home so that he can sail round the world in a sloop with four other blokes and five birds: 'Look, it's not my fault. It's like what they said in the *Guardian* the other week. You are a victim of the failure of Western Society in not knowing how to take care of their old people.' The episode deals with one of the stock themes of the genre: the futility of the individual who tries to change anything. Attempts to seek different answers and new life-styles begin as parody and end as failure, as they have ever since Hancock denounced the world and went to live on Clapham Common in *The*

Wild Man of the Woods. Despite similar outbursts of hubris by Harold Steptoe or Terry Collier it is likewise the *status quo* which defines for them the bounds of the possible, even if not always of the acceptable.

So it is with *Porridge.* The programme works within the assumption that prisons are there to be coped with rather than challenged, a necessary and even inevitable part of the scheme of things. Ronnie Barker's hero Fletcher, is first and foremost one who accepts the system and works within it. His scorn is reserved less for the warders than for those of his fellow prisoners who try to fight the system. Much of the humour comes from Fletcher's witty answering back to those in authority, but he is no more a *threat* to authority than Alfie Bass's Bootsie was years ago. Prison indeed is conceived of as a kind of national service stint where repression at least breeds an admirable wit and resourcefulness in the men. The liberal prison warder is a weakling and the prisoners, who are basically lazy, shiftless column-dodgers, take advantage of any attempt to treat them as human beings. Far from undermining authority, the political implications of *Porridge* are almost entirely reactionary. Prisons are 'natural', we are assured and providing that one doesn't try to fight it, prison life can be quite a lot of fun – entertaining, amusing and never, never boring.

f. Stand-up comedians

The sources of laughter   The analysis of stand-up comedians and their jokes may proceed in a number of ways. Iconographic analyses based upon the techniques outlined in Chapter 4 might be attempted. The results achieved by this method could then be usefully compared with the analyses and additional historical material presented in Fisher.[25] Another approach is to look more closely at the jokes themselves and to explore some of the psychological mechanisms of laughter. Among a number of possible erudite explanations, one which is very accessible to pupils has been provided by Desmond Morris:

> Crying is present at birth, but laughing does not appear until the third or fourth month. Its arrival coincides with the development of parental recognition. It may be a wise child that knows its own father, but it is a laughing child that knows its own mother. Before it has learnt to identify its mother's face and to distinguish her from other adults, a baby may gurgle and burble, but it does not laugh. What happens when it starts to single out its own mother is that it also begins to grow afraid of other, strange adults. At two months any old face will do, all friendly adults are welcome. But now its fears of the world around it are beginning to mature and anyone unfamiliar is liable to upset it and start it crying. (Later on it will soon learn that certain other adults can also be rewarding and will lose its fear of them, but this is then done selectively on the basis of personal recognition.) As a

result of this process of becoming imprinted on the mother, the infant may find itself placed in a strange conflict. If the mother does something that startles it, she gives it two sets of opposing signals. One set says, 'I am your mother – your personal protector; there is nothing to fear,' and the other set says, 'Look out, there's something frightening here'. This conflict could not arise before the mother was known as an individual, because if she had then done something startling, she would simply be the source of a frightening stimulus at that moment and nothing more. But now she can give the double signal: 'There's danger but there's no danger'. Or, to put it another way: 'There may appear to be danger, but because it is coming from me, you do not need to take it seriously'. The outcome of this is that the child gives a response that is half a crying reaction and half a parental-recognition gurgle. The magic combination produces a laugh.

So the laugh says, 'I recognize that a danger is not real', and it conveys this message to the mother. The mother can now play with the baby quite vigorously without making it cry. The earliest causes of laughter in infants are parental games of 'peek-a-boo', hand-clapping, rhythmical knee-dropping, and lifting high. Later, tickling plays a major role, but not until after the sixth month. These are all shock stimuli, but performed by the 'safe' protector. Children soon learn to provoke them – by play-hiding, for example, so that they will experience the 'shock' of discovery, or play-fleeing so that they will be caught.

The naked ape, even as an adult, is a playful ape. It is all part of his exploratory nature. He is constantly pushing things to their limit, trying to startle himself, to shock himself without getting hurt, and then signalling his relief with peals of infectious laughter.

Laughing *at* someone can also, of course, become a potent social weapon among older children and adults. It is doubly insulting because it indicates that he is both frighteningly odd and at the same time not worth taking seriously. The professional comedian deliberately adopts this social role and is paid large sums of money by audiences who enjoy the reassurance of checking their group normality against his assumed abnormality.[26]

Morris's location of laughter as a response to the potentially frightening provides a useful tool for analysing particular jokes and an entree to understanding the function of humour as defence mechanism, both through its ability to defuse frightening situations and as a method of diverting attention away from one's own shortcomings. These uses of humour should I think be made clear with reference to the class group itself – who are the comedians? and why? – though it goes without saying that this should be treated with great sensitivity by the teacher, the objective, as always, being to increase understanding and not to embarrass individuals. These understandings can now be fed back into analyses of particular comedians, so many of whom are physically abnormal (very small, unusually fat or simply unprepossessing; there are few handsome comedians) and more than usually insecure and depressive.[27]

Stereotyping Stereotyping is such a common source of humour that it is worth isolating and discussing with pupils in some detail. It is not a difficult task for a group to compile lists of racial, national or sexual stereotypes, perhaps using jokes as reference points.

Of all of the texts available to us, it was Trevor Griffiths' play *Comedians* which provided the best analysis of the technique. In the play, Eddie Waters, an ex-professional comedian runs a night-school class for would-be stand-up comics. Here is part of one of his lessons. Of his students, McBrain and Connor are Irish and Samuels, Jewish:

Waters: (*finally, mild, matter of fact*) I've never liked the Irish, you know. Dr Johnson said they were a very truthful race, they never spoke well of each other, but then how could they have? (*They look around, faintly puzzled, amused.*) Big, thick, stupid heads, large cabbage ears, hairy nostrils, daft eyes, fat, flapping hands, stinking of soil and Guinness. The niggers of Europe. Huge, uncontrollable wangers, spawning their degenerate kind wherever they're allowed to settle. I'd stop them settling here if I had my way. Send 'em back to the primordial bog they came from. Potato heads.
  (*Pause. McBrain clenches and unclenches his fist on the desk, watches them carefully.*)
Connor: (*slowly*) Would that be Southern Irish or Northern Irish, Mr Waters?
Waters: Or Jews, for that matter.
Samuels: What you staring at me for?
  (*Uneasy laughter, dying fast.*)
Waters: (*still very matter of fact*) They have this *greasy* quality, do Jews. Stick to their own. Grafters. Fixers. Money. Always money. Say Jew, say gold. Moneylenders, pawnbrokers, usurers. They have the nose for it, you might say. Hitler put it more bluntly: 'If we do not take steps to maintain the purity of blood, the Jew will destroy civilisation by poisoning us all.' The effluent of history. Scarcely human. Grubs.
Samuels: (*unfunnily*) He must've met the wife's family.
Waters: Negroes. Cripples. Defectives. The mad. Women. (*Turning deliberately to Murray's row.*) Workers. Dirty. Unschooled. Shifty. Grabbing all they can get. Putting coal in the bath. Chips with everything. Chips and beer. Trade unions dedicated to maximising wages and minimising work. Strikes for the idle. Their greed. And their bottomless stupidity. Like children, unfit to look after themselves. Breeding like rabbits, sex mad. And their mean vicious womenfolk, driving them on. Animals, to be fed slops and fastened up at night.

What's wrong with stereotyping? As one of the characters in *Comedians* says, what's so bad about 'a few crappy jokes'?

Waters: It's not the jokes. It's not the jokes. It's what lies behind 'em. It's the attitude. A real comedian – that's a daring man. He *dares* to see what his listeners shy away from, fear to express. And what he sees is a sort of truth, about people, about their situation, about what hurts or terrifies them, about what's hard, above all, about what they *want*. A joke releases the tension, says the unsayable, any joke pretty well. But a true joke, a comedian's joke, has to do more than release tension, it has to *liberate* the will and the desire, it has to *change the situation*. (*Pause*.) There's very little won't take a joke. But when a joke bases itself upon a distortion – a 'stereotype' perhaps – and gives the lie to the truth so as to win a laugh and stay in favour, we've moved away from a comic art and into the world of 'entertainment' and slick success. . . . a joke that feeds on ignorance starves its audience. We have the choice. We can say something or we can say nothing. Not everything true is funny, and not everything funny is true. Most comics *feed* prejudice and fear and blinkered vision, but the best ones, the best ones . . . illuminate them, make them clearer to see, easier to deal with. We've got to make people laugh till they cry. Cry till they find their pain and their beauty. Comedy is medicine. Not coloured sweeties to rot the teeth with.[28]

Comedians encourages the analysis of particular jokes using the criteria established here. The second act of the play consists of the 'turns' performed by Waters' protegees in a working-men's club. Their jokes are inevitably filtered through to us via the evaluative framework suggested here by Waters. But this framework can also be used by the class to analyse jokes of their own choice. Does the joke 'feed prejudice and fear and blinkered vision' or does it illuminate them? Pupils should recognise that what is at issue here is of some importance. For behind the stereotype lies a distortion; behind the distortion lies fear, and ultimately behind both lies the possibility of the joke becoming real, of its preparing the ground for inhumanity and even persecution which are far from funny.

4. Mediated education

In Chapter 2 it was argued that the educational process should be the subject of a great deal of discussion within television studies, both because it represented the point at which mystification was most closely woven into the experience of pupils and because education was itself the subject of a good deal of attention by the medium. The following notes on three programmes which judiciously add more than a dash of entertainment to an ostensibly 'educational' content – *Tomorrow's World*, *The Burke Special* and *Master-*

mind – demonstrate the extent to which a pupil's understanding of television can be directly fostered through the discussion of the educational processes in which he is involved. The section on *Tomorrow's World* consists principally of a student hand-out based upon group discussion and analysis of the programme; the pieces on *The Burke Special* and *Mastermind* are representative of my own attempts to write about the medium alongside my pupils.

a. *Mediated science*: '*Tomorrow's World*' (*BBC1*)

Tomorrow's World represents one of television's most successful incursions into the fields of science and technology. Its attempts to render the mysteries of its subject-matter intelligible and even pleasurable to a mass audience, are generally considered, even by people who distrust the medium, to be worthwhile and educationally valuable. Murdock and Phelps for example, found that while 'negativeness was perhaps the most important characteristic of the overwhelming proportion of teachers' responses to the question of the effects of mass media on pupils' behaviour . . . the general tone of science teachers' remarks was definitely positive and they tended to view the mass media's effects on their pupils in terms of increased scientific knowledge and interest in science subjects.' Many teachers specifically picked out *Tomorrow's World* for its educational value:

> They gain a good deal of factual content from the more informative and educational programmes like *Tomorrow's World*.
>
> Television science programmes (e.g. *Tomorrow's World*) stimulate interest in a few pupils and reach more pupils than would be the case with science literature.
>
> I feel that *Tomorrow's World* type programmes are stimulating a genuine interest in scientific and technological achievement.[29]

Close viewing of two programmes from the *Tomorrow's World* series produced some surprising results however as the following hand-out based upon group discussion and analysis reveals. The structure of the hand-out follows the pattern of analysis already undertaken in *Cartoons* and *Young Scientists of the Year*.

---

b. '*Tomorrow's World*': hand out

Title sequence
Description: The title *Tomorrow's World* appears on the screen, but it is then blotted off by an explosion. Each letter of the title reappears in order. The

letters are cleverly made up from everyday objects – an egg, some nails, a fire, some pills – until finally the fully reconstructed title appears again on the screen. Suggestions as to what this sequence signified were varied:

It is saying that science has many facets and is about everyday objects.
Science covers many kinds of activity from cookery to engineering.
Shows how everyday objects can appear in an unusual futuristic manner.
It shows you what Tomorrow's World is going to be like.

There is a suggestion too in this sequence that science is capable of creating order and meaning from chaos, but that initial explosion, as well as the ambiguity of some of the other images (the fire and the pills for example) suggests another, less optimistic view of science. Science can either be used to solve real problems (to eliminate poverty, for example, to provide necessities for those who lack them, to make 'two ears of corn grow where only one grew before' as Swift put it), and to serve the welfare of the whole of the community. Or it can be used for other purposes: to destroy, kill and maim more effectively, or to increase the profits of industry through the introduction of 'new models' of cars, toothpaste or furniture, which make the type everyone else is using obsolete. What has happened in these two instances is that science and scientists have been appropriated or taken over by the state (enabling it to arm and 'defend' itself more efficiently) and by industry (enabling it to keep ahead of its competitors and make bigger profits). There are overwhelmingly more scientists working to create more sophisticated weapons of destruction, or to increase profits than there are engaged upon work whose results might benefit everyone. The technology mediated to us via *Tomorrow's World* is only one possible technology and not necessarily the most honourable and worthwhile. The show presents it as the only technology however, never pointing to alternatives or placing the view it offers into any kind of critical perspective.

Some of the group disagreed with this, using a counter-argument which may be summarised thus:

Scientists who work for industry *do* contribute towards progress and *do* provide us with a more comfortable and pleasant world within which to live, as well as helping to increase profits. Just because an article is profitable doesn't mean to say that it isn't of any social value. Indeed, the fact that an article is profitable does indicate both its usefulness and its general popularity.

The problem with this argument is that so very often the greatest needs lie with people who are poor, starving and homeless. Profits cannot be made by catering for their needs, and so the scientist's energy tends to go into those projects which will provide facilities and services for those people who *do* have the money to afford them. This is the reason why so-called 'technological innovations' tend to be small and trivial (a new kind of garden spade to make digging easier, or a rucksack which incorporates a seat, to take two recent examples from *Tomorrow's World*). Far from meeting people's needs, this use of science tends to make them dissatisfied and unhappy with what they already have.

Scientific advance is now so locked into industrial production that it is very difficult to think of other ways in which it might operate to perform a more social and humanitarian function. One way in which it might be done would be to concentrate attention upon *needs* (and how to meet them) rather than *products* (and how to make them more efficient). *Look at the needs of some of the lower-income groups in your community (old age pensioners, the sick, single-parent families). Find out about and define particular problems which might be solved by either science or technology, then bring your ideas back for discussion next week.*

Theme *Tomorrow's World* attempts to make science and technology more accessible and explicable to a mass audience. Among the techniques noted for achieving this were:

1. a concentration upon the familiar and domestic in choice of subject and location;
2. the use of presenters who are not white-coated professionals, but 'intelligent laymen';
3. scientific explanations which are brief and to the point;
4. a concentration upon the practical usefulness of technological innovation;
5. introducing the new by way of the familiar;
6. lack of objects and images usually associated with science (test-tubes, laboratories, etc.);
7. humour, informal language, well-known anchor man, unstuffy presentation, visually appealing introductions and illustrations to convince us that science can be 'fun' as well as interesting.

Structure The programme is built around an anchor man and featured reporters, and consists of a number of stories each of which centres upon a particular technological innovation. The stress, however, tends to be less upon the *processes* of science and technology than upon its *objects*, and the presentation of these tends to be through *demonstration* in the mode of a shop assistant or car salesman. Indeed, the language and imagery of advertising permeate the whole programme. The objects which give the programme its coherence and continuity have a number of characteristics.

1. They tend to belong to the more prosperous end of the consumer market (a

speed-boat; a central-heating system for a caravan; a new recording device; a calorie-counting machine in the shows we watched).
2. They make current objects and systems obsolete. This is often graphically illustrated by detailed comparisons between the old and the new.
3. They are approved of and uncritically endorsed by the presenters rather than carefully evaluated in terms of their advantages and drawbacks.
4. They are considered fascinating and worthwhile in their own right.
5. They often embody small, even trivial 'improvements' — that is, they tend to be gadgets rather than real innovations.

Attitudes and values   *Tomorrow's World* is generally considered to be a very worthwhile, even educationally valuable programme because, as we have seen, it seems to be attempting to demystify science — to be making it easier for ordinary people to understand. At the end of the programme ask yourself what you have learned about science that you did not know before. The answer will probably be 'very little'. But why is this?

As we have seen, the programme pays far more attention to *objects* than it does to the scientific principles and processes which led to the development of the innovation. The nature of scientific investigation isn't really communicated at all, and remains as much a mystery as it ever was. It is the *end-products* of science which the programme celebrates.

Furthermore, the 'scientific' explanations which do occur in each item in the show are dealt with quickly and not always clearly. The main emphasis within the programme clearly lies not here but in the presentation of 'new models' which we may one day have the opportunity of owning. Far from being an interesting, rewarding field in its own right, or from being an activity which might satisfy important human needs, science is strictly subordinated to industrial production and the continuous consumption which is necessary for its survival. The mass audience, however, needs to be constantly 'educated' and 're-educated' to consume at an ever-increasing rate. This 'education' is provided by advertisements, by films which conspicuously draw attention to consumer goods, and by programmes like *Tomorrow's World*.

---

c. 'Burke's master-class': 'The Burke Special'

The essence of *The Burke Special* is encapsulated in its credit sequence. The screen is dominated by images of Burke's head which rotate to the rhythm of the show's up-tempo signature tune. The images prepare us for a show in which Burke himself will be the central and most important feature. He is the star who will dominate both the screen and the material he presents. Indeed, it is he who will transform the material into something 'special', so that subjects will become important or interesting or worth thinking about because they pass through his hands.

The nominal content of each programme is of so little importance that we have little or no idea of what each show is to be about before we switch on. What we can be assured of is that it will receive the special treatment and that Burke, who alone gives the series its continuity, and is the one permanent rock in a sea of unrelated but vitally important topics, will be back next week with something else.

The music which accompanies the images cryptically introduces us to the notion that there is to be an instructional element in the programme. The keen-eared may discern it is based upon the chord sequences of the hoariest of all school hymns, 'Jerusalem'. It is a suitable emblem for a programme which, for all its style, its visual pyrotechnics and verbal adroitness, is presented in terms of formal educational structures.

Burke is closely related to the open-necked casual figure who introduces most schools' television programmes, and is a close cousin of the epilogue vicar who appears in collar and tie in the hope that we won't penetrate his disguise and switch him off. He is the teacher whose informal language and mode of dress promise not teaching but dialogue, and the studio audience, who listen quietly and do as they are told, are his class.

Each programme is presented as a kind of master-class, an exemplar of what might be possible in education if resources and technicians were plentiful, classes well-behaved, and teachers entertaining and intelligent. Add to this the fact that the topic presented each week is infallibly relevant, important and up-to-the-minute, that each point is graphically illustrated and that there is a good deal of class participation, and you have the ingredients for what most people would describe as a worthwhile educational experience. Certainly it is true to say that hundreds of thousands of pounds are currently being poured into education to give it just these qualities. Why is it then that the show is finally so disappointing, leaving one, at its end, with so little of substance?

Perhaps the reason is that *The Burke Special* has a fundamentally cynical view of its audience. The principle upon which it is based is a kind of primitive behaviourism. Its *modus operandi* is the stimulus–response mechanism, which is applied in the kind of fragmented and random way which suggests that little thought has been given to the ways in which stimuli can relate to and reinforce one another. More significantly, the audience's responses to the stimuli are ultimately irrelevant, since they are not allowed to affect the nature of later experiences in the show.

In spite of all the gestures which are made towards the notion of participation, the programme has been too carefully planned and packaged to allow it to happen. The rhetoric of participation, which plays such an important part in *The Burke Special*, is as hollow as the avowed importance of the subject. In this context Burke's informal language and casual dress can be seen as further attempts to postulate qualities by presenting their signs. They imply an attempt to relate to the audience in as human a way as possible. But the promise is never carried out. Studio audience and television viewers alike are stimulus-fodder, left to pick their way as best they can through a confused succession of experiences, and Burke's relationship to them is both hierarchical and manipulative. The significance of *The Burke Special* is that it embodies in transparently clear form a modern myth whose potency is spreading within education but which already suffuses politics, industrial relations, bureaucracies and international – and even social and personal – relations. For the programme dramatises a view of progress in which the rhetoric of participation, communality and relationship is employed in the service of yet more subtle forms of manipulation.

d. Education as inquisition: 'Mastermind'

Mastermind opens with ominous, impersonal, futuristic music, strongly reminiscent of Kubrick's *2001*. The scene is set by Magnus Magnusson, who carries with him a distinct whiff of intellectuality from his association with a number of cerebral programmes on BBC 2. He reinforces the information of the caption and introduces the first contestant giving the minimum of necessary information about him. The proceedings are deliberately dehumanised: there is no welcome for the contestants, no smile, no setting at ease. Right answers are given the clipped response of 'correct'.

Mastermind's key metaphor is the interrogation, and through its mode of presentation it invites a particular response in the viewer. This response is dictated not only by the *mise-en-scene*, but also by the patterning of the programme's editing and camera movements. A full-length shot of the contestant walking to the central chair is followed by a medium shot as he answers the first questions, and then by progressively tighter close-ups of his face. We are invited, that is, to objectify each contestant, who only begins to engage our closer attention when he is under stress. Our complicity is thus induced in the strong element of public (albeit voluntary) humiliation within *Mastermind*. Again, the mode of presentation heightens the effect. Magnusson, for example, does not tell us, the viewers, the answers to the questions which were fluffed; he tells the contestant, upon whom, squirming and embarrassed, the camera is fully turned.

What makes this device particularly interesting in *Mastermind* is its kinship with the viewers' collective experience of the processes of education and schooling. The link between the quiz show and formal education, between, for example, success in the programme and academic excellence, is specifically made by a number of shows. The titles of *Mastermind* and *Top of the Form* embody this and Magnus Magnusson speaks of his semi-finalists as 'having graduated with honours' from a previous round. The academic professions are well represented among *Mastermind's* contestants and the fact that the show takes place within a university gives the impression that the institution is in some way endorsing the proceedings. Viewers might be forgiven for believing that what goes on during the programme – the rapid regurgitation of unrelated facts, often upon some such absurd specialism as mushrooms, or European mountaineering before 1914 – is not unrelated to the kind of pursuit which takes place within that same institution when the cameras and lights have been packed away.

Some of the other assumptions which a programme like *Mastermind* makes about learning are perhaps worth elaborating: learning is fundamentally a doggedly serious business, it thrives through competition; it is unpleasant – the main pleasure to be derived from it is in triumphing over others; the rewards of learning are extrinsic to it; the results of learning can be quantified; the only things worth knowing about are either academic disciplines or middle-class leisure pursuits; far from being a natural human function, learning is a semi-mystical experience best undertaken by eccentrics; it involves being judged by others; it is, above all, a dehumanising experience, closely associated with humiliation and failure.

Quiz shows are important for they project to millions of people a deeply reactionary view of what education really ought to be about. They are important, too, because many of our institutions take them as seriously as the medium itself does. Some schools, for example, go to great lengths when preparing for *Top of the Form*, holding eliminating contests to choose their team, and going in for elaborate preparatory coaching. An important visual element in *Top of the Form* is the sight of the whole school turned out, immaculately uniformed, in the school assembly hall, thus converting a piece of television trivia into 'A Very Important Occasion' at which the honour and reputation of the school is clearly held to be at stake.

The reason for this attitude is not difficult to discern. For the messages which quiz shows transmit about learning are also largely the messages of our schools and universities. The final irony of a programme like *Mastermind* is that cheap and trivial though it is, it can stand as a powerful Swiftian metaphor for the values and assumptions of our educational system.

5. 'Classic' serials

Studying the television adaptation of a literary work is a time-consuming, but very worthwhile and rewarding exercise. It may take a full six weeks work, or even longer, but a great deal of challenging and rigorous activity can be crammed into that time. My own experience has been that the stimulus to reading offered by this exercise is such that pupils will be prepared to tackle with some enthusiasm novels normally considered to be far too difficult and sophisticated for them. The fact that one is expecting fifteen-year-olds to accomplish the reading tasks of eighteen-year-olds is, of course, the greatest of incentives for them to do it. My own work with pupils was concerned with BBC 2's prestigious adaptation of Thomas Hardy's *Wessex Tales*. The group contained nobody who regarded reading with any enthusiasm and not one of them had read a book for pleasure in the previous eighteen months. I explained that it had seemed a good idea to me to look at a television adaptation of a novel at some stage of the course. Not only would it illuminate for all of us the detailed ways in which the two media worked, but it might be a good way of introducing them to a writer who might have something to say to them. As I talked to them about Hardy I was reminded of John Holt's story of the young girl who looked at him in amazement when she was told that he wrote books. She seemed to be aware for the first time that *people* write books, and the realisation that they write them because they have something which they think is important to communicate certainly proved to be a breakthrough with my own secondary school pupils, used as they were to deadeningly impersonal school textbooks. Drawing attention to the writer behind the book represented a shift in emphasis which the group responded to with an immediate commitment; each pupil voluntarily bought a copy of *Wessex Tales* which had just hit the local bookstalls – two weeks of concerted publicity by the BBC and *Radio Times* helped too of course – and we were ready to begin.

It is impossible to re-create in print the kind of detailed reading, viewing and discussion which occupied our time during the following six weeks. Any teacher undertaking this kind of project will find himself and his class similarly engrossed. But it is possible to draw a number of general conclusions which might be helpful to a teacher undertaking detailed cross-media analysis. Since this is a comparatively new kind of exercise it is important that the teacher should think about new and imaginative ways of managing the materials at his disposal. To adopt a stereotyped formula each week of reading–viewing– discussion would probably kill interest very quickly. At the same time there *is* a lot of material to read, view and discuss and one constantly has to keep moving on – it isn't possible to allow every interest to be developed, every point covered to be explored in depth, or each individual initiative to be fully carried through. The important thing is to try to approach the material in a slightly different way each week. In the first few weeks it will be enough to notice the surface discrepancies between written and visual texts. In later episodes more challenging questions can be considered and the group can begin to move from the details of the text to its broader thematic concerns. When pupils consider the problems of adapting a text to the television screen, they are compelled to see through details to their significance, and to distinguish between details that are important (and which will need emphasis in the adaptation) and those that are less so. As the stories progressed, the sweep of our discussion became necessarily broader; themes became clearer and cross-connections could be made between stories. If the story were read first the group could think about the generalised techniques and broad sweeps of production which would be appropriate to its television adaptation. And this inevitably led them to view the actual adaptation in a new and very different way – in terms of the total impact actually achieved and of what its details seemed to add up to.

This approach was usually complemented the following week by moving through the work's larger structures back again to its detail. A paragraph was taken at random from the literary text and pupils were given this exercise to work upon.

Read the selected passage carefully and try to estimate its importance in relation to the whole story (or chapter). If you were adapting the story/chapter for television, what incidents and details from this paragraph would you include? Write a shooting script suitable for television covering these details.

Many teachers will be sceptical about the possibility of their students responding to this and in terms of a polished and finished response, their doubts will probably be justified. But there are a number of factors which make the exercise well worth trying. To begin with, the problem encountered is a real and not an academic or spurious one; it is one which has been faced by the professional writer responsible for the television adaptation and which he will have solved according to his understanding, both of the text and of the potentialities of the medium. His solution is one which the class will soon be able to see and discuss. The teacher should try the exercise himself along with the rest of his class and have his ideas subjected to their comments and criticisms. Whatever the value of his contribution (and it may be of very little value) it should enable him to see that the point of the exercise lies as much in identifying problems as in solving them. Some students may produce very inventive and imaginative scripts, but I would be very pleased with a student who had done nothing more than thought about and clarified some of the problems involved, for his understanding of and interest in the following week's adaptation will be that much greater.

In fact, the work produced by pupils in response to the series was impressive even by the most traditional standards. Within a week everyone in the group had read all of the stories and they re-read them as we studied each one in detail. There were substantial written contributions from all pupils and a 3000 word study from a young man who, until that point, had been the least responsible and mature member of the group. One of the girls read everything by Hardy she could lay her hands on, and everyone watched the film of *Far from the Madding Crowd* which was shown on television on Christmas Day. Some followed this up by reading the novel itself. In short, the sheer volume of reading, writing and discussion prompted by the series was impressive evidence of the medium's potentialities as an educational stimulus, judged by even the most traditional and formal criteria.

My advice to teachers who wish to look closely at a televised adaptation of a novel, but who doubt their students' stamina and ability to undertake the necessary concentration of reading, is to try it. They will, I think, be pleasantly surprised.[30]

10

Social, Political and Aesthetic Education through Television

All teaching is necessarily both a social and political activity. The fact that the social and political functions of teaching generally remain implicit should not blind us to the fact that all educational practice inevitably proceeds from assumptions about how people ought to relate to each other, and postulates the preferability of certain kinds of human behaviour over others. The processes of social and political education begin when the assumptions upon which the practice of education is based are made explicit to pupils. More needs to be said however, and this chapter, in attempting to clarify the processes of social and political education and to show how these processes may be carried out within the study of television, draws together a number of strands of central significance to this book. Finally, the role which television might legitimately play in the aesthetic development of school pupils is examined.

1. Social education

The term 'social education' covers so many diverse educational practices that it is necessary to clarify what is meant by the expression throughout this book. *Social education is most fundamentally an enabling process through which pupils may acquire an understanding of the social groupings and relationships of which they are a part, and social abilities through which they can act as change-agents within those groups and relationships.* Social education then, as it is conceived here, is not a subject with a specific content, but a process which can be developed within the teaching of each and every subject. It is important to recognise that implicit social education takes place in all schools at all times. Uniforms, assemblies, house- and prefect-systems, the way pupils are grouped, and the way they are spoken to by teachers all carry implicit social messages, ingested by pupils and teachers alike, which tell them what they are, what is expected of them, and what their place within the institution is. Every teacher whether he likes it or not is a teacher of social education and, as we have seen, it is the social messages of education which are the most potent and long-lasting of all. As one highly experienced teacher expressed it: 'For over twenty years I worked under the delusion that I was teaching maths. The social pressures I put upon the kids were designed to make my maths teaching more effective. I now realise that I was really teaching social passivity and conformity, academic snobbery, and the naturalness of good healthy competition, and that I was using maths as an instrument for achieving these things.' The revelation caused this teacher to change, after almost twenty-five years, the whole orientation of his teaching and to regard himself as primarily a teacher of social education, who nevertheless still taught maths on the school time table.

Since the implicit social education carried out by most schools tends to hinder rather than develop the social sensitivity, effectiveness and responsibility of its pupils, to teach social education and make explicit the values underpinning the social organisation of the school is the first step towards changing it. Once this first step has been taken what further elements are necessary to the development of social education?

a. Group awareness

From the outset social education will need to involve an awareness of the potentialities of the group in generating observations, ideas and knowledge, and will stress the importance of co-operative rather than competitive learning. Most classes have never been encouraged to think of themselves as groups at all. They therefore exhibit the characteristics of a *crowd* culture of accidentally linked independent individuals rather than a group culture with a strong sense of its own identity and the interdependency of its members. Specific examples of activities in which the group functions as the most important learning resource are given throughout this book, but the teacher should continually encourage his pupils to think of themselves as a group which is capable of making its own rational and autonomous decisions. As we have seen, simple devices such as the abolition of marks and competition can be important steps in encouraging this recognition.

b. Teacher participation

Social education is not something which the teacher passes on (or down) to his pupils but rather a dynamic process in which he himself is involved. Teachers learn just as much from social education as pupils do, and the teacher's social education will begin just as soon as he sees any difficulties he may encounter not as *his* problems with which he must cope alone, but as blockages to effective *group* progress which need full and open discussion, and ultimate resolution by the group. In doing this the teacher will be playing his part in breaking down classroom hierarchies and resolving the pupil–teacher dichotomy, which undermines the liberating potentialities of most educational transactions.

c. Group skills

Apart from encouraging an awareness of the value of co-operative learning, the teacher will need to help his pupils to acquire abilities enabling them to function effectively within groups. The simulations described in this book provide contexts within which a number of group skills might grow and develop with increasing sophistication. It may be helpful to delineate a few of these skills:

the sensitivity not to dominate or be too egocentric (especially important for articulate or quicker thinking pupils).
an openness to the ideas and suggestions of others.
the confidence of shy members to find a voice and make a contribution, and the ability of others to value it.
a greater willingness to express positive feelings than hostile ones.
the ability to initiate group action.
the ability to collaborate and find a suitable role within a group activity.

d. Observation and communication

Acuteness of observation and sensitivity in interpreting what is observed underpin most social skills. Sharpening pupils' powers of observation — inevitably a central objective in the study of any visual medium — is also the first step towards achieving greater social awareness. The observational and interpretative abilities developed by the kind of activities described in Chapter 3 could almost be said to define social sensitivity. Sensitivity to the range of signals through which people express their feelings is part of what it means to relate to and really understand other people. It is an integral part of sustaining very close personal relationships as well as more generally social ones. But human relationships depend to an even greater extent upon a willingness and ability to communicate with others. A television studies course which is also concerned with a pupil's social development will therefore encourage speaking and writing in a variety of situations and linguistic registers, and provide opportunities for consciously communicating meanings through a whole range of non-verbal signals. For example, a subtle amalgam of observational sensitivity and communication skill was demanded by the work described on interviewing in which pupils were called upon to approach a stranger on the basis of preliminary observations, effect an introduction, put him at his ease and initiate and control a conversation with him.

e. Pupil participation and control

Social education is preconditioned by a willingness on the part of the teacher to hand over much of his decision-making power to his pupils. A group of pupils can only be expected to respond seriously to school work if it has serious rather than spurious decisions to make. One of the most appealing aspects of studying television is that it allows for real pupil participation from the outset. Pupils need have little fear of the burdens of cultural heritage, teacher expertise and rigid syllabus which render them so passive and impotent in other subjects. Advanced syllabus planning by the teacher would forfeit a great deal of the spontaneity which can be given to a course when current interests within the group are seized and shaped by the teacher, and general preoccupations respected and developed as real growth points. Apart from exercising a great deal of control over course content, pupils can be given responsibility in the following areas:

defining questions which they wish to explore
course evaluation and self-assessment
the removal of learning blockages and the resolution of class problems and
    conflicts
devising homework schedules, responsibility for files, etc.
shaping their own response to visual material.

2. Political education

a. Introduction

We know, at the moment, precious little about how to foster effective political education and understanding. Indeed the very definition of what might constitute political education is far from generally agreed upon. A current Hansard Society/Politics Assoc. Project on Political Education has revealed diverse opinions amongst the project team on the possible aims and objectives of a political education. Summarising the often complex arguments in a very general way, one may say that a conflict exists between those who see political education as a kind of up-dated 'civics' and others who would argue for models which would encourage participation and action.[1] In the former the teacher is seen as passing on to his pupils 'political' information, concepts, skills and attitudes which are themselves value-free, a kind of 'banking' concept of political education, designed to produce aware spectators, capable of critical consumption of their political system. On the other hand those who posit a participatory/action model of political education with a meth-odological emphasis upon simulations, decision-making skills, and school and community action are not slow to recognise that this version of political education will be anathema to many teachers and schools, conflicting as it does with the traditional role of both as purveyors of received wisdom.

In spite of these differing perspectives there *is* some agreement that political education at school level is best regarded, not as a discrete discipline, but, like social education, as a process to which different school subjects might contribute. What then can be said of the nature of the political development which might be encouraged through the study of television?

b. Implicit political education

As with social education, the first thing that needs to be recognised is that implicit political education already takes place within schools. Neil Postman expresses the point succinctly:

> all educational practices are profoundly political in the sense that they are designed to produce one sort of human being rather than another – which is to say, an educational system always proceeds from some model of what a human being ought to be like. In the broadest sense, a political ideology is a conglomerate of systems for promoting certain modes of thinking and behaviour. And there is no system I can think of that more directly tries to do this than the schools. There is not one thing that is done to, for, with or against a student in school that is not rooted in a political bias, ideology or notion. This includes everything from the arrangement of seats in a classroom, to the rituals practised in the auditorium, to the textbooks used in lessons, to the dress required of both teachers and students, to the tests given, to the subjects that are taught and, most emphatically, to the intellectual skills that are promoted.[2]

Postman's position would be strenuously denied by many educationalists. It is one of our most cherished traditional precepts that education as it is commonly practised is a-political and that its proper purposes are in danger of subversion by those who are 'politically motivated'. This position is itself a form of political illiteracy – an inability to recognise the political dimensions of 'normal' situations – which it is one of the purposes of overt political education to overcome.

It is a persistent assumption of this book that pupil development in any sphere must evolve from an understanding of the material conditions which most closely impinge upon him – this indeed is the *prima facie* case for the very study of television itself. The beginnings of any authentic political development will lie in pupils' willingness and ability to reflect upon their own school structures. The process of implicit political education, that is – like the process of implicit social education –needs to be made explicit. Chapter 2 provides examples of ways in which this work might be begun by teachers.

c. The political dimensions of social and aesthetic education

In many of the activities advocated in this book, political, social and aesthetic awarenesses coalesce. The relationship between political and social education is often self-evidently close (see for example the stress placed upon the potency of group action, and the ability to act effectively within groups); between political and aesthetic development, the relationship may seem less clear, and in need of further elaboration.

Chapter 3 explored the meanings of objects, modes of dress, gestures, postures and the like, not in purely 'aesthetic' terms, but as expressions of values and beliefs, for the purpose was not to create a hived-off, internally coherent aesthetic which only marginally impinged upon criteria and values external to it, but to demonstrate that communication, even at a subconscious level, is not innocent, but reflects belief. It is assumed throughout this report that no rigid divisions exist between modes of communication, and the values and beliefs of the societies or individuals who employ them. Aesthetic and political understandings then are mutually reinforcing, and an increasing aesthetic sensitivity to television images and programmes will be coincident with the development of a more complex political awareness.

d. Imagining alternatives

Integral to any political understanding is the ability to see in societal forms not the laws of nature but the hand of man; to see that reality could be other than it is; to have experienced, or even to have imagined other alternatives. The emphasis upon alternative structures – in the analysis of television programmes, in television practical work, and in negotiating appropriate classroom learning strategies – has been a consistent one throughout this book. The deliberate exclusion of alternative values in some programmes – in *Tomorrow's World* or *The Flintstones*, for example – is so perverse that analysis most logically proceeds from a consideration of those alternatives which continue to obtrude even at the very point at which they are most strenuously denied. As a *consistent* method of interrogating the television image however this approach has obvious limitations. It is, for the most part, not only impossible to know what has been excluded or rejected, but difficult to sustain – once a particular image or programme has been projected – the necessary belief that it could indeed have been otherwise. Simulation as a method of working within television studies represents an important way in which attention can be drawn 'through the pores' to the hidden act of selection, and restores to the study of the medium a dimension easily lost in an unwavering concentration upon the television image.

e. Political issues and events

Politics itself is such an important part of the *explicit* content of television that the study of the medium will inevitably entail at some point the discussion and clarification of a wide range of political concepts and issues. Since many investigators[3] have established the existence within our own society of a mass political ignorance, this by-product of studying the medium is perhaps not without some significance. This is a minimum claim. In practice one can often say much more. Political issues and events (a General Election for example, or coverage of events in Northern Ireland) might legitimately be the subject of specific and detailed investigation within television studies. In this sense the 'systematic, coherent and critical study of political language, arguments and issues',[4] which Ian Lister has described as being the most fruitful area for investigation by schools can be more easily accomplished within television studies than in any other curriculum subject.

f. The significance of structures

An important ingredient of political literacy – the ability to see beyond social phenomena to their structural determinants – has received constant emphasis throughout this book in relation to both education and television. Attention was drawn to structural questions at an early stage of television analysis and because a great number of analytical structures could be postulated for a particular television programme a hierarchy of structures was suggested which was based upon the universality of their application to television material (see Chapter 1). Since a prime objective of television studies is to provide pupils with an understanding of programmes which they will see in the future, the most significant structures were taken to be those which applied to the entire output of television and not just part of it. Hence the attention paid to those structures which illuminated the medium's *non-transparency* – the philosophical/ideological frameworks within which agendas were set, the characteristic cultural and televisual codings employed, the concept of programmes as constructs, and the range and variety of mediating structures – rather than say purely 'aesthetic' structures, important though they might be in the study of particular programmes. And, as we have seen, attention to television's non-transparency, the exposure of 'the window on the world' myth, is simultaneously an exposure of the medium's ideological function (Chapter 1). When pupils move from seeing programmes as 'the way the world is' to seeing them as 'the way the world has been constructed or interpreted' they have taken a profound political step. American news broadcasts often end with a newscaster's cliché: 'And that's the way it is this Thursday evening'. Our pupils will take the road towards political literacy when they begin to ask of such statements the two questions posed by Stuart Hall 'Who says?' and 'Why does he see life like that?'[5]

It needs to be emphasised that this represents a higher developmental stage than the 'systematic, coherent, and critical study of political language, arguments and issues' as they are presented by television. For given explicitly 'political' material, the most pertinent ideological questions are not 'Is this well argued?', 'Has he falsified the issues?', 'Who got the better of the debate?', but 'Who says these are the issues?', 'Within what assumptions and frameworks are the arguments presented?' and 'What other possible agendas might be set?'

Finally, it should be observed that such structural determinants of television images themselves as institutional practices and professional codes have received a good deal of attention in this book, while structural determinants in the field of education, and methods of bringing them to the attention of students were fully discussed in Chapter 2.

g. The process of political education

To conclude: political education almost universally tends to be seen in terms of content – of the specifics of what can be done during lessons – rather than process. But what precisely is this process of political education? As I have described it, it is the development of political core concepts and abilities (e.g. observation and communication, which move through description to analysis; the development of group skills and awarenesses; an understanding of the significance of structures; an ability to imagine alternatives; and above all a willingness and ability to control and change one's own environment) through their application to material which is at first unitary, and concrete (see Chapter 3), and which, through something resembling Bruner's spiral curriculum, becomes progressively more complex and abstract.

3. Aesthetic development

a. Posing the question

What can be positively done to foster aesthetic development within the classroom? The first necessity is for the teacher to ask himself this very question and then to attempt to answer it bearing in mind the pupils, area, resources and organisational constraints within which he is working. Robert Witkin in a research report on the Schools' Council's *Arts and The Adolescent* project came across little evidence that teachers were placing their curricular activities within any kind of personal developmental framework at all. Speaking specifically of his research into the attitudes of English teachers, Witkin noted:

> When it comes to the organization of the curriculum it is more often the concept of 'academic' development rather than personal development which guides the teacher's structuring of material . . . When the teacher attempts to move outside the developmental framework provided by the examination syllabus he has considerable difficulty in formulating developmental objectives clearly . . .[6]

Allowing that it is the teacher himself, knowing his own pupils, who can best work out the details of a developmental programme for their aesthetic education, what general principles and guidelines can be established to help him formulate his developmental objectives more clearly and coherently? It is this question which the rest of this chapter seeks to answer.

b. *Eliciting a response*

The precondition for any aesthetic growth is the necessity of a response to aesthetic stimuli. One asks only of this response that it should be, however crudely formulated, *felt* and *authentic*. The teacher's primary task is to promote cultural engagement using whatever material he thinks fit so as to make this kind of response possible. He will need to counteract two principal blockages to authenticity of response: (i) communication blockages; and (ii) pupil conviction of the irrelevance or unimportance of his own responses.

(i) If a text does not speak directly to a pupil, perhaps because of vocabulary or conceptual difficulties or because it does not seem to impinge in an important way upon his experience, he will find difficulty in responding personally to it and become reliant upon the hand-me-down responses of others. The most appropriate material for aesthetic growth, particularly in its early stages, is, therefore, material which has as few blocks to direct communication as possible. This constitutes one important reason why visual material, and television material in particular, may be more appropriate than literature for encouraging those first tentative steps in independent judgement by pupils.

(ii) Pupils become convinced of the uselessness of personal response early on in their school careers when it becomes clear that success is gauged in terms of the fast production of right answers. Clarifying what is going on in your mind is less important than guessing what is going on within the teacher's. Within the context of television studies, however, guessing what is going on within the mind of the teacher becomes less of an imperative since there are few right or wrong answers in either television theory or practice. And when the medium for the discussion of judgements and ideas becomes the peer-group forum rather than teacher—pupil dialogue, it becomes possible to transform the relationship between pupil and text. The pupil can now be liberated to scan the text, not to discover what the teacher may think, but to clarify his own responses to it. It needs to be emphasised that this process will not take place spontaneously, immediately or easily. Pupils have too long been trained in another school. Having had their own responses undervalued, they will undervalue them themselves. And it will need a good deal of effort on the part of the teacher and the mature shouldering of responsibility by pupils if this situation is to be changed.

It may be argued at this point that good teachers of English, art, music or drama are already involved in this kind of practice. Indeed there can be no doubt that the high priority often given within these subjects to artistic *practice*, and the significance of personal responses within this practice are highly conducive to aesthetic development. But it does need to be stressed that all of these subjects carry with them notions of a cultural heritage and a critical tradition in relation to which the teacher carries the legitimised status of expert or adept. This, in relation to analysis leads almost inevitably to the hierarchical transmission of knowledge, with the attendant reception of second-hand values by the student. The danger is that what becomes of importance is not the student's response to a poem or painting but his understanding of the place in a tradition assigned to it by those who know better. Discrimination or appreciation – the avowed aims of most aesthetic education – can become acts of obeisance rather than a sharpening or clarification of responses. As we have seen (Chapter 1) the very notion of 'discrimination' is founded upon a distrust and rejection of what many pupils actually like, while the response implicit in 'appreciation' is essentially one of passive humility before an awesome tradition.[7] Both words suggest acts of accommodation to an established culture rather than the honing of individual or group awareness. Indeed our literary, artistic and musical cultures can become lethal and terrifying weapons for *undermining* the opinions, feelings, responses and language – the individuality and group identity – of our pupils. Within the study of television however where, as we have seen, notions of discrimination and appreciation are quite inappropriate, where there is neither a weight of established tradition nor a critical consensus, and where the role of the teacher as expert would be difficult to sustain, the necessity for students to make and clarify their own responses to a medium which is quite familiar to them becomes obligatory.

c. The process of aesthetic development

Aesthetic development then cannot take place unless pupils are willing to take responsibility for shaping their own responses to the texts they encounter. It is worth emphasising the extent to which conventional pedagogic practices discourage pupils from taking this crucial step. The most common method of eliciting pupils' responses to a text is through teacher questioning; this may take the form of a Socratic dialogue which many teachers can conduct with great sensitivity or it may take the written form of a comprehension exercise, an essay or an examination paper. The difficulties here go beyond the possibility that teacher questions in whatever form may be of the 'guess-what-is-in-my-mind' variety. They centre upon the fact that the constant necessity of having to *answer* questions actually short-circuits the difficult but essential act of judgement by relieving the pupil of the burden of having to *ask* questions himself. The absolute importance of framing one's own questions has been pointed to by Postman and Weingartner:

> Knowledge isn't just *there* in a book, waiting for someone to come along and 'learn' it. Knowledge is produced in response to questions. And new knowledge results from the asking of new questions; quite often new questions about old questions. Here is the point: once you have learned to ask questions – relevant and appropriate and substantial questions – you have learned how to learn and no one can keep you from learning whatever

you want or need to know . . . The most important and intellectual ability man has yet developed – the art and science of asking questions – is not taught in schools . . . We believe that the school must serve as the principal medium for developing in youth the attitudes and skills of social, political and cultural criticism.[8]

In framing questions one imposes limitations and order upon inchoate material. Intellectual and aesthetic development depend vitally upon this practice of shaping and making sense of his experience by the individual. Given only the ability to answer questions the individual remains a mere receiver, dependent upon the frameworks and perceptions of others in making sense of his experience.

The point can best be illustrated by asking you, the reader, to reflect upon a recent aesthetic or intellectual experience of some significance to you – a film, book or television programme perhaps, whose effect upon you was something out of the ordinary. Pause for a short while before reading on and reflect upon the precise nature of the mental processes involved.

It seems probable that, like most forms of change, aesthetic development is a dialectical process, conditional upon a psychological dissonance or uneasiness which is ultimately synthesised into a heightened or more complex awareness. Crudely, any aesthetic experience will have predominantly one of three effects upon us. It is most likely – because we tend to seek out those aesthetic experiences which will confirm our own vision of the world – to leave us perhaps a little more comfortable and self-satisfied but basically unchanged. It is least likely – because we are adept at avoiding such experiences – to project a world with which we can in no way empathise and which we reject. I suppose that in these days of ambiguous film titles there is just a possibility that your maiden aunt might find herself in a cinema watching a film called *Lip Service*. Unless she is a good deal livelier than mine however she will effectively tune out most of its messages. The aesthetic experience which changes us however works dialectically, inextricably binding our own ideas and interpretations of situations with others which are new to us, which we have previously rejected or which we have simply failed to reflect upon. It is the experience whose validity we accept yet which forces us to ask questions of our own attitudes and beliefs because it points to contradictions and inconsistencies within them. This kind of experience, which needs to be lived with and thought through over a period of time until we reach our own synthesis of it, is crucial to the process of aesthetic or indeed intellectual development.[9]

I am less concerned at this point to draw attention to the nuances of aesthetic change however than to emphasise the extent to which conventional classroom procedures actually prevent the primary confrontation between the mind of the student and the raw text from ever taking place. 'Socratic' teaching has its value of course, and by astute non-directive questioning the teacher can help his pupils to clarify their own responses to a text. However the limitations of asking questions of others and the function of questions in necessarily predefining discussion parameters and pre-empting other structurations, placing their recipients in a passive relation to text rather than an active and creative one, has rarely been made explicit to teachers. Within a Socratic dialogue the pupil does not need to take note and make sense of his own responses to a piece of imaginative work; he does not need to wrestle through his confusion to his own synthesis; he does not need to clarify his own interpretive frameworks, or formulate his own questions. The teacher will do all of this for him. He simply needs to answer the teacher's questions, and in doing so he accepts the way in which another makes sense of the world. Traditional literary comprehension tests, still in widespread use in schools, provide the *reductio ad absurdum* of the method. Most pupils devote their attention not to the written text, but to the questions asked of it, and then to those *aspects* of the text to which the questions have directed them.[10] The very stuff of aesthetic activity – the clarification of one's own responses, and the formulation of one's own significant questions – being of little consequence to this activity, goes unexercised. Any teacher who really wishes to foster literary comprehension might begin by asking his pupils to frame their own questions to the text under consideration, a stratagem which forces attention back upon the work itself and compels pupils to structure their own response to it.

Many teachers will have objections to the plea that their pupils be allowed to grapple in their own way with literary and visual texts. Many will see it as an invitation to chaos, though in practice the checking of individual responses against peer-group and teacher reactions is a powerful antidote to this. Others, knowing the apathy of their pupils, will think it supreme optimism to hope for any positive reaction. The likelihood of a creative pupil response can be increased if the ground is thoroughly prepared. First of all exercises and discussions on the nature of questions, and the vast range of possible structurations may be undertaken by the group (see Chapter 4). Secondly pupils need to be made aware of their own paramount responsibility for responding to the texts they encounter and for shaping their own responses to them. Without pupils taking on responsibility – and this should be made absolutely clear to them – very little progress is possible. Conventional classroom practice, rarely asking for this degree of responsibility, does not get it, and is content to perpetuate the pretence that progress is possible through surmounting obstacles placed there by the teacher rather than through a genuinely creative input by the pupil.

Doubts may persist. A common fear is that 'less-able' pupils are less able to handle freedom than their more academic counterparts. Here are the comments of a teacher-colleague on an 'open' practical criticism paper on 'unseen' television extracts, which I had set a mixed-ability group of pupils:

I wonder if pupils really are best served by being told to write freely about

'aspects of the extracts which interest them'. Might not such freedom be
their undoing? Might this not be true of pupils who might be expected to
achieve the lower examination grades? Is it not very likely that in dealing
with each extract they might limit themselves to a very pedestrian account
of the plot of the extract or a very general account of the plot-line or
characters in the series without any mention of the significance of these
things in relation to the extract or the genre or without any attempt at
evaluation? Might they not have a *better* chance of doing well if directed by
definite questions?

The 'doing well' of that last sentence makes evident the real business of
schools – the achievement of illusory standards by means of teacher guidance
through examinations; a confusion, in Illich's phrase, of 'process and
substance'. For in what sense can any person unable to formulate the kinds of
questions of significance and importance to him raised by a television extract
be said to have made any progress at all in developing an understanding either
of himself or of the medium?

There is one important respect however in which my colleague's reser-
vations were well justified. It is true that at the present time the vast majority of
university and sixth-form students, let alone pupils of average and below-
average ability, would find great difficulty in articulating a coherent response
to an unseen television extract. Indeed to give this kind of exercise to bright,
sophisticated, succeeding students and to witness the triteness and hollowness
of their response is to see how naked the emperor really is when deprived of his
second-hand clothes. The most constructive reaction to this reality is not to
disguise it by presenting students with tasks which they *can* perform, but to
recognise the situation for what it is – an indictment of where our students
really are in their aesthetic development. The examples of work in this book
by children deemed to be of average and below-average ability by their school
are I believe quite convincing evidence that practice in discussing and writing
about television in an open way over a two-year period can induce both an
ability to confront new material freshly, imaginatively and divergently and a
willingness to exercise and stand by one's own individual critical judgement.
The understandings reached here by pupils are personal and organic, when
compared with the spurious ventriloquisings of their master's voice usually
mouthed by pupils in the classroom. Finally, the relevancy of their aesthetic
training to the concrete out-of-school aesthetic experiences of pupils at least
opens out the possibility of an ever-increasing refinement of understanding
which can continue into post-school experiences of watching and thinking
about television.

4. Social, political and aesthetic education: a final note

Emphasis must finally be placed upon the assumptions which lie behind all of the developmental processes outlined in this chapter: that the relationship of the pupil to his world should be an active and critical one, rather than passive and domesticating; that this 'world' is not static, closed or God-given, but open to critical intervention and change; that every pupil, through dialogue with others, is capable of looking critically at his world; that the teacher as much as the pupil is the subject of each process; and finally that development and growth in each area will be dependent upon the degree of power, freedom and self-direction which the teacher – within the institutionalised context of the school – is able to negotiate for his pupils.

Appendix 1

Periodicals of Interest to the Television Teacher

Broadcast   The broadcasting industry's weekly magazine. Up-to-the-minute news, information, rumour and gossip with useful longer critical articles. An invaluable source for the teacher wishing to keep abreast or even ahead of current developments in broadcasting. (111A Wardour Street, London W1)

Independent Broadcasting   Quarterly journal of the Independent Broadcasting Authority. Occasionally carries articles of interest both on programmes and educational developments. (Free from the IBA, 70 Brompton Road, London SW3)

Journal of the Centre for Advanced TV Studies   Contains abstracts and reviews of recent books on television. (48 Theobalds Road, London, WC1 8NW)

Journal of Educational Television   Journal of the Educational Television Association. Mainly devoted to educational technology but an increasing number of articles discuss the place of television within the curriculum. (80 Micklegate, York)

The Listener   Published weekly by the BBC. Contains transcripts of programmes and background articles on broadcasting.

Media, Culture and Society   A new journal published by the Polytechnic of Central London (309 Regent Street, London W1)

Media Reporter   Quarterly journal, mainly devoted to journalism, but also carrying articles on media education. (Brennan Publications, 148 Birchover Way, Allestree, Derby)

Media Studies Association Newsletter   Contains conference reports, articles, news and reviews relating to media education. (Forster Building, Sunderland Polytechnic, Sunderland)

Screen   Quarterly. Mainly devoted to film, but there are occasionally critical articles on television.

Screen Education   Quarterly. Aimed specifically at media teachers and the most useful journal currently available for television teachers. Both *Screen* and *Screen Education* are published by the Society for Education in Film and Television. (29 Old Compton Street, London W1)

Sight and Sound   Recent issues are devoting much more space to critical articles on television, though this remains primarily a popular film magazine. Published by the British Film Institute. (127 Charing Cross Road, London WC2)

Teaching London Kids   A very lively and attractively presented magazine for teachers. Always topical and stimulating, TLK often features articles on media and image teaching. Three times each year from 79 Ronald Road, London N5.

Visual Education   The official magazine of the National Committee for Audio-Visual Aids in Education. Mainly concerned with educational technology, but occasional articles deal with media teaching. News items and reviews on a wide range of multimedia resources also make the journal worth looking at for the television teacher. (254 Belsize Lane, London NW6)

Working Papers in Cultural Studies An invaluable source of radical and intelligent ideas from one of the few institutions in Britain engaged in rigorous thinking about media, the Centre for Contemporary Cultural Studies, Birmingham University.

Appendix 2

Organisations with an Interest in Television Education

Educational Advisory Service
The British Film Institute
81 Dean Street
London W1

The Educational Television Association
National Co-ordinator, Patricia Kelly
86 Micklegate
York

The Media Studies Association
c/o Leigh College
Railway Road
Leigh
Lancashire

Society for Education in Film and Television (SEFT)
29 Old Compton Street
London W1

Appendix 3

CSE Mode III Syllabus for Television Studies – East Midlands Regional Examination Board

A. Aims and Objectives

1. To enable pupils to decode television pictures by involving them in a structured developmental *process* of analysis. This process begins with the study of non-verbal means of communication, develops through the analysis of particular objects and images, and the study of language as it is used by the media, and culminates in the perception of the television programme as an agglomeration of people, objects, words, gestures and movements which need to be
   a. *observed* and *described* as closely as possible, and
   b. *interpreted* in terms of the values which they embody.
2. To foster the general aesthetic development of the pupil through television.
3. To demystify the television medium by
   a. encouraging the widest possible use of television and videotape recording equipment, and
   b. making pupils aware of its *mediating* influence – its tendency to present *constructed* events as 'real'.
4. To examine the characteristics of the principal television genres (television drama; quiz shows; documentaries; police series, etc.)
5. To examine possible critical methodologies for the analysis of television programmes.
6. To develop an understanding of the specificity of television as a medium of communication.
7. To develop, through the mode of learning, group and social skills.

B. Content

1. Term one. Decoding images

a. Introduction to television. Comparison with other media. The specificity of the medium.
b. The nature of visual perception. Visual illusions and puzzles.
c. Observing and interpreting the denotations and connotations of
   (i) physical objects
   (ii) gestures
   (iii) eye-contact
   (iv) people as complex communication networks
   (v) body language
   (vi) still photographs
   (vii) soundless television pictures

d. Examining the denotation and connotations of language used in advertising and television.
e. The perception and decoding of one television programme as a complex agglomeration of objects, sounds, people, movements and relationships.

2. Term two. *Ways of seeing*

a. An introduction to the wide variety of ways in which the television picture may be perceived. Critical and analytical methodologies are defined in terms of the kinds of questions they ask. The kinds of questions explored will include the following, and they will be applied to a wide variety of programmes:
(i) Is this programme like real life? How does it differ? (Mediation/realism.)
(ii) What conventions are operating here? What other programmes is this one like? (Genre.)
(iii) What connections can be made between this programme and others featuring the same actor/star/production team/writer? (Auteur/star system.)
(iv) What is the function or purpose of this programme? Why have it at all? (Social functions of TV; BBC/IBA as institutions.)
(v) What insights does this programme give us into the problems/people it deals with? (Content examination.)
(vi) How does this programme compare with the novel or play of the same name? (Cross-media analysis; specificity of television.)
(vii) Does this programme appeal to you personally? (Autobiography/personal taste.)
(viii) What systems of signs and symbols are operating here? How can these systems be decoded? (Semiology.)
(ix) Does the programme have a serious theme? Are the techniques used appropriate to the content? Does the programme/drama have any kind of organic unity? Is it of greater or less value than comparable programmes? (Television 'appreciation'; Literary/Leavisite approaches to the medium).
b. An introduction to television *genre*. The concept will be introduced and discussed
(i) *in general terms* – the conventions, techniques and assumptions of a wide variety of programmes will be examined
(ii) *in detail* – in relation to one of the simplest of TV genres, the television cartoon.

3. Terms three–six

The order and duration of topics covered cannot be predicted with any precision since topicality, programme transmissions and group enthusiasms will all be important factors in determining syllabus content. Indeed, there will be little emphasis placed upon the acquisition of information or factual material. The focus of attention will rather be upon the development and increasing sophistication of the observational and interpretive skills introduced during Term One.

It is possible, however, to indicate in general terms the topics which will be covered during these four terms.

(i) *Genre and mediation*   Programmes as constructs. The conventions, techniques and political and social assumptions of
a. Pop music shows
b. Variety spectaculars
c. Comedy shows
d. Documentaries

e. Current affairs/news broadcasts
f. Sports programmes
g. Quiz shows
h. Domestic dramas
i. Police series

(ii) *Cross-media analysis* The examination of serialised novels or plays adapted for television. At least one televised novel will be considered in depth, and this will constitute at least one half-term's work.

(iii) *Practical work* Making news programmes using simulations; practising interviewing techniques; familiarisation programme with vtr equipment and cameras; group video work.

(iv) Analysis of particular programmes of topical or aesthetic interest.

C. Assessment

Students will be assessed on:

a. A file of:
   (i) *Ten pieces of work* Though it is expected that most of the entries in the file will consist of critical analyses of television programmes, examples of creative writing, taped work, original research may be included (40 per cent of the marks).
   (ii) *One assignment or project* (*approximately 1000 words*) An assignment may take the form of a long critical study or essay on any of the topics covered by the course. Original research (surveys, polls etc.) or creative writing (a TV script, a short play for TV, etc.) may be included. A tape, lasting for 15–25 minutes may also be included as an assignment (10 per cent of the marks).
b. A two-hour practical criticism examination in which the students will be required to comment upon and analyse three short extracts from television programmes. (The practical criticism paper will carry 40 per cent of the marks.)
c. A fifteen-minute oral examination in which the student will be expected to talk about and answer questions upon aspects of the course, as well as any topical issues which may arise. (The oral examination will carry 10 per cent of the marks.)

Note on assessment

It is proposed that the student's file be graded as an entity and not as the sum of a number of grades for different pieces of work. Individual pieces of written work will be assessed in the sense that they will be fully commented upon so that each student will receive a precise indication of the progress he is making, and of the weaknesses to which he will need to pay particular attention. Continuous assessment will, therefore, not be defined as continuous grading, for it seems important to us that the student should chart his progress in terms of the skills he acquires, and the sensitivity of response he develops, rather than in the necessarily cruder terms of a numerical grade.

Notes and References

Chapter 1

1. Report of the British Film Institute/Society for Education in Film and Television Conference on *Film and Television Studies in Secondary Education*, York University, 1976, pp. 39–40 (available from the British Film Institute).
2. Ibid., p. 29.
3. At the York conference cited above.
4. See G. Murdock and P. Golding, 'Communications: the continuing crisis', *New Society*, 25 April 1974, for a more detailed study of patterns of ownership and control.
5. My own classroom experience of the excellent *Viewpoint* series (Thames), for example, was that the programme dealing specifically with the business side of the media (Programme 8: *Show Business*) was one of the least popular with pupils.
6. See *Screen Education*, no. 16 (Autumn 1975).
7. R. Exton and H. Hillier, 'Film as industry in the ILEA 6th form film study course', *Screen Education*, no. 16 (Autumn 1975).
8. I. Gilmour and M. Walker, 'Film as industry in the G.C.E. mode III O level in film studies', *Screen Education*, no. 16 (Autumn 1975).
9. More light has been thrown on these matters by M. Alvarado and E. Buscombe, *Hazell: the Making of a TV Series*, (BFI/Latimer, 1978). If anything, the conclusions to be drawn from this study should make the reader even more circumspect in drawing his own conclusions. Alvarado and Buscombe, after covering every aspect of the production of the Hazell series, can say that 'in the process of production . . . They [the production team] were trying to produce a show which they thought was entertaining, and then hoping that the audience would like it too. Doubtless there are people producing television programmes which they believe to be rubbish, but who do it because they can make a lot of money. As a general rule we did not think that this was the case on *Hazell* . . . A model of popular television which sees it either as cynical manipulation or a straightforward identity of tastes between producers and audience (though there must be cases of both) would be, based on our experience of Hazell, an oversimplification' (pp. 250–1).
10. The ILEA for example is making an outstanding attempt not only to co-ordinate but to develop television work in schools, whilst in Lincolnshire co-operation between the local authority and two local colleges of education has resulted in the setting up of television facilities which are widely used by local schools.
11. J. Bruner, *The Process of Education* (Harvard, 1960) pp. 12–13.
12. N. Keddie, 'What are the criteria for relevance?', *Screen Education*, no. 15 (Summer 1975) p. 4.

13. J. D. Halloran, 'Understanding television', *Screen Education*, no. 14 (Spring 1975).
14. S. Hood, 'Visual literacy examined' in B. Luckham (ed.), *Audio-Visual Literacy* (Proceedings of Sixth Symposium on Broadcasting Policy) University of Manchester, 1975.
15. R. Barthes, *The Rhetoric of the Image*, Working Papers in Contemporary Cultural Studies, Spring 1971, Birmingham University.
16. The precise nature of the media's ideological function has been the subject of much debate. Some writers – following Marx's, 'the ideas of the ruling class are in every epoch the ruling ideas' – identify the dominant ideology as the pattern of ideas and beliefs of the dominant class, a position which leads to a view of media products as monolithic expressions of ruling-class values. But as Sylvia Harvey has observed, 'The notion of a single ruling class ideology organising and uniting the organs of mass communication ignores both the presence of divisions within the ruling class and the extent to which the ideology of free speech does open up a space for progressive journalists and media practitioners' (*May 1968 and Film Culture*, BFI 1978). More recent Marxist thinking has therefore suggested a more complex view of ideology as a process through which ruling-class ideas become transmuted into 'natural' representations and common-sense notions. This development has been clarified by Barthes' concept of Myth, but owes most to a resurgence of interest in the work of Gramsci whose concept of *hegemony* moved beyond notions of imposition of ruling-class ideas to an understanding of how a dominant class's definitions of reality come *by consent* to constitute the lived reality of a subordinate class and to define the limits of common-sense for that class and for society as a whole. Common sense is, as Geoffrey Nowell-Smith has suggested, 'the way a subordinate class in society lives its subordination'. This view of ideology involves an obvious paradox. For common-sense is, in its own terms, by definition, un-ideological, a-political. The process of ideology, therefore, works most crucially in the very area where its existence is most strenuously denied. It is to be understood, in Stuart Hall's words, 'not as what is hidden and concealed but precisely as what is most open, apparent, manifest . . . the most obvious and "transparent" forms of consciousness which operate in our everyday experience and ordinary language: common-sense'.
17. See N. Postman and C. Weingartner, *Teaching as a Subversive Activity* (Penguin, 1971) for a detailed discussion on the importance of questions in the school curriculum.
18. G. Murdock and G. Phelps, *Mass Media and the Secondary School* (Macmillan, 1973) Chapter 5.
19. *A Language for Life* (The Bullock Report) (HMSO, 1975) Chapter 2, Para. 5. The *difference* between viewing and classroom hours may surprise even television teachers. Bullock gives the average figure of 25 hours viewing per week for pupils between the ages of 5 and 14. This gives an annual total of 1300 viewing hours. Assuming that pupils between 5 and 14 are in the classroom for $4\frac{1}{2}$ hours each day (rounding down to discount time spent in assemblies, sports, etc.) and for 40 weeks each year, this gives an annual total of 900 hours spent in the classroom. *Children between 5 and 14 therefore on average spend 44 per cent more time watching television than they do in the classroom.*
20. P. Hartmann and C. Husband, 'The mass-media and racial conflict' in S. Cohen and J. Young, *The Manufacture of News*, (Constable, 1973).
21. *Report on Secondary Education* (Spens Report) (HMSO, 1938) pp. 222–3.
22. *15–18* (The Crowther Report) (HMSO, 1959) vol. I, para. 65–6.
23. F. R. Leavis and D. Thompson, *Culture and Environment* (Chatto and Windus, 1948) pp. 3–5.

24. D. Thompson, 'Introduction' to D. Thompson (ed.), *Discrimination and Popular Culture* (Penguin, 1964) p. 20.
25. S. Hall and P. Whannel, *The Popular Arts* (Hutchinson, 1964) p. 15.
26. Ironically in *The Popular Arts*, popular films (i.e. British and American films), invariably described as having major flaws, are generally seen as works to be discriminated against. Cinematic art resides not in the popular cinema at all but in foreign language films. The book is littered with sentences such as 'No one has to be defended against de Sica, Bergman or Antonioni' or '. . . we can understand the claims of Renoir, Bunuel, Kurosawa and Antonioni to this area of "high culture"'. And following a brief analysis of the films of John Ford we read that 'He is essentially a poet/craftsman rather than an intellectual, and he does not bring to the cinema the cultural equipment of a Bergman or a Bunuel. It is partly this which prevents him from being a major director' (p. 109).
27. *Half Our Future* (The Newsom Report): *A Report of the Central Advisory Council for Education (England)* (HMSO, 1963) paras. 475–6.
28. Newsom cannot be held solely responsible for this paradox. As I have suggested the report simply reflects the most progressive thinking about media in the early 1960s. Hall and Whannel's enormously influential *The Popular Arts*, for example, simply treats television as a crude and inferior form of cinema. See their analysis of *Z Cars* (esp. p. 127), the only popular series to receive even a qualified endorsement.
29. R. Hoggart in the *Observer*, 14 May 1961, reprinted as 'Culture – dead and alive' in *Speaking to Each Other*, vol. One: *About Society* (Chatto and Windus, 1970) pp. 131–3.
30. R. Williams, *Keywords* (Fontana, 1976) p. 75.
31. Ibid.
32. See P. Abrams, *Radio and Television* in D. Thompson *Discrimination and Popular Culture* for a reminder and dramatisation of the difficulties involved in arriving at discriminatory criteria within broadcasting.
33. For 'each class has its own political and artistic criteria' (Mao Tse Tung).
34. For two recent examples see R. Cathcart, *Education through Time Machines: Dr. Who and Star Trek* in B. Luckham *Audio-Visual Literacy*; and M. L. Scarborough, *The Educational Value of Non-Educational Television* (Independent Broadcasting Authority Research Report, 1973) p. 2.
35. G. Murdock and G. Phelps, *Mass Media*, p. 148.

Chapter 2

1. J. Henry, *Culture Against Man* (Random House, 1963) p. 27.
2. Ibid., pp. 295–6. For a further interesting discussion on the anecdote see R. D. Laing, *The Politics of Experience* (Penguin, 1967) p. 59ff.
3. D. H. Hargreaves, *Interpersonal Relations and Education*, revised student edition (Routledge, 1975) pp. 155–6.
4. D. Holly, *Beyond Curriculum* (Paladin, 1974) p. 27. For the views of students on this problem see School of Barbiana, *Letter to a Teacher* (Penguin, 1970) p. 27.
5. Holly, ibid., pp. 27–8.
6. A. Hunt, *Hopes for Great Happenings* (Eyre Methuen, 1976) p. 16.
7. R. F. Mackenzie, *State School* (Penguin, 1970) p. 61.
8. P. Freire, *Pedagogy of the Oppressed* (Penguin, 1972) p. 46ff.
9. E. Reimer, *School is Dead* (Penguin, 1971). See Chapter 4: 'How schools work'.
10. The model suggested here is one which worked very successfully in the Schools' Council Social Education Project; see J. Rennie, E. A. Lunzer, and W. Williams,

Social Education: An Experiment in Four Secondary Schools, Schools' Council Working Paper 51 (Evans/Methuen, 1974).

11. See D. H. Hargreaves, *Social Relations in a Secondary School* (Routledge and Kegan Paul, 1967).
12. The remarkable work of American psychotherapist Carl Rogers in the field of self-evaluation and non-directive learning is worth at least a footnote here. Indeed his *Freedom to Learn* (Merrill, 1969) and *On Becoming a Person* (Constable, 1961) are indispensable texts for the teacher more interested in facilitating learning than depositing knowledge.
13. All quotations are from J. Mack, 'Education and the media', *New Society*, 2 Nov 1978.
14. See P. Hooton, *Humanities Curriculum Project: 3 Years On*, Dialogue no. 14 (Schools' Council), Summer 1973.
15. Hunt, *Hopes for Great Happenings*, p. 6.
16. See Rennie, Lunzer and Williams, *Social Education*, pp. 95–6 for an account of how one teacher changed from his conventional authoritarian role to the role advocated here.

Chapter 3

1. R. L. Gregory, *Eye and Brain* (Weidenfeld and Nicolson, 1966) p. 7.
2. See A. Melnik and J. Merritt (eds), *The Reading Curriculum* (University of London Press in association with the Open University Press, 1972) esp. pp. 222–66: 'Comprehension: skills and levels'.
3. E. A. Lunzer and W. K. Gardner, *The Effective Use of Reading*, Chapter 2, (The Schools Council, 1979).
4. Ibid.
5. The phrase is originally Andrew Wilkinson's. See 'Total communication', *English in Education*, vol. 6, no. 3 (Winter 1972) p. 55ff.
6. See M. Argyle, *The Psychology of Interpersonal Behaviour* (Penguin, 1972) pp. 80–93.
7. For a detailed analysis of eye-contact patterns see Argyle, ibid., pp. 80–93.
8. *Startline*, Schools Council Moral Education 8–13 Project (Longmans, 1978).
9. D. Vaughan, *Television Documentary Usage*, British Film Institute Monograph no. 6 (BFI, 1976) p. 16.
10. Quoted in N. Garnham, *Structures of Television*, British Film Institute Monograph no. 1 (BFI, 1973) p. 27.
11. Ibid., p. 8.
12. S. M. Jourard, 'An exploratory study of body accessibility', *British Journal of Social and Clinical Psychology*, vol. 5 (1966) pp. 221–31.
13. Ibid.
14. R. Barthes, *Mythologies* (Cape, 1972).
15. G. Facetti and A. Fletcher, *Identity Kits* (Studio Vista, 1971).
16. A. E. Scheflen, *Body Language and the Social Order* (Prentice Hall, 1972).
17. In *Communication*, Social Sciences Foundation Course: *Making Sense of Society*, Block 3 (The Open University Press, 1975).
18. Barthes, *Mythologies*.
19. J. Berger, *et al.*, *Ways of Seeing* (BBC and Penguin, 1972).
20. J. Berger, 'From today art is dead', *Times Educational Supplement*, 1 Dec 1972.
21. Argyle, *The Psychology of Interpersonal Behaviour*.
22. S. Hall, 'The determinations of news photographs' in S. Cohen and J. Young, *The Manufacture of News* (Constable, 1973) and *Working Papers in Cultural Studies*, no. 3, Birmingham University (Autumn 1972).

23. *Humanities Curriculum Project* (Heinemann, 1970–3).
24. *Startline.*
25. G. Gauthier, *The Semiology of the Image* (British Film Institute, Advisory Document, 1976).

Chapter 5

1. The figures are taken from *News Broadcasting and the Public in 1970*, (BBC, 1971).
2. The attitudes cited here are taken from GCE Advanced Level examination answers in General Studies, 1976.
3. *Front Page* and *Radio Covingham* are two of twelve communications simulations devised by Kenneth Jones. The simulations may be obtained from Management Games Limited, 11 Woburn Street, Amptill, Bedford, MK45 2HP. Some of the *Front Page* material has been reproduced in J. L. Taylor and R. Walford, *Simulation in the Classroom* (Penguin, 1972) Chapter 7. Some of the *Radio Covingham* material appears in M. Alvarado, 'Simulations as method' in *Screen Education*, no. 14 (Spring 1975). An excellent and more recent simulation which extends and elaborates some of the basic ideas of *Front Page* is *Choosing the News* by Michael Simons and Andrew Bethell. This is obtainable from the ILEA English Centre, Sutherland Street, London, SW1V 4L11.
4. P. Willis, 'What is news? A case study'. *Working Papers in Cultural Studies* (Spring 1971) p. 9.
5. S. Hall, 'The determinations of news photographs' in Cohen and Young, *The Manufacture of News*, p. 178.
6. N. Ryan, quoted in J. Bakewell and N. Garnham, *The New Priesthood* (Allen Lane, 1970) p. 146.
7. J. Whale, *The Half-Shut Eye* (Macmillan, 1969) p. 30.
8. T. Burns, *The BBC* (Macmillan, 1977) pp. 194 and 196.
9. For a detailed description of what goes on inside a television news room see Glasgow University Media Group, *Bad News* (Routledge and Kegan Paul, 1976) Chapter 3.
10. E. McCann, 'The British Press and Northern Ireland' in Cohen and Young, *Manufacture of News*, pp. 259–61.
11. A. Smith, 'Internal pressures in broadcasting', *New Outlook*, no. 4 (1972) pp. 4–5 quoted in T. Burns, *BBC*, p. 195.
12. Burns, *BBC*, pp. 195–6.
13. R. Williams, *Television: Technology and Cultural Form* (Fontana, 1974) pp. 97–118.
14. Burns, *BBC*, pp. 158–9.
15. J. Galtung and M. Ruge, 'The structure of foreign news', *Journal of International Peace Research*, no. 1 (1965). Reprinted in Cohen and Young, *Manufacture of News*, p. 62ff.
16. Ibid., p. 63.
17. M. Frayn, *The Tin Men* (Collins, 1965) Chapter 13. In Cohen and Young, *Manufacture of News.*
18. C. Cockburn, *Nine Bald Men* (Hart-Davis, 1956).
19. The first quotation is from a BBC Television News broadcast in August 1976; the second from ITN's *News at One*, 12 Oct 1978.
20. J. Galtung and M. Ruge, 'The structure of foreign news', in Cohen and Young, *Manufacture of News*, p. 65.
21. P. Rock, 'News as eternal recurrence', ibid., p. 77.
22. G. Murdock, 'Political deviance: the press presentation' in Cohen and Young, ibid., p. 169.

23. R. Collins, *Television News*, BFI Television Monograph no. 5 (1976) pp. 30–1. Collins makes use of Michael Barratt's autobiography to establish this point:

> The papers arrive and I read them with tonight's programme in mind. It seems a pretty thin day for news – the usual industrial unrest, a soldier killed in Northern Ireland, constituency reports on the new county council election campaigns, nothing that we've not covered again and again in Nationwide . . .
> On the way along the M4 I switch radio channels to catch all the new bulletins, but there is still nothing which prompts an idea for tonight's programme. After nearly four years of Nationwide, 50 minutes a night, fresh topics are hard to come by. What a voracious medium we work in!

Collins comments,

> It's clear here how important is the process of the mass media of communication taking in each other's washing. Each 'arm' – radio, television, the press – scrutinises the presentation of the world, the news, the others offer and incorporates it into its own.

24. G. Murdock, 'Political deviance', p. 168.
25. B. Groombridge, *Television and the People* (Penguin, 1972) Chapter 6; K. Nordenstreng and T. Varis, 'International flow of TV programmes' in J. Caughie, (ed.), *Television: Ideology and Exchange* (British Film Institute, 1978).
26. Murdock, 'Political deviance', p. 164.
27. D. Potter, 'Lost horizons', *New Statesman*, 20 Feb 1976.
28. Galtung and Ruge, 'The structure of foreign news', p. 68.
29. H. M. Enzensberger, 'Constituents of a theory of the media' in *New Left Review*, no. 64 (Nov/Dec 1970) p. 20.
30. Bakewell and Garnham, *New Priesthood*, p. 173.
31. Hood, *A Survey of Television*, Chapter 7.
32. *Protest for Peace* is available from EMI Film Distributors Ltd, Film House, 142 Wardour Street, London W1V 4AE.
33. Collins, *Television News*, p. 30.
34. S. Hall, 'A world at one with itself', in Cohen and Young, *Manufacture of News*, p. 89.
35. Quoted in Glasgow University Media Group, *Bad News*, p. 235.
36. Collins, *Television News*, p. 21.
37. Hall, 'A world at one', in Cohen and Young, *Manufacture of News*, p. 88.
38. For a particularly good example of the 'soft' technique see the transcript of an interview between Robin Day and Lord Hailsham in T. Pateman, *Television and the 1974 General Election*, British Film Institute Television Monograph no. 3 (1974) pp. 65–9.
39. Hall, 'A world at one', p. 88.
40. One of the clearest accounts is offered by J. Young, 'The myth of the drug-taker in the mass-media' in Cohen and Young, *Manufacture of News*, pp. 314–15.
41. Burns, *BBC*, pp. 200–2.
42. See Glasgow University Media Group, *Bad News*, pp. 82–3.
43. C. Curran, 'Broadcasting and public opinion', *The Listener*, 20 June 1974.
44. J. Dearlove, 'The BBC and the politicians', *Index on Censorship*, vol. 1 (1974).
45. J. D. Halloran, G. Murdock and P. Elliott, *Demonstrations and Communications: A Case Study* (Penguin, 1970).
46. Hall, 'A world at one', p. 90.
47. Ibid., p. 92.
48. The complex nature of 'the collusion . . . with the Establishment' against

'pressure from without' has been most effectively explored by Burns, *BBC*, Chapter 6.

49. Halloran, Murdock and Elliott, *Demonstrations and Communications*, p. 223.
50. P. Hartmann and C. Husband, 'The mass media and racial conflict', *Race*, vol. xii, no. 3 (1971). Extract in Cohen and Young, *Manufacture of News*, pp. 273–4.
51. P. Rock, 'News as eternal recurrence' in Cohen and Young, ibid., p. 77.
52. Collins, *Television News*, p. 9.
53. Ibid., p. 37.
54. See for example J. Baggaley, *TV Codes and Audience Response* (British Film Institute Education Advisory Document, 1978).
55. Hood, in Luckham, *Audio-visual Literacy*.
56. Glasgow University Media Group, *Bad News*, p. 26.

Chapter 6

1. E. Buscombe (ed.), *Football on Television* British Film Institute Monograph, no. 4 (1975).
2. Murdock and Phelps, *Mass Media and the Secondary School*, p. 20.
3. D. H. Hargreaves, *Interpersonal Relations and Education*, pp. 120–2.
4. For notes on the programme see E. Buscombe, 'Match of the day' in *Screen Education Notes 3* (Summer 1972).
5. A. Tudor, 'The panels' in Buscombe, *Football on Television*, p. 61.
6. C. M. McArthur, 'Setting the scene: Radio Times and TV Times', Buscombe, ibid., p. 8ff.
7. R. Williams, 'There's always the sport' in *The Listener*, 16 April 1970.
8. C. Barr, 'Comparing Styles: England v. W. Germany', and T. Ryall, 'Visual Style in Scotland v. Yugoslavia' in Buscombe, *Football on Television*.
9. Barr, ibid., p. 47ff.
10. Tudor, 'The panels', p. 56 and p. 59.
11. Bakewell and Garnham, *New Priesthood*, pp. 120–2.
12. Ibid., pp. 233–4.

Chapter 8

1. A. Padfield, 'Put them in the picture', *Cog*, no. 1 (Summer 1976, Nottingham Teachers' Centre).
2. G. Wade, 'TV rules OK?' in *Libertarian Education*, no. 9 (1976).
3. P. Cooper, 'Keeping your cool in the communications business', *Times Educational Supplement*, 8 Aug 1975.
4. Ibid.
5. Padfield, 'Put them in the picture'.
6. Cooper, 'Keeping your cool'.
7. Ibid.
8. E. Carpenter, *Oh, What a Blow that Phantom Gave Me* (Paladin, 1976) p. 165.
9. A. Girard, 'Cable television and cultural policy' in J. Caughie (ed.), *Television*.
10. See *Report of the Committee on the Future of Broadcasting* (The Annan Report) (HMSO, 1977) Ch. 14, paras. 37 and 38. For the full account see P. M. Lewis, *Community Television and Cable in Britain* (BFI, 1978).
11. Cooper, 'Keeping your cool'.
12. Enzensberger, 'Constituents of a theory of the media', p. 22.
13. For further examples see Baggaley, *TV Codes and Audience Response*.

Chapter 9

1. C. Brunsdon and D. Morley, *Everyday Television: Nationwide*, BFI Monograph no. 10 (BFI, 1978) pp. 65–6.
2. For specific examples of such frameworks and links see Brunsdon and Morley, ibid., pp. 45–51. The links are analysed on pp. 58–60.
3. For an analysis of this effect in one interview see S. Heath and G. Skirrow, 'Television: a world in action' in *Screen*, vol. 18, no. 2 (Summer 1977) pp. 44ff.
4. T. Pateman, *Television and the 1974 General Election*, pp. 65ff.
5. S. Hall, I. Connell and L. Curti, 'The "unity" of current affairs television', *Working Papers in Cultural Studies*, 9 (Spring 1976) pp. 64ff.
6. Heath and Skirrow, 'Television: a world in action'.
7. G. Dyer, 'Teaching about television interviews', *Screen Education*, no. 27 (Summer 1978).
8. Brunsdon and Morley, *Everyday Television*.
9. Collins, *Television News*, p. 21.
10. Hall, 'A world at one with itself', p. 88.
11. Glasgow University Media Group, *Bad News*, pp. 26ff.
12. *Teachers' Protest*, devised by Michael Simons and Cary Bazalgette, with additional material by Andrew Bethell and Simon Clements, is obtainable from the Society for Education in Film and Television, 29 Old Compton Street, London W1V 5PN, and for ILEA teachers only from the publishers, The English Centre, Sutherland Street, London SW1V 4L11.
13. The second caption is the correct one. Interestingly enough this example was used by *The Sunday Times* as incontrovertible visual evidence of the Dutch team's superiority over England.
14. Acknowledgements are due here to Alan O'Shea and Bob Osgerby of Furzedown College of Education, London, whom I first saw using these simple exercises with great effectiveness with their students.
15. *Protest for Peace*, EMI Film Distributors Ltd, Film House, 142 Wardour Street, London W1V 4AE.
16. Heath and Skirrow, 'Television: a world in action'.
17. S. Bennett, 'A television documentary course', *Screen Education*, no. 25 (Winter 1977/78).
18. Bakewell and Garnham, *New Priesthood*.
19. D. Vaughan, *Television Documentary Usage*, British Film Institute Monograph no. 6 (BFI, 1976).
20. The two most well received approaches not mentioned in this chapter were (i) the study of 'low' comedy series such as the Hylda Baker vehicle *Nearest and Dearest* via George Orwell's study of vulgar postcards in 'The Art of Donald McGill' (in *Decline of the English Murder* (Penguin, 1965)) and (ii) a case study of writers Ray Galton and Alan Simpson in which a new series *Casanova 73* was examined in the light of their previous work. The approach is outlined in L. Masterman, 'The writer revealed', *Times Educational Supplement*, 26 Oct 1973, p. 94.
21. M. Esslin, *The Theatre of the Absurd* (Penguin, 1970).
22. Entr'Acte is obtainable from the British Film Institute, 81 Dean Street, London W1V 6AA; *Un Chien Andalou* and *Cul-de-Sac* from Contemporary Films, 55 Greek St, London W1; *Two Men and a Wardrobe* from Connoisseur Films, Glenbuck House, Surbiton, Surrey. For an account of the surrealist elements in Polanski's films see L. Masterman, 'Cul-de-Sac: Through the mirror of surrealism', *Screen*, vol. 11, no. 6 (1970).
23. L. Rhinehart, *The Dice Man* (Panther, 1972).
24. A. Hunt, 'When to say no', *Times Educational Supplement*, 4 April 1975, p. 102.

25. J. Fisher, *Funny Way to be a Hero* (Paladin, 1976).
26. D. Morris, *The Naked Ape* (Cape, 1967) pp. 116–19.
27. See Fisher, *Funny Way to be a Hero* for many examples.
28. T. Griffiths, *Comedians*. (Faber and Faber, 1976) pp. 23ff.
29. G. Murdock, and G. Phelps, *Mass Media and the Secondary School*, pp. 21ff.
30. For a detailed discussion of the problems of adapting *Wessex Tales* for television see my own article 'BBC – the eternal acolyte', *Times Educational Supplement*, 21 Dec 1973.

Chapter 10

1. *A Programme for Political Education*, Political Education Research Unit Document no. 1 (York University, July 1974).
2. N. Postman, 'The politics of reading' in N. Keddie (ed.), *Tinker, Tailor* . . . (Penguin, 1975) p. 86.
3. See for example I. Lister, 'The political vocabulary test: a negative document', *The Bulletin of the General Studies Association*, no. 12 (Winter 1968) and R. Stradling, *The Political Awareness of the School Leaver* (Hansard Society, 1977).
4. I. Lister, *The Aims and Methods of Political Education in Schools* (Paper presented to the conference on the Development of Democratic Institutions in Europe) April 1976, p. 4.
5. S. Hall, 'Television and culture', *Sight and Sound*, vol. 45, no. 4 (Autumn 1976) p. 249.
6. R. W. Witkin, *The Intelligence of Feeling* (Heinemann, 1974) p. 70.
7. J. Berger, 'From today art is dead'.
8. N. Postman and C. Weingartner, *Teaching as a Subversive Activity*, p. 34.
9. Parallels to this process can be found in the fields of psychological and intellectual change. See for example Festinger's cognitive dissonance theory (L. Festinger, *The Theory of Cognitive Dissonance* (Row, Peterson, 1957)), and Piaget's concepts of equilibration, accommodation and assimilation (J. Piaget and B. Inhelder, *The Early Growth of Logic in the Child* (Routledge and Kegan Paul, 1964)).
10. See the findings of L. Thomas and S. Augstein, that better results were obtained from pupils who read a passage in the expectation of a request to summarise it than from pupils who read the same passage in the expectation of receiving a comprehension test upon it ('An experimental approach to learning from written material', *Remedial Education*, 8 (1972)).

Select Annotated Bibliography

The following bibliography includes books and articles referred to in the text as well as other sources of interest to the television teacher.

Three voluminous categories of literature about television have been excluded: sociological research literature, particularly that relating to the 'effects' debate; books and articles written by professional broadcasters themselves (though teachers may occasionally find these of value); and literary spin-offs from popular television series.

Sources marked with an asterisk * are those which are particularly recommended for use on initial and in-service teacher training courses.

Abercrombie, M. L. J., *The Anatomy of Judgement* (Hutchinson, 1960). An excellent account of the implications for teaching and learning of studies in perception, and a useful source of visual puzzles and ambiguities.

Abrams, P., 'Radio and television' in D. Thompson (ed.), *Discrimination and Popular Culture* (Penguin, 1964). A rare and conspicuously unsuccessful attempt to establish clear criteria for evaluating television programmes.

Alvarado, M., 'Eight hours are not a day' in T. Rayns (ed.), *Fassbinder* (British Film Institute, 1976). Comparison of *Coronation Street* with a similar, yet strikingly different 'family series' directed by Fassbinder for German television.

Alvarado, M., 'Simulation as Method', *Screen Education*, no. 14 (Spring 1975). Contains a description and evaluation of the simulation, *Radio Covingham*.

*Alvarado, M. and Buscombe, E., *Hazell: The Making of a TV Series* (BFI/Latimer, 1978). Detailed account of the production of a popular television series, and one of the few available sources for teachers wishing to examine 'TV as Industry'. One of the best programmes from the series, 'Hazell Meets the First Eleven' may be hired from the BFI, and should be used in conjunction with the book.

Argyle, M., *The Psychology of Interpersonal Behaviour* (Penguin, 1972). A useful general introduction to the field of non-verbal communication.

Attneave, F., 'Multistability in perception', in *Readings from Scientific American, Recent Progress in Perception*, Chapter 14. Originally in *Scientific American* (December 1971). Well illustrated article on pictures and geometric forms which 'spontaneously shift in their principal aspect when they are looked at steadily'. A good source of practical examples for the classroom.

Baggaley, J., *TV Codes and Audience Response* (BFI Advisory Document, 1979). Interesting account of practical television work with undergraduates designed to explore the precise effects of particular visual codings in the medium.

Baggaley, J. and Duck, S., *Dynamics of Television* (Saxon House, 1976). Examines the conventions and forms of television, and their effects upon the individual viewer.

Bakewell, J. and Garnham, N., *The New Priesthood* (Allen Lane, 1970). Potted but illuminating interviews with producers, writers and executives in television. Enjoyable reading. Sections on News, Documentary, Current Affairs, Drama and Light Entertainment.

Barr, J. C., 'Comparing styles: England v W. Germany' in Buscombe, E. (ed.), *Football on Television.* Comparison of styles of football presentation on English and W. German television. Unconvincing since two different *types* of presentation are compared.

Barr, C., Hillier, J. and Perkins, V. F., 'The making of Upstairs, Downstairs', *Movie*, no. 21 (Autumn 1975). Interviews with the makers of the television series.

*Barthes, R., *Mythologies* (Cape, 1972). Analytical vignettes on aspects of popular culture along with an important theoretical essay, *Myth Today*. A key work.

Barthes, R., 'The rhetoric of the image', *Working Papers in Cultural Studies*, no. 1 (Spring 1971). Semiological analysis of an advertising photograph, with a useful discussion of different levels of analysis of visual material.

Bazalgette, C., 'Regan and Carter, Kojak and Crocker, Batman and Robin', *Screen Education*, 20 (Autumn 1976). Account of a rare attempt to teach about popular detective series.

Beharrell, P. and Philo, G. (eds), *Trade Unions and the Media* (Macmillan, 1977). Essays which too often cover very familiar ground. Most interesting, because most original, are two short studies of media coverage of students and farmworkers.

*Benjamin, W., *The Work of Art in the Age of Mechanical Reproduction* in *Illuminations: Essays and Reflections* (Cape, 1970). Important and recently re-discovered article which argues that art loses its 'aura' in the age of mechanical reproduction and that 'creativity, genius, eternal value and mystery' become 'outmoded concepts'. Film is constituted by 'the sequence of positional views which the editor composes from the material supplied him', while the audience 'can take the position of a critic . . . Filmed behaviour lends itself readily to analysis . . . and manages to assure us of an immense and unexpected field of action. Our taverns and our metropolitan streets, our offices and furnished rooms, our railroad stations and our factories appeared to have us locked up hopelessly. Then came the film and burst this prison-world asunder.'

Bennett, S., 'A television documentary course', *Screen Education*, no. 25 (Winter 1977/78). The most detailed account available of teaching about documentary. The course described was taught to undergraduates at City University, London.

Bennett, S., *Unesco Survey of Media Studies in Europe*. Extracts from this invaluable report may be found in *Screen Education*, no. 18 (Spring 1976).

*Berger, J., 'From today art is dead', *Times Educational Supplement*, 1 Dec 1972. Clarion call for a new approach to visual education. An important and seminal article.

*Berger, J., et al., *Ways of Seeing* (BBC and Penguin, 1972). Radical perspectives on art and popular culture based on the television series.

Bigsby, C. W. E. (ed.), *Approaches to Popular Culture* (Arnold, 1976). An assortment of essays by diverse hands, unrelated either to each other or to any meaningful containing structure. Of little value to teachers.

BBC, *News Broadcasting and the Public in 1970* (BBC, 1971). Useful source of data on audience attitudes to television news programmes.

BBC, *The Task of Broadcasting News* (BBC, 1976). Smug BBC pamphlet, designed to allay anxieties about its news coverage.

British Film Institution Television Monographs (BFI).

1. *Structures of Television* by Nicholas Garnham.
2. *Light Entertainment* by Richard Dyer.

3. *Television and the February 1974 General Election* by Trevor Pateman.
4. *Football on Television* edited by Ed. Buscombe.
5. *Television News* by Richard Collins.
6. *Television Documentary Usage* by Dai Vaughan.
7. *Broadcasting and Accountability* by Caroline Heller.
8. *Television and History* by Colin McArthur.
9. *Television: Ideology and Exchange* edited by John Caughie
10. *Everyday Television: Nationwide*, by Charlotte Brunsdon and David Morley.

Essential reading for teachers, the monographs represent one of the few current sources of extended analysis on different aspects of television. Details of each monograph are given under their authors.

British Film Institute and Society for Education in Film and Television, *Report of 1976 Conference on Film and Television Studies in Secondary Education* (BFI, 1976). The report offers a useful survey of progress in and attitudes towards film, television and media studies in the mid-1970s.

*Brunsdon, C. and Morley, D., *Everyday Television: Nationwide* (BFI, 1978). Television Monograph No. 10. Excellent analysis of the *Nationwide* programme. Perhaps the most directly useful and relevant of all of the BFI Monographs to the teacher.

Bruner, J., *The Process of Education* (Harvard, 1960). Important in establishing education as process rather than content orientated, and for its advocacy of a 'spiral' curriculum.

Brunt, R., 'The spectacular world of Whicker' in *Working Papers in Cultural Studies*, no. 3 (Autumn 1972). Important and detailed analysis of *Whicker's World* – 'a conditioned world of constant fascination where the possibility of boredom is unremittingly denied'.

Buckhout, R., 'Eyewitness testimony' in *Scientific American* (Readings from) Chapter 20. Originally in *Scientific American*, December 1974. An account of a number of experiments which demonstrate how remarkably subject to error eyewitness testimony can be. Useful for classroom work on perception.

*Burns, T., *The BBC: Public Institution and Private World* (Macmillan, 1977). Long awaited study of the Beeb based on interviews in the early 1960s and early 1970s. Essential background reading.

Buscombe, E., *Films on TV* (Society for Education in Film and TV, 1971). Excellent pamphlet on how films are presented on television, including analyses of programmes about the cinema.

*Buscombe, E. (ed.), *Football on Television* (BFI Monograph No. 5, 1975). See Chapter 10.

Buscombe, E., *Match of the Day*, Screen Education Notes No. 3, Summer 1972. An early, but nevertheless useful analysis of the programme.

*Buscombe, E., 'Television studies in schools and colleges', IBA Report in *Screen Education*, no. 12 (Autumn 1974). An earlier exploration of some of the ground covered in this book. Sections on 'Why study television?' and 'What should one teach about television?' are followed by descriptions of seven different television courses and a 'model' course.

Cardiff, D., Cram, D. and Dyer, G., 'The broadcast interview'. Useful unpublished paper offering possible structures for interview analysis.

Carpenter, E., *Oh, What a Blow that Phantom Gave Me!* (Paladin, 1976). Extraordinary collection of media anecdotes and illuminations by an anthropologist (and former colleague of McLuhan) who demonstrates how print and the electronic media 'swallow cultures'.

Cathcart, R., 'Education through time machines?': Dr Who and Star Trek' in

Luckham, B. The reductio ad absurdum of discriminatory approaches to the medium. Cathcart argues, without conviction, the educational value of *Dr Who* and *Star Trek*.

Caughie, J. (ed.), *Television: Ideology and Exchange* (BFI, 1978). Television Monograph No. 9. Seven disparate but extremely useful essays from foreign sources. 'Underlying the collection is the assumption that television does function broadly as an Ideological Apparatus'.

Cirino, R., 'Bias through selection and omission' in S. Cohen, and J. Young. Classic account of how bias in newspapers is used to manipulate public opinion in favour of powerful business and political interests and away from areas of genuine public concern.

Cockburn, C., *Nine Bald Men* (Hart-Davis, 1956).

*Cohen, S. and Young, J., *The Manufacture of News* (Constable, 1973). A collection of important, and often indispensable texts on the news media's treatment of deviancy and social problems. Cross-media in content, but an important in-service text for television teachers.

*Collins, R., *Television News*; BFI Monograph no. 5 (BFI, 1976). A useful study of some of the assumptions and practices of British televised news.

Cooper, P., 'Keeping your cool in the communications business', *Times Educational Supplement*, 8 August 1975. An account and justification of school video work.

Curran, C., 'Broadcasting and public opinion', *The Listener*, 20 June 1974. Reflections by the BBC's Director–General on BBC Election Coverage. A bureaucratic concoction of myth-making ('The BBC is committed to a policy of avoiding a point of view of its own') and complacency ('It was remarkable to hear that our *Election Call* programmes . . . produced "overflow calls" from between 5,000 and 10,000 people for every programme').

Curran, J., Gurevitch, M. and Woollacott, J. (eds), *Mass Communication and Society* (Arnold, 1977). Excellent reader for the Open University course on *Mass Communication and Society*. Contains overview articles designed to summarise current discussion and research.

Dearlove, J., *The BBC and the Politicians* in Pateman, 1974, and the *Index on Censorship*, vol. 1 (1974). Analysis of the BBC's treatment of politics and politicians.

Dennett, T. and Spence, J., 'Photography, ideology and education', *Screen Education*, no. 21 (Winter 1976–7). Practical ideas on how photography may be used in schools and colleges to make explicit the concept of ideology.

Deregowski, J. B., 'Pictorial perception and culture' in *Scientific American* (Readings from) Chapter 21. Originally in *Scientific American*, November 1972. Short cross-cultural study of perceptual differences between Africans and Europeans.

Disch, R. (ed.), *The Future of Literacy* (Prentice Hall, 1973). Valuable anthology on the crisis of literacy with contributions from McLuhan, Marcuse, Goodman, Ionesco, Artaud, Kampf, Wellek, Steiner and Carpenter.

Dorfman, A. and Mattelart, A., *How to Read Donald Duck* (International General, 1975). A detailed study of Donald Duck comics and how they embody capitalist–imperialist ideology.

*Dyer, G., 'Teaching about television interviews', *Screen Education*, no. 27 (Summer 1978). Valuable account of teaching about interviews with Polytechnic students.

*Dyer, R., *Light Entertainment*, BFI Television Monograph no. 2 (BFI, 1973). The starting point for any teacher wishing to work in the area of pop and variety shows. The monograph does not examine 'light entertainment' as it is normally thought of within the BBC (i.e. comedy shows, quiz programmes, etc. are not included).

Dyer, R., *The Meaning of Tom Jones* (Working Papers in Cultural Studies no. 1, Spring 1971). Analysis of 'the public personality of Tom Jones'. Uses publicity booklets and newspaper articles as well as Jones's television show as source material. Good discussion on the nature of stardom.

Elliott, P., *The Making of a Television Series* (Constable, 1972). Somewhat disappointing sociological account of the making of a documentary series from the original planning stages to the final production.

*Enzensberger, H. M., 'Constituents of a theory of the media', *New Left Review*, no. 64 (November–December 1970). A seminal paper which moves beyond still current theories of the media (including 'manipulative' theories) towards the necessary constituents of any socialist media strategy. 'Marxists have not understood the consciousness industry and have not been aware of its socialist possibilities.'

Esslin, M., *The Theatre of the Absurd* (Penguin, 1970). Still the best text on the origins and development of the absurd tradition.

Exton, R. and Hillier, H., 'Film as industry in the ILEA 6th form film study course', *Screen Education*, no. 16 (Autumn 1975). Two practising teachers report on some of the problems of teaching about film as industry in a London comprehensive school.

*Facetti, G. and Fletcher, A., *Identity Kits: A Pictorial Survey of Visual Signals* (Studio Vista, 1971). A profusely illustrated guide to signs and signals, and an invaluable pupil introduction to the field of semiology.

15–18 (The Crowther Report) (HMSO, 1959).

*Fisher, J., *Funny Way to be a Hero* (Paladin, 1976). Excellent study of stand-up comedians with invaluable lengthy extracts from their old music-hall routines. Many of the comedians included (Max Bygraves, Ken Dodd, Frankie Howerd, Les Dawson, Morecambe and Wise) are now established television stars.

Fiske, J. and Hartley, J., *Reading Television* (New Accents Series) (Methuen, 1978). Heavy-handed semiotics based approach to the medium. Sometimes idiosyncratic (it argues that television serves a 'bardic' function), often lumpily eclectic, its potential usefulness to readers in summarising the work of other writers is vitiated by a general lack of facility in handling their ideas.

Frayn, M., *The Tin Men* (Collins, 1965).

*Freire, P., *Pedagogy of the Oppressed* (Penguin, 1972). Difficult going, but one of the most important educational texts published this decade. Freire argues that education is necessarily either liberating or oppressive, never neutral, and that it can enable men either to act upon and transform their world or to adjust to it. Through a process of dialogue, which resolves the dichotomy between teacher and taught, every man can become capable of looking critically at his world, acting upon it, and transforming it.

*Galtung, J. and Ruge, M., 'The structure of foreign news' *Journal of International Peace Research*, no. 1 (1965). Reprinted in Tunstall. A lengthy extract is also available in Cohen and Young. Classic essay on news values.

Garnham, N., *Structures of Television*, BFI Monograph no. 1 (BFI, 1973; revised 1978). An examination of the ideological assumptions behind the organisational structures of British television.

*Gauthier, G., *The Semiology of the Image* (BFI Advisory Document, 1976). An important paper which proposes a semiological approach to the study of images in the classroom. This may not be a realistic approach in most secondary schools, but Gauthier's paper does offer readers many fruitful ideas on teaching about images. Slides accompanying the paper may be bought or hired from the British Film Institute.

Gilmour, I. and Walker, M., 'Film as industry in the GCE mode III 'O' level in film studies', *Screen Education*, no. 16 (Autumn 1975).

Glasgow University Media Group, *Bad News*, vol. 1 (Routledge & Kegan Paul, 1976). Volume One of a somewhat disappointing research study on television news broadcasts with particular reference to the coverage of industrial news. If the teacher can skate through the masses of data he will find a useful review of the literature on television news, a valuable subjective account of life inside a television newsroom, a helpful analysis of the relationship between trade unions and the news media and short case studies of television news coverage of two different strikes.

Goodman, P., *Growing Up Absurd* (Vintage, 1956). Why the young find it difficult to grow up in organised society. 'The disaffection of the young is profound and it will not be remediable by better techniques of socialising. Instead, there will have to be changes in our society and its culture, so as to meet the appetites and capacities of human nature, in order to grow up.'

Gregory, R. L., *Eye and Brain* (Weidenfeld and Nicolson, 1970).

Gregory, R. L., *The Intelligent Eye* (Weidenfeld and Nicolson, 1970). Two hand-books on perception with illustrations and discussion of a large number of illusions.

Griffiths, T., *Comedians* (Faber, 1976). Script of Griffiths' successful West End play. Griffiths' analysis of comedy and humour can usefully be applied both to the many jokes contained in the play and to any offered by the class.

Groombridge, B., *Television and the People* (Penguin, 1972). Argues for participatory democracy and for the importance of television's role in helping create it. Contains useful insights on news presentation.

Hain, P., *Mistaken Identity* (Quartet, 1976). An account of how Hain was arrested on eye-witness testimony for a crime he did not commit. A terrifying reminder that perceptual problems are not simply of academic interest.

Half our Future (The Newsom Report). A Report of the Central Advisory Council for Education (England) (HMSO, 1964). A liberal and influential document which legitimised the film study movement of the following decade, but unwittingly held back the development of television studies (see Chapter 1).

* Hall, S., 'The determinations of news photographs', *Working Papers in Cultural Studies*, no. 3 (Autumn 1972). Birmingham University. Reproduced in Cohen and Young. Excellent analysis of the function of photographs in newspapers. Required reading for teachers.

* Hall, S., 'Television and culture' in *Sight and Sound*, vol. 45, no. 4 (Autumn 1976). Examines the 'deeply manipulative' nature of television particularly in relation to programmes which appear to be transmitting 'raw' events. The second part of the article contains a useful commentary upon Benjamin.

*Hall, S., 'A world at one with itself', *New Society*, 18 June 1970. Argues that the consensus assumptions of news programmes mystify rather than clarify 'real events in the real world'.

Hall, S., Connell, I. and Curti, L., 'The unity of current affairs television', *Working Papers in Cultural Studies*, no. 9 (Spring 1976). Detailed analysis of political interviews in one *Panorama* programme, using many of the ideas argued in Hall, S., *ibid*.

Hall, S. and Whannel, P., *The Popular Arts* (Hutchinson, 1964). Classic text of the 1960s with many illuminating analyses. Argues that many aspects of popular culture are worthy of consideration as 'serious' art, a view which gives the authors little that is constructive to say about television.

Halloran, J. D., 'Understanding television', *Screen Education*, no. 14 (Spring 1975). Future television analysis and research, by concentrating upon and clarifying social needs, could become an instrument for determining broadcasting policy and be a necessary counterbalance to vested interests, political expedience and the needs of existing institutions.

* Halloran, J. D., Murdock, G. and Elliott, P., *Demonstrations and Communications: A Case Study* (Penguin, 1970). Excellent case study on newspaper and television coverage of an anti-Vietnam march and demonstration. Events tended to be fitted

into a preconceived formula by the media, and the formula itself provided the media's frame of reference in subsequent news stories.

Hargreaves, D. H., *Interpersonal Relations and Education*, revised student edition (Routledge & Kegan Paul, 1975). Usefully summarises and evaluates the work of the most interesting writers on education since the mid-1960s.

Hargreaves, D. H., *Social Relations in a Secondary School* (Routledge & Kegan Paul, 1967). Classic study of a 'delinquescent' subculture in a northern secondary modern school. Demonstrates graphically the disastrous social consequences of streaming.

* Hartmann, P. and Husband, C., 'The mass media and racial conflict', *Race*, vol. XII, no. 3 (1971). Reprinted in Cohen and Young. '[The media] play a major part in defining for people what the important issues are and the terms in which they should be discussed . . . The way race-related material is handled serves both to perpetuate negative perceptions of blacks and to define the situation as one of intergroup conflict.' Essential reading for teachers handling race-related issues in television.

Harvey, S., *May 1968 and Film Culture* (BFI, 1978). Clearly written and intelligent account of developments in film culture since 1968 with excellent chapters on 'Notions of cultural production' and 'Ideology and the impression of reality' which are directly relevant to issues facing television theory and practice.

Heath, S. and Skirrow, G., 'Television: a world in action', *Screen*, vol. 18, no. 2 (Summer 1977). Excellent analysis of a typical programme from the television documentary series.

Heller, C., *Broadcasting and Accountability* (BFI, 1978). Television Monograph No. 7. An examination of how far broadcasting institutions are, and ought to be, accountable to the public.

Henry, J., *Culture against Man* (Random House, 1963). Influential sociological account of American schools and culture in the early 1960s.

Higgins, A. P., *Talking about Television* (BFI, 1966). One of the few sources which reveals pupil responses to the medium, but pupil discussion rarely moves beyond low-level chat, and the teaching lacks even an ill-defined conceptual framework.

Hoggart, R., *Speaking to Each Other. Vol. One: About Society* (Chatto & Windus, 1970). Somewhat dated collection of articles by the author of *The Uses of Literacy*, including a number on television (*The Uses of Television; Television as the Archetype of Mass Communications*, etc.) See Chapter 1.

Holly, D., *Beyond Curriculum* (Paladin, 1974). Valuable sociological account of British schools in the 1970s with critical evaluations of recent curriculum projects and innovations.

Holt, J., *How Children Fail* (Penguin, 1969). How school looks from the pupils' perspective. Holt draws attention to pupil strategies for pleasing the teacher, producing right answers and keeping out of trouble. 'For children the central business of school is not learning.'

Hood, S., *The Mass Media* (Studies in Contemporary Europe) (Macmillan, 1972). Clear survey of patterns of ownership and control of the broadcasting media and the press in Europe since the war. Particularly valuable for teachers who wish to develop 'television as industry' work, and an easy guide for those who wish to discover who owns what.

Hood, S., *A Survey of Television* (Heinemann, 1967). Still a first-rate introduction to many aspects of the medium by a seasoned professional. Differences between Charter and Act, and video and film are spelled out, and there are insights into problems of programme planning, and the roles of producer, director, engineers and others involved in the process of making television programmes.

* Hood, S., *Visual Literacy Examined* in Luckham, (1975). Admirably simple and concise paper on the premisses underlying recent critical work in television.

Hooton, P., 'Humanities curriculum project: three years on', *Dialogue*, no. 14

(Summer 1973). Schools Council. A teacher from a trial school evaluates the project.

*Horrox, A., Lowndes, D. and Skirrow, G., 'Viewpoint – mass communication in society', *Teacher's Notes* (Thames Television, 1975). The teacher's booklet accompanying the controversial television series, *Viewpoint*, includes numerous suggestions for classroom activities, many relating to television.

Howell, G., *The Penguin Book of Naughty Postcards* (Penguin, 1977). Useful source book of postcards by McGill and others. Relevant to the study of 'broad' television comedy.

Huff, D., *How to Lie with Statistics* (Penguin, 1973). Includes sections on how visual depictions of statistical information can be used to deceive.

Hunt, A., *Hopes for Great Happenings* (Eyre Methuen, 1976). First-rate critique of our alienating educational system by one who attempted to create alternative frameworks within it. Some interesting insights on the problems involved in teaching about film, and the difficulties in video-work of getting students to think beyond the reproduction of 'real' television.

Hunt, A., 'When to say no', *Times Educational Supplement*, 4 April 1975. Comparison of *Porridge* and *Within These Walls* (see Chapter 9).

Husband, C. (ed.), *White Media and Black Britain* (Arrow, 1975). Essays examining the role of the media in race relations.

Independent Broadcasting Authority, *Television and Radio*. Published annually. The IBA's annual guide to independent television and independent local radio. Useful source of current information.

Jourard, S. M., 'An Exploratory Study of Body Accessibility', *British Journal of Social and Clinical Psychology*, 5 (1966). Early study of touch taboos.

Keddie, N., 'What are the criteria for relevance?', *Screen Education*, no. 15 (Summer 1975). A tortuous analysis of the film studies movement.

A Language for Life (The Bullock Report) (HMSO, 1975). Demonstrates the significance of television viewing in the child's experience and urges teachers to use this experience constructively in educating their pupils.

Laing, R. D., *The Politics of Experience* (Penguin, 1967). Laing's superb essay on the absolute validity and significance of each individual's experience has important implications for the television teacher.

Laurenson, D. and Swingewood, A., *The Sociology of Literature* (Paladin, 1972). An introduction to a fast expanding field. The contributions of Taine, Marx and Engels, Lukacs and Goldmann to the field are all discussed.

Leavis, F. R. and Thompson, D., *Culture and Environment* (Chatto and Windus, 1948). First published in the 1930s, *Culture and Environment*, for all its 'high cultural' and moralistic tone, was instrumental in bringing media texts out from the cold and into the classroom.

Lewis, P. M., *Community Television and Cable in Britain* (BFI, 1978). A doggedly optimistic account of the short and largely disastrous history of British cable television. For a more jaundiced (or realistic?) view see Girard, A., *Cable Television and Cultural Policy* in Caughie (ed.).

Lister, I., *The Aims and Methods of Political Education in Schools*, Paper presented to the Conference on the Development of Democratic Institutions in Europe 1976. An excellent summarising paper on the main trends and likely future developments in the field of political education by one of its leading advocates in this country.

Lister, I., 'The political vocabulary test: a negative document', *The Bulletin of the General Studies Association*, no. 12 (Winter 1968). Early evidence of political illiteracy amongst school pupils.

Lloyd, B. B., *Perception and Cognition* (Penguin, 1972). A cross-cultural study of perception and cognition which contains a review of cross-cultural perceptions of colour, orientation, space and visual illusions. Some interesting illustrations but somewhat dry and academic.

* Lowndes, D., 'The Unesco survey and the British situation', *Screen Education*, no. 18 (Spring 1976). Because the enormous resources of the consciousness industries far outstrip those of education, 'liberal' teaching approaches to the media are now in fact repressive. Media studies should include a totalising conceptual framework which would expose the implicit and explicit beliefs pumped out by the mass media, and of which the concept of ideology would be a central part. Lowndes goes on to discuss the few texts available for developing in teachers a radical theoretical background to media studies. An important article.

Luckham, B., *Audio-Visual Literacy*, Proceedings of the Sixth Symposium on Broadcasting Policy. University of Manchester 1975. An attempt to clarify the concept of audiovisual literacy with reference to *Dr Who* and *Star Trek*. Apart from contributions by Buscombe and Hood an extremely weak collection with little insight offered into either of the programmes chosen and even less into the nature of audiovisual literacy.

Lunzer, E. A. and Gardner, W. K. (eds), *The Effective Use of Reading* (The Schools Council, 1979). An important report on reading and comprehension abilities. Many of the strategies and conclusions apply with equal force to the field of visual literacy and comprehension.

Lusted, D., *Television Genre Study* (BFI, 1976). Helpful BFI paper describing a further education course on television detective series.

Mack, J., 'Education in the media', *New Society*, 2 Nov 1978. A survey of recent press coverage of schools, demonstrating how they survive scrutiny which is often very unfair.

Mackenzie, R. F., *The Sins of the Children* (Collins, 1967).

Mackenzie, R. F., *State School* (Penguin, 1970). The experiences of a Scottish headmaster totally committed to the pursuit of excellence and uncompromisingly opposed to traditional elitist conceptions of education for the masses. Sensitive writing and excellent reading.

MacLaine, Shirley, *You Can Get There from Here* (Corgi, 1976). By no means a typically 'ghosted' star autobiography. Forceful views on both American television and society.

MacLuhan, M., *Understanding Media* (Routledge and Kegan Paul, 1964). Chapter 31 is on television; Chapter 20 is on photography.

Masterman, L., 'BBC – the eternal acolyte', *Times Educational Supplement*, 21 Dec 1973. An analysis of the television adaptation of Hardy's *Wessex Tales*. Should be of some value for teachers studying adaptations of novels with their classes.

Masterman, L., 'Cul-de-Sac: through the mirror of surrealism', *Screen*, vol. 11, no. 6 (1970). Draws attention to the surrealist elements in Polanski's film.

Masterman, L., 'The writer revealed', *Times Educational Supplement*, 26 Nov 1973. Attempts to place Galton and Simpson's *Casanova '73* within the context of the writers' previous work.

Masterman, L., Rennie, J. and Williams, W., *An Introduction to Social Education* (Nottingham University, 1972). Social education defined in terms of its processes and as a way of teaching in *all* subjects.

McArthur, C. M., 'Setting the scene: Radio Times and TV Times' in E. Buscombe, *Football on Television*. Excellent article on how the two magazines act as important mediating agents for the viewer.

McArthur, C. M., *Television & History*, Television Monograph no. 8 (BFI, 1978). Usefully points to the ways in which the presentation of the past, both in fictionalised and factual television programmes, is dominated by a bourgeois conception of history and of television forms. Both the general theoretical stance and the discussion of particular programmes (*Upstairs, Downstairs; Days of Hope*, etc.) should be of considerable interest to teachers.

McCann, E., 'The British press and Northern Ireland' in˙Cohen and Young. Interesting study demonstrating *inter alia* the institutional pressures placed upon practising journalists.

Morris, D., *The Naked Ape* (Cape, 1967). Contains sections on the origins of laughter and humour.

Murdock, G., 'Understanding television drama production', *Screen Education*, no. 26 (Spring 1978). A review of Alvarado and Buscombe, which crystallises some of the principal issues involved in understanding television drama production, and contains a valuable annotated guide to further reading on television drama.

Murdock, G. and Golding, P., *Communications: the Continuing Crisis* (25 April 1974). The 'crisis' is constituted by the ever increasing concentration in ownership and control of the media.

Murdock, G. and Phelps, G., *Mass Media and the Secondary School*, Schools Council Research Studies (Macmillan, 1973). Important research study examining differences in teacher and pupil perceptions of the mass media. Raises most of the important issues about mass-media education, though rather more concerned with the field of pop music than television.

The Open University, *Communication*, Social Sciences Foundation Course Block 3 Units 7–10 (The Open University Press, 1975). Unit 7 on *Interpersonal Communication* by Richard Stevens provides a valuable survey of the field with usable illustrations.

The Open University, *Mass Communication and Society*, a third-level Social Sciences course of fifteen units (The Open University Press, 1977). The following units of this course are the most relevant to the television teacher:

Unit One: *Issues in the Study of Mass Communication and Society* by Michael Gurevitch and Carrie Roberts.
Unit Four: *Popular Culture and High Culture: History and Theory* by John Hartley and Terence Hawkes.
Unit Six: *Messages and Meanings* by Janet Woollacott.
Unit Ten: *Patterns of Ownership; Questions of Control* by Graham Murdock.
Unit Thirteen: *The Media as Definers of Social Reality* by Tony Bennett.
Unit Fourteen: *The Definition of Social Problems: Violence and Race* by Peter Braham.

Orwell, G., 'The art of Donald McGill' in *Decline of the English Murder* (Penguin, 1965). Well-known analysis of postcards. Relevant to a good deal of 'low' television comedy.

Orwell, G., 'Boys' weeklies' in *Inside the Whale* (Penguin, 1962). Classic discussion of pre-war comics. Still usable with today's pupils.

Padfield, A., 'Put them in the picture', *Cog*, no. 1 (Summer 1976). Nottingham Teachers Centre. A teachers centre warden looks at the possibilities of video work for schools.

Pateman, T., *Television and the February 1974 General Election*, Television Monograph no. 3 (BFI, 1974). Written specifically with the teacher in mind, though not classroom orientated. The appendices are longer than the text itself and perhaps more valuable. They include transcripts of two Robin Day interviews.

Perls, F. Hefferline, R. F. and Goodman, P., *Gestalt Therapy* (Delta, 1951). Includes examples and analyses of a number of now well-known perceptual problems.

*Pirsig, R. M., *Zen and the Art of Motor-Cycle Maintenance* (Corgi, 1976). Extraordinary multi-layered novel, one of whose concerns is the whole question of values in education. Excellent on the dilemmas facing the radical teacher with a realistic depiction of the narrator's attempts to dispense with grades and introduce self-evaluation.

Postman, N., 'The politics of reading' in Keddie, N. (ed.), *Tinker, Tailor . . .* (Penguin, 1975). Polemical attack upon the 'reading lobby' in education. 'A school that put electric circuitry at its centre would have to be prepared for some serious damage to all of its bureaucratic and hierarchical arrangements.'

Postman, N., *Television and the Teaching of English* (Appleton–Century–Crofts, 1961). An early American attempt to encourage teachers to think about the television education of their students.

Postman, N. and Weingartner, C., *Teaching As A Subversive Activity* (Penguin, 1971). Suggests basing the school curriculum on questions defined by and important to the students.

Potter, D., 'Lost horizons', *New Statesman*, 20 Feb 1976.

Register of Research on Mass Media and Mass Communication (Centre for Mass Communication Research, University of Leicester, since 1976). Annual register of mass-media research with a large section devoted to current research in television. An invaluable document for media researchers.

Reimer, E., *School is Dead* (Penguin, 1971). Simple exposition of the main principles of the de-schooling movement by a colleague of Ivan Illich. Easier going than most of Illich's work, but less original.

Rennie, J., Lunzer, E. A. and Williams, W., *Social Education: An Experiment in Four Secondary Schools*, Schools Council Working Paper 51 (Evans/Methuen, 1974). An account of one of the most interesting and radical Schools Council projects, though its impact is somewhat modified by the circumspection of its title. 'Social Education is an enabling process through which children may acquire skills which will allow them both to achieve a greater understanding of society and to effect change within it.'

* *Report of the Committee on the Future of Broadcasting* (The Annan Report) (HMSO, 1977). Obligatory reading. Its twenty-nine chapters raise almost all of the arguments and issues in current debates about broadcasting. Unfortunately its price will put it out of the reach of most students and teachers.

Report on Secondary Education (The Spens Report) (HMSO, 1938).

Rhinehart, L., *The Dice Man* (Panther, 1972).

Rock, P., 'News as eternal recurrence' in Cohen and Young. Very useful essay on news gathering as routine and news as ritual.

Rock, I., 'The perception of disoriented figures' in *Readings from Scientific American*. Numerous examples of the way in which familiar objects become unrecognisable when their orientation is changed.

* Rogers, C. R., *Freedom to Learn* (Merrill, 1969). 'Teaching is a vastly over-rated function . . . I see the facilitation of learning as the aim of education.' Real learning is dependent upon a context of freedom; it 'has a quality of personal involvement, is self-initiated, pervasive and is evaluated by the learner'. An important book for teachers who wish to encourage self-directed and self-evaluated learning in their pupils.

Rogers, C. R., *On Becoming a Person* (Constable, 1961). One becomes a person ('actualises' oneself) through making rewarding and productive choices within an environment which is accepting, understanding and consistent. An important book and a milestone in humanistic psychology – but the locus of change is placed firmly within the individual rather than society.

Ryall, T., 'Visual style in Scotland v. Yugoslavia' in E. Buscombe (ed.). Examines patterns of editing within a particular televised football match.

Scarborough, M. L., *The Educational Value of Non-educational Television* (Independent Broadcasting Authority Research Report, 1973). Primary school children's responses to popular television programmes. Very limited in its perspectives and conclusions.

Scheflen, A. E., *Body Language and the Social Order* (Prentice Hall, 1972). Somewhat jargon-bound American introduction to kinesics, but containing usable illustrations.

*Schlesinger, P., *Putting 'Reality' Together* (Constable, 1978). Intelligent and clearly written sociological study of BBC News. Published too late for inclusion in Chapter 5, but developing many of the issues raised there. Contains a chapter on 'The reporting of Northern Ireland'. The best study currently available in the well-researched field of broadcast news. Essential reading.

*Scientific American (Readings from) *Recent Progress in Perception* (Freeman, 1976). Twenty-five articles from *Scientific American* on different aspects of perception. Excellent source material and profusely illustrated.

Seymour-Ure, C., *The Political Impact of Mass Media* (Constable, 1974). Well written study of the political effects of the mass media. Principally concerned with newspapers but included here for its excellent case studies (on Enoch Powell, *Private Eye*, etc.) – good examples of the kind of original work which students might try for themselves – and a general survey of mass media coverage of general elections from 1945–1970.

Shamberg, M. and Raindance Corporation, *Guerrilla Television* (Holt, Rinehart & Winston, 1971). Alternative video handbook from the USA. Great disparity between the inflated claims made for alternative video and the results actually achieved. Of little value to teachers.

Shubik, I., *Play for Today: The Evolution of Television Drama* (David-Poynter, 1975). An account of the development of television drama with useful insights (not all of them intentional) into the role of the producer.

Simon, B. (ed.), *The Radical Tradition in Education in Britain* (Lawrence and Wishart, 1972). An unusual book – an historical radical reader. The extracts from Robert D. Owen and William Lovett are especially relevant to many of the issues raised in Chapter 2.

*Smith, A., *British Broadcasting* (David and Charles, 1974). Valuable source of important documents in the history of broadcasting, including Acts of Parliament, codes of practice and key statements by broadcasters and politicians.

Smith, A., *The Shadow in the Cave* (Quartet, 1976). Lengthy study of broadcasting structures in Britain, USA, France, Japan and Holland. Chapter 3 deals with news presentations.

Smith, J. M., 'Making do – or better?: the American TV film', *Movie*, no. 21 (Autumn 1975). Unconvincing attempt to evaluate films made for television by 'tracking down the work of particular directors', i.e. to carry over to television a mode of analysis derived from film study.

* *Startline*: The published material of the Schools Council Moral Education 8–13 Project (Longmans/Schools Council, 1978). The Startline materials contain large numbers of excellent photographs and posters, designed 'to increase children's awareness of the verbal and non-verbal aspects of behaviour' and 'to heighten their perception and sensitivity to other people's needs, attitudes and feelings'. Although intended for 8–13-year-old pupils, the materials represent a rich resource for studying non-verbal communication at any educational level. The suggested activities and games relating to the material are imaginative and appealing.

Stradling, R., *The Political Awareness of the School Leaver* (Hansard Society, 1977). Contains evidence of low levels of political awareness among school leavers. (e.g. 44 per cent believe the IRA is a Protestant organisation, etc.)

Tansey, P. H. and Unwin, D., *Simulation and Gaming in Education* (Methuen, 1969).

Taylor, J. L. and Walford, R., *Simulation in the Classroom* (Penguin, 1972). Two of the most accessible introductions to the use of simulations in the classroom.

Teuber, M. L., 'Sources of ambiguity in the prints of Maurits C. Escher' in *Scientific American* (Readings from). Originally in *Scientific American* (July, 1974). Excellent study of the work of the Dutch artist which traces the influence of experiments on visual perception upon his work. First-class illustrations.

Thompson, D. (ed.), *Discrimination and Popular Culture* (Penguin, 1964). A collection of essays which made an influential contribution to the popular culture debate of the 1960s. Now largely of historic interest though the attitudes and arguments they embody still linger on.

Thompson, J. O., Baggaley, J. P. and Jamieson, G. H., 'Representation, review and the study of communication', *Journal of Education Television*, no. 1 (March 1975). Research article indicating the possible modes of analysis for television within communication studies. Kinesics, and perceptual and information theory are examined within the framework of the medium's dual facility for representation and review.

Took, B. *Laughter in the Dark* (Robson/BBC, 1976). 'An informal history of British Radio Comedy' from 1922 to the present day, which contains extracts from the scripts of numerous shows. Useful background reading for pupils studying television comedy.

Tracey, M., *The Production of Political Television* (Routledge, 1978). A study of the determinants of political television is followed by a potpourri of case studies on the General Strike and the BBC, the retiring of Sir Hugh Greene, the *Yesterday's Men* affair, and ATV's coverage of the 1974 General Election. Of value as background reading.

Tudor, A., 'The panels' in E. Buscombe (ed.). Analysis of the role played by panels of experts in soccer coverage.

Tunstall, J., *The Media are American* (Constable, 1977). Wide-ranging historical survey of the international flow of communications. Rejects any simple notions of 'media imperialism'.

Tunstall, J. (ed.), *Media Sociology: A Reader* (Constable, 1970). Curiously dated collection of essays, though the contributions of Burns, and Galtung and Ruge still have much relevance.

*Vaughan, D. *Television Documentary Usage*, BFI Television Monograph no. 6 (BFI, 1976). Written by someone who has worked extensively within the medium, 'this monograph is more an autobiography than a work of research'. Difficult going at times but some useful material on the working assumptions of documentary practice and on the pervasiveness of 'mannerism' – 'the attempt by film to approximate to the condition of verbal prose'.

Vernon, M. D., *The Psychology of Perception* (Pelican, 1962). Straightforward introduction to some of the problems of perception. Especially useful for the theoretical impetus it gives to the study of visual material throughout the school curriculum.

Wade, G., 'TV rules OK?', *Libertarian Education*, no. 9 (1976). A teacher's account of his experience of video-work.

Whale, J., *The Politics of the Media* (Fontana, 1977). Worth noting as possibly the worst book on media currently available, offering as insights every conceivable establishment myth about the press and broadcasting.

White, P. and White, J., *A Programme for Political Education: A Critique* (York University, 1975).

Wilkinson, A., 'Total communication' in *English in Education*, vol. 6, no. 3 (Winter 1972). Argues for the classroom study of all aspects of non-verbal as well as verbal communication.

*Williams, R. *Keywords* (Fontana, 1976). An essential source. Culture, art, media, mediation, ideology, hegemony, standards, taste, sensibility and image are just a few of the words whose derivations, development and modern meanings are explored in depth.

Williams, R., *Television: Technology and Cultural Form* (Fontana, 1974). Examines technology and social change, the characteristic 'forms' of television and the concept of 'planned flow' ('The defining characteristic of broadcasting') with an original and useful analysis of television in terms of its flow rather than its discrete programme units.

Williams, R., 'There's always the sport', *The Listener*, 16 April 1970. Television coverage of sporting events makes 'the ante-room the arena, the reaction the event and the commentators the real agents'. Discussed in Chapter 10.

Willis, P., 'What is news? A case study', *Working Papers in Cultural Studies*, no. 1 (Spring 1971). Includes a helpful discussion on the nature of bias in news presentations.

Winston, B., *The Image of the Media* (Davis-Poynter, 1973). A slim volume which summarises the principal issues and arguments in sociological and cultural studies of the media and then turns to information theory as 'the only approach which really talks the same language as the new media'.

York University, *A Programme for Political Education*, Political Education Research Unit Document no. 1 (York University, July 1974). Critical examination of current notions of what might constitute a political education programme.

Index